NORTHERN

FRONTIER

NORTHERN

HOMELAND

THOMAS R. BERGER

NORTHERN

FRONTIER

NORTHERN

HOMELAND

THE REPORT OF THE MACKENZIE VALLEY PIPELINE INQUIRY

REVISED
EDITION

Douglas & McIntyre
Vancouver/Toronto

Revised edition 1988
88 89 90 91 92   5 4 3 2 1

Douglas & McIntyre Ltd.
1615 Venables Street, Vancouver, British Columbia V5L 2H1

Canadian Cataloguing in Publication Data

Mackenzie Valley Pipeline Inquiry (Canada)
Northern frontier, northern homeland

Originally published 1977 as the report of
the Mackenzie Valley Pipeline Inquiry.
ISBN 0-88894-601-5
1. Mackenzie Valley Pipeline (N.W.T.) -
Environmental aspects. 2. Mackenzie Valley
Pipeline (N.W.T.). 3. Indians of North
America - Canada, Northern. I. Berger,
Thomas R. II. Title.
HD9580.C33M33 1988   388.5'09719'3   C88-091081-X

Design by Alexandra Hass

Map by Department of Geography
Trent University
Typeset by The Typeworks
Printed and bound in Canada by Webcom

The author and publisher gratefully acknowledge the co-operation of the Frost Centre, Trent University, where, as the first occupant of the chair of Northern Studies, Thomas R. Berger delivered the 1986 Northern Lecture Series, on which the introduction to the revised edition is based.

CONTENTS

Introduction to the Revised Edition   1

Letter to the Minister   14

1 The North   31

    Northern Frontier, Northern Homeland   31

    The Northern Biome   33

    Northern Peoples   40

2 Engineering and Construction   46

    The Pipeline Project: Its Scope and Scale   50

3 The Northern Environment   53

    Environmental Attitudes and Environmental Values 53

    Wilderness   55

4 The Northern Yukon   58

    A Unique Heritage   58

    Man and the Land: Old Crow   62

    Porcupine Caribou Herd   66

    A National Wilderness Park for the Northern Yukon 74

    An Alternative Route Across the Yukon   77

5   The Mackenzie Delta–Beaufort Sea Region   80

Man and the Land   81

Region and Environment   85

Industry's Plans   93

Delta Region Impacts   95

Whales and a Whale Sanctuary   99

Offshore Concerns   103

Spill Clean-up   109

6   The Mackenzie Valley   115

The Region   115

The People and the Land   116

Environmental Concerns   118

Corridor Development   123

Balancing Development with the Environment   124

7   Cultural Impact   127

Cultural Impact: A Retrospect   127

The Persistence of Native Values   136

The Native Economy   145

8   Economic Impact   163

The Development of the Northern Economy   166

Objectives of Economic Development   171

The Mixed Economy   174

Employment and the Pipeline   179

If the Pipeline Is Not Built Now   183

9   Social Impact   187

The Northern Population   188

Social Impact and Industrial Development   196

Specific Impacts   202

The Limits to Planning   210

10   Native Claims   213

History of Native Claims   214

Self-Determination and Confederation   231

Native Claims: Their Nature and Extent   237

The Claim to Renewable Resources   240

Native Claims and the Pipeline   247

11   Epilogue: Themes for the National Interest   257

Index   265

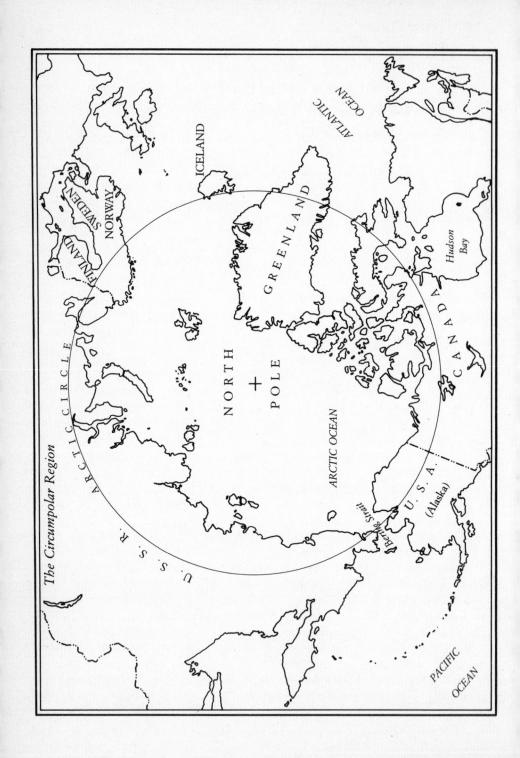

The Circumpolar Region

ARCTIC CIRCLE

U.S.S.R.

FINLAND

SWEDEN

NORWAY

ICELAND

ATLANTIC OCEAN

GREENLAND

NORTH + POLE

ARCTIC OCEAN

Bering Strait

CANADA

Hudson Bay

U.S.A. (Alaska)

PACIFIC OCEAN

INTRODUCTION TO THE REVISED EDITION

ONE DAY IN JANUARY 1974, I RECEIVED A TELEPHONE CALL FROM Jean Chrétien, Canada's Minister of Indian Affairs and Northern Development.

"Would you be willing," he asked me, "to conduct an inquiry into the proposed Mackenzie Valley pipeline?" A consortium of twenty-seven Canadian and American companies had proposed the greatest construction project ever to be undertaken by private enterprise, a gas pipeline some 2,600 miles (3860 km) long from Prudhoe Bay, Alaska, across the Northern Yukon, then south from the Mackenzie River delta to mid-continent.

Without any hesitation, I agreed. Between 1974 and 1977, as Commissioner of the Mackenzie Valley Pipeline Inquiry, I travelled in the Mackenzie Valley, and in fact throughout Canada's Western Arctic region, to listen to what the peoples of the North had to say about the impact of the proposed pipeline on their lives. More than a thousand witnesses gave evidence in these hearings. My report, *Northern Frontier, Northern Homeland,* came out in April 1977.

I think that the Mackenzie Valley Pipeline Inquiry was unique in the Canadian experience; it was the means by which the nation examined the future of the North and of its peoples. More than a decade later, the Inquiry's report is still relevant to the future of the North, for it is there that Canadians have the opportunity to realize an idea of progress that has a place not only for industrial advance but also for native rights and environmental values.

Ever since my report came out in 1977, I have followed closely events in the North. It is a long way from my home in Vancouver, but I have been back there many times. Indeed, in 1983, I went to Alaska, under the sponsorship of the Inuit Circumpolar Conference, to conduct the

Alaska Native Review Commission. For two years, I travelled throughout Alaska, taking testimony from witnesses, repeating in many ways the
experience of the Mackenzie Valley Pipeline Inquiry.

My travels have taken me to the constellation of native villages extending across the top of North America from Bering Strait to Hudson Bay. I
have slept under the open sky, in tents and log cabins, on schoolroom
floors, and, of course, in more ordinary accommodations. Travelling
mostly by small chartered aircraft, occasionally by freighter canoe, my
journey from one village to another, then another, then another, seemed,
sometimes, as though it would never end—yet always, on arrival, another
warm welcome made me forget the temporary hardships of incessant
travel.

The intensity of the experience made an impression on my mind that
has stayed with me ever since. Long after I had left those far-off villages
in Canada's Arctic and sub-Arctic, memories of real persons with real
problems in real places—many of them recorded in these pages—
lingered in my mind and continued to trouble me.

When I wrote *Northern Frontier, Northern Homeland,* I wanted to
help Canadians to discover the true North. To be sure, there is another
North, a land that never was, except in popular tales that have per-
petuated misconceptions down through the ages. To many who write
about the northern landscape, its impact on the eye and the imagination
overwhelms the mind. How could anyone survive in this cold and un-
forgiving climate?

We had had a steady diet of heroic tales of European navigators and
explorers who did survive. They were supposed to have discovered the
arctic and sub-arctic regions of North America. We celebrated their
achievements, and those of the fur traders and priests who followed
them, as if the exploration of the North had been nothing more than a
challenge to European courage, endurance and technology. Almost inci-
dentally, we were told of the indigenous peoples they encountered; the
Inuit of the barren lands and the Indians of the northern forest were
no more than a curiosity. To chroniclers of exploration by sea, the Inuit were faceless people peeping through the icebergs. Even to those
who came by land, guided by Indians of the northern forest, the natives
were irrelevant. Yet in the North, as throughout the Americas, the
native people had their own history, their own culture and their own
technology.

We think of the explorers and navigators as the cartographers of the
Arctic, but now we realize that the North was already mapped by the Inuit and the Indians—traced all over by their hunting patterns. It was the
Indians and the Inuit who showed the early explorers, navigators,
traders and priests how to survive. We think of the fur trade as a white

man's undertaking; but the native people, who gathered the furs, were their partners in the venture.

All of this lay, however, in the past. Now Canada was going to open up the North. The Mackenzie Valley Pipeline would be to the North what the Canadian Pacific Railway had been to the West.

Who could be against such an undertaking? It had progress written all over it. I went to the North assuming that the pipeline represented the means of bringing northerners into the mainstream of the Canadian economy. My assumption was shared by most Canadians. But as the hearings went on, I realized that the environmental losses would be severe, the opposition of the native people unyielding, and the issues we faced far more difficult than we had thought.

By the time the hearings concluded, I realized that it would be necessary in my report to recommend against the pipeline. How was I to make such a recommendation meaningful to Ottawa? How to portray the North, its peoples and the issues we faced there in a way that would persuade legislators to do more than a quick and dirty compromise? How to show that the assumptions that guide us in the south do not hold good in the North? How to make all this clear to decision-makers in Ottawa surrounded by executive assistants and copying machines? That was my job.

As my work in Canada's North drew to a close, I met with Prime Minister Pierre Trudeau; I outlined the issues that my report would raise. I spoke in particular of the Porcupine caribou herd ranging between Canada and Alaska, a herd of 110,000 animals on which native villagers in both countries depend, and of the likelihood that the establishment of a pipeline and an energy corridor would drive the herd from its calving grounds on the arctic coast. I summarized the evidence, in this and other issues, indicating that choices had to be made. He followed closely, often saying "Good point." I reiterated that, whatever I might recommend, the final decision would rest with the government; there was every reason for him and his colleagues to begin to think about the issues. Trudeau said, "You've got a very interesting job." I replied, "It's the best job in the country."

As we parted, I returned to the subject of the Porcupine herd, urging Trudeau to visit the Northern Yukon in June. I told him that the herd, migrating from the Ogilvie Mountains to the arctic coast, reaches the Coastal Plain, like clockwork, at the beginning of June. I had been there and seen the herd on its migration back into the mountains in late summer. I confess the sight of this magnificent aggregation of animals—there is nothing like it on the earth, except perhaps the migration of the wildebeest on the Serengeti—had helped me to make up my mind to recommend that no pipeline be built along the coastal plain. A year later, after my report had been handed in, I read in the newspapers that Trudeau and his sons were camping in the Northern Yukon. I said to my wife, "That's it." "How do you know?" she asked. I replied, "No one can visit the Porcupine herd, and then decide to build a pipeline that would drive them from their calving grounds. How could you face yourself at the shaving mirror each morning for the rest of your life?"

I wanted the prime minister to see the North. For other Canadians, I would have to make the case in writing. In my report, I had to convey the truth about the North. Caught up in the idea of progress, we sought to replicate in the North life as we know it in the metropolitan centres of North America. For many years our firm belief was that in the Arctic, native people should live as we do, that they should share our values. Their own values we regarded as quaint, of merely anthropological interest.

Progress meant absorption and assimilation of the native peoples. Confronted with what we conceived to be the poverty and the backwardness of the Inuit and the Dene (the Indians of the Mackenzie Valley), we sought to make them over into white people with brown skins.

Our actions had resulted not only in the usual bureaucratic muddle but in enormous social upheaval. In the 1950s native people in the North were living off the land. We evacuated them and clustered them in settlements—the villages in which native people live today—where they were to begin a new life, cut off from the land. The traditional native subsistence economy, based on hunting, fishing and trapping, which had maintained them for centuries, had to be abandoned if they were to enter the new age.

But in these villages there were few jobs. We spent millions of dollars to create jobs, but most of these jobs went to white people. The state of dependence of native people, their sense of powerlessness, increased.

To be sure, many native people wanted to leave the land, to live as we do. Many others wondered which way was best. But virtually all of them wanted to maintain their identity as natives.

The difficulty was not simply one of sorting out native aspirations. It had to do with the nature of the North itself. It was unwise, indeed fraudulent, to claim that wage and salaried employment awaited these villagers. It does not. To say this is not patronizing—it is simply facing the facts. The farther North you go, the more limited is the prospect of conventional economic opportunity. The climate, the distances, the sparse population, are all against it. So the subsistence economy had to be preserved, not destroyed.

Yet public policy in Canada proceeded on the assumption that wage and salaried employment for everyone could be provided in these villages. This was the assumption made by government, by industry, and half-adopted by the native people themselves—though they realize now what perhaps they sensed all along, that it could not be achieved.

No one who travels in the Arctic can be unaware of the social pathology that disfigures northern life—family violence, alcoholism, and, most tragic of all, suicides by young people, usually in their teens and early twenties, and usually males. I believe that these lamentable statistics are the tragic outcome of the policies we pursued for so many years. In the midst of this pathology, social workers, nurses, counsellors—many of them native, but most of them white—do the best they can.

The fact is, however, that the causes are not treatable by a short stay in a detoxification centre, by counselling, or by any conventional means. They stem from individual demoralization and the demoralization of whole communities. Too often in the past, the representatives in northern Canada of powerful social and economic institutions in southern Canada—government administrators, representatives of industry, missionaries and clergy, policemen, social workers and teachers, supplemented by invasions of academic and commercial scientists in season—were united in their dismissal of native languages, cultures and traditions, and in their condemnation of ways of life different from their own. Young natives were taught to reject their own people, their own past, their own sense of identity. Young natives, inadequately educated to enter a white middle-class world that is, in any case, largely closed to them, feel cornered, frustrated and hostile. Most often, they have turned their violence inward, against themselves.

Government and industry believed that the nation needed the pipeline and that the best hope of northern natives lay in construction of the pipeline. If we did not build the pipeline, the president of the pipeline consortium declared, Canadians would experience "serious consequences in the mid-80s." Furthermore, there would be no jobs for natives and other northerners. Careers in industry and government depended on the construction of the pipeline, so it is not surprising that, to a large extent, this view was shared throughout industry and government.

Both wanted the pipeline to be built. Government and its bureaucracy had always sought to diminish the importance of subsistence hunting and fishing, of living off the land. Industry and their public relations men joined in: if subsistence is dying, if it is an anachronism, all the more reason for large-scale frontier development. The object was to bring native people into the market economy, at the very least into the welfare economy.

But all of this took place against a background of rising native consciousness and against the emergence of the land claims movement. Native leaders, and virtually all the native people who testified at the hearings, said that land claims must be settled before the pipeline was built. Many Canadians thought, however, that to allow the native people to hold up the pipeline until their claims were settled would give them the means, in the phrase popular at the time, "to hold the country to ransom." It was a contest between two cultures, between two quite distinct ideas of progress for the North. In the end I recommended that no major pipeline should be built along the Mackenzie Valley for ten years, to give us time to settle native claims.

Well, we did not build the Mackenzie Valley pipeline; we are now past the mid-1980s and there have been no serious consequences. Canada and the U.S. are still well supplied with natural gas. In fact, had the Mackenzie Valley pipeline been built, it would have entailed shutting in natural gas in Alberta in order to transport expensive gas from the Arctic to markets in the mid-continent. (In the early 1980s a pipeline was built to carry oil from Norman Wells to Alberta; the Norman Wells pipeline is in no way comparable in scope and scale to the proposed Mackenzie Valley pipeline.) The Mackenzie Valley pipeline's time may come, but it is not here yet.

Nothing illustrates so well as the pipeline the tendency for conventional wisdom to be wrong. The way of the future for these arctic villagers does not lie in large, capital-intensive frontier projects. This is not to say that the idea that inspired the pipeline was not praiseworthy or to deny that we are all often wrong in our forecasts. But what has happened in the North should make us less certain about accepting the preference of bureaucratic and economic power for large-scale, capital-intensive development. Bureaucracy and industry usually share the same priorities: their interests are interlocked, and they usually lie far from the interests of native northerners.

I devoted much of *Northern Frontier, Northern Homeland* to present-day concerns of the native peoples of northern Canada. Urban, mobile, southern Canadians who have lost any binding sense of family, place or tradition can barely comprehend the depth of feeling natives express for their northern homeland. It is their fate that is tied up with the future of the North. They were born there, they will spend their lives there, they will die there. So what are native people in the North to do? Well, they can do what they've always done—they can hunt and fish and trap. But does this not consign them to a life of backwardness, of stagnation? Only if we believe there is no place in the world for the maintenance of a hunting and fishing economy. Of course, many native northerners want wage and salaried employment. And where jobs can be provided, they should have them. We can do more than we are doing to make jobs in government and in industry available to native people. All agree on such an objective. My concern is that in the Arctic and sub-Arctic there will never be the prospect of anything like full employment for native people. So, unless they are going to emigrate from the North, the subsistence economy must be strengthened. This is not for sentimental reasons, to preserve it as a souvenir of a past long since dead, but rather as the means of ensuring the greatest measure of self-sufficiency for native northerners. In the North, the strengthening of the subsistence economy is one way to achieve the Bruntland Commission's goal of sustainable development.

Evidence I heard during the Mackenzie Valley Pipeline Inquiry on the strength of the native subsistence economy in northern Canada genuinely surprised me, although the three-volume report of the Inuit Land Use and Occupancy Project, published by the Department of Indian and Northern Affairs in 1976, had to some extent prepared me for it. This report demonstrates that, by adapting southern technologies to traditional purposes, the Inuit of the Northwest Territories continue to use today all of the land their ancestors used for hunting, fishing and trapping.

Even after the completion of a similar survey by the Dene in the Western Arctic, we in Canada should have known. Yet there remained a seed of skepticism. I thought, when I went to Alaska, a decade after the completion of the Trans-Alaska Pipeline and the extinguishment by Congress of aboriginal rights, that the subsistence economy of Alaska natives would have shrivelled. But no, in fact it is still the mainstay of village life. Native harvests there, as in northern Canada, have increased, not diminished.

Quietly, in the midst of the talk of development, the subsistence economy of the North has survived and remains the best hope of self-sufficiency for the majority of the native inhabitants of the Arctic and sub-arctic. According to the 1980 Report of the Northwest Territories Science Advisory Board, the fish and wildlife of the Northwest Territories could provide enough protein to support a human population twice its present size.

Why have we consistently and persistently underestimated the importance of the subsistence economy? I think it is because there is no place in our ideas of progress for the idea of a viable hunting and fishing economy. We were not merely indifferent to the idea, we vehemently opposed it. The attack on the subsistence economy has come from every quarter: from those who wanted to change the native people, from those who wanted their land, and now from those who regard their way of life as cruel to animals. Enthusiasts for animal rights have now joined the missionaries, bureaucrats and entrepreneurs in their rejection of subsistence activities.

When promoters of animal rights began to campaign during the 1960s to stop Newfoundlanders from clubbing, then skinning, baby harp seals or whitecoats, no one anticipated a generalized prohibition of seal products in Europe. The banning of seal products in Europe has devastated the economies of Inuit in the Canadian Arctic and Greenland who have probably never seen a harp seal pup. They harvest adult ringed seals. Inuit had depended on the sale of ringed-seal skins for the cash that

enabled them to buy equipment they need to feed their families by hunting, fishing and trapping. The animal rights activists, ethnocentric and
ignorant of northern conditions, wanting to impose their own values and
attitudes on northern natives, have aggravated existing hardships. By destroying the market for ringed-seal skins, they have substantially reduced
incomes in many northern communities and deepened feelings of frustration and despair.

Is our record in the North then one of complete failure and frustration? Of course not. In many ways, Canada's achievements in the North
are unsurpassed. We have overcome the difficulties of distance and
climate. We have willingly paid what it cost to build northern airfields,
highways, meteorological and scientific stations, radar-warning systems
and other military installations. We have mined the region's gold,
uranium, iron ore and other minerals. We have harnessed its water to
produce hydroelectric power. All Canadians may take pride in the fact
that the Canadian oil and gas industry and its engineers lead the world in
the development of technology for the recovery of oil and gas in arctic
waters. But the paradox is that we are limited in our ideas of northern
development.

We need a broader definition of development, one that encompasses
not only industrial activity but also the strengthening of the traditional
subsistence economy. It is not an either/or proposition. In the North, the
vast open spaces are not required as in the West for agriculture; the subsistence economy can still thrive.

Behind the story of the mines and the oil rigs lies the question: are the
native peoples merely a curious cultural backdrop to the activities of
Western man, or are they the peoples for whom the North was made? A
lack of understanding and of sensitivity to native peoples and native
values is endemic to European-derived political systems. What is remarkable is that despite the attempts to separate native people from their
language, history and culture, they have retained their distinctive
identity.

The Dene, the Inuit and the Metis are advancing land claims
proposals and proposals for new political arrangements in the Northwest
Territories. Whatever the outcome of these proposals, they are evidence
of a renewed determination—and a new capacity—on the part of native
peoples in the North to defend what they believe is their right to a future
of their own. They are engaged in a search for self-determination and in
the development of new political institutions. As well, they have undertaken the defence of the northern environment.

It was the native people who insisted most strenuously—and still do—
on the preservation of the Porcupine caribou herd. If there had not been
native people opposed to a pipeline across the Northern Yukon, we
might have lost a herd of 110,000 caribou, for the evidence made it plain

that construction of a pipeline across the calving area would mean that the herd would be reduced to a remnant by the end of the century.

In *Northern Frontier, Northern Homeland* I recommended that, in order to protect the Porcupine herd, no pipeline should ever be built across the arctic Coastal Plain and that an international wilderness area should be established comprising nine million acres (3.6 million hectares) in the Northern Yukon and, on the American side, the nine-million acre Arctic National Wildlife Range. Together these two areas, nine million acres on each side of the international boundary, would preserve critical habitat for the long-term well-being of the Porcupine herd and other wildlife. It was my view that in the Northern Yukon, preservation of the wilderness and of the caribou herd would plainly be in keeping with the interests of the native peoples on both sides of the border. Certain essential conditions had to be observed: native people would have to be guaranteed the right to live, hunt, trap and fish within the park. I also suggested that they should play an important part in the management of the park, and in particular, of the caribou herd.

In 1980, the U.S. established a wilderness designation for much of the Arctic National Wildlife Range. In Canada the environmental interest was united with the native interest. The Inuvialiut—the Inuit of Canada's Western Arctic—urged that the establishment of a national park be included in the final resolution of their claim. On 25 July 1984, as part of the Inuvialiut Claims Settlement Act, the Northern Yukon National Park was established with special management and hunting, fishing and trapping provisions for native peoples. This makes the point I want to emphasize: the native peoples have been in the forefront in devising measures to protect the arctic and sub-arctic environment. Almost forgotten just a few years ago, they have re-emerged in the history of the North, not as figures of folklore but as actors on the modern stage.

Today the administration of President Ronald Reagan wants to open up the coastal plain of the Arctic National Wildlife Range to oil and gas drilling activity. This is lunacy; it threatens the future of 110,000 caribou (in fact, the herd is even larger now). For what? To provide what is in the long run a trivial volume of oil—two years' supply—to grease the North American industrial machine. Congress has refused to go along with the president. But we may be sure that in due course other attempts will be made to drill on the Coastal Plain.

Destruction of the Porcupine herd would mean, in its turn, destruction of the subsistence economies of native villages on both sides of the international boundary; at what cost in suffering to the natives themselves, at what cost in dollars to taxpayers for their relief, no one can reckon; but there can be no doubt both would be great. There is a line below the bottom line, and it is for value judgments that anyone can read. It is impossible and undesirable to separate scientific, technical and economic considerations from their social and environmental context. We must always consider the untidy web of moral and ethical considerations into which these judgments inevitably lead.

Our ideas of progress are industrial and technological. Since the Industrial Revolution we have thought of industrialization as the means to prosperity and well-being. And so it has been, to many people, and to many parts of the world. But the rise of the industrial system has been accompanied by a belief in an ever-expanding cycle of growth and consumption, a belief that conditions our capacity and our willingness to reconsider or even to contemplate the true goals of the industrial system. There is a feeling that we cannot pause to consider where we are headed, for fear of what we shall find out about ourselves.

Even our terminology has become eccentric. Those who seek to conserve the environment and traditional values are often regarded as radicals, and those who are undertaking radical interventions in the natural world that threaten the future of existing communities and wildlife populations think of themselves as conservatives. Thus the debate about the future of the North often tends to become a barren exchange of epithets. This debate, now raging, now waning, goes on in Canada and the United States; it illustrates one of the basic facts about the North: international co-operation is needed, between the United States and Canada to preserve the Porcupine herd, and among all the circumpolar countries to preserve the arctic and sub-arctic environment.

Our belief that we can reproduce our own values, industry and technology in the North, a belief that has inspired our policies towards the people of the North, now inspires our attitudes towards the northern environment. But the Arctic is vulnerable. The old stories of the taming of the frontier, of the triumph of Western technology, cannot be repeated there without immense danger, for our experience in the temperate zone does not apply in the Arctic.

The Arctic and sub-Arctic lie beyond the reach of agricultural advance, in many ways beyond the reach of industrial advance. They are cold places, dark throughout much of the winter. In the arctic winter, the tundra recedes for miles on the horizon—a forlorn, endless white landscape, relief coming only with a squall of snow. It is the only place in North America where we have not yet completed the cycle of progress: made permanent settlements, subdued the landscape and transformed the surface of the earth. But we are attempting to do so; the attempt, however, cannot succeed, and it will incur great risk.

We should not draw the wrong conclusions. There is oil and gas in the North, and if we can develop technologies to bring them out economically and safely, no doubt in due time we should. It is the rational application of industry and technology that we must pursue; an order based on the human scale and directed to human needs. In the North this means the maintenance of the subsistence economy, and political institutions to defend subsistence. It means an examination of the environmental consequences of industrial activity in the North and on the North, throughout the circumpolar basin.

Offshore drilling in arctic waters, diversion and damming of arctic rivers, and the accumulation of acidic particles in the arctic atmosphere, all may threaten the polar ice cap, arctic waters and arctic weather systems, perhaps even the earth's weather system. The possibility of catastrophe, gradually revealing itself to us, exists as surely in the Arctic as does the hole in the ozone layer over Antarctica. A concept of collective stewardship must be developed if we are to ensure the protection of the arctic environment.

It is right that we Canadians should wish to take measures to protect the Arctic. But we should wish to do so for the right reasons. The United States has disputed Canada's claim to sovereignty over the Northwest Passage. The Soviet Union and the United States now deploy nuclear submarines under the arctic ice, *our* arctic ice. Canada argues that we must, at whatever cost, deploy our own nuclear submarines there, too. We must assert our sovereignty.

Why should we permit the concept of national sovereignty to define the terms of debate over the future of the northern environment? Whether the world as we know it ends with a bang or a whimper hardly matters. The real dangers of mutually assured nuclear destruction are, comparatively speaking, well understood, but people everywhere seem to find difficulty in grasping the real dangers of mounting global pollution and environmental degradation.

Here, once again, the idea of the expansionary role of nation-states on the European model dominates our thinking. So the debate about the Arctic is cast in terms of sovereignty, of national ambition. Why allow the sterile goals of the nation-state to define the future of the North?

National sovereignty is a limited and limiting concept. Beyond sovereignty lies stewardship. Sovereignty is a national issue; stewardship an international issue. Surely the Arctic is a place where an attempt ought to be made to transcend the particularities of the Cold War.

Our policy ought not to consist merely of noisy assertions of sovereignty over our arctic waters, assertions to the grandstand of public opinion that we may be in no position to enforce.

Nations that encompass arctic lands and waters face common challenges. But they are not grappling with these challenges in concert.

The Inuit Circumpolar Conference has taken a first step towards the creation of a unified approach to common problems within a common environment. They have urged that the Arctic be a nuclear-free zone. Is it too much to ask that nation-states also should be prepared to tackle these issues on an international basis? We can, at least, point to the precedent of the Antarctica Treaty.

On 1 December 1959, the United States, the Soviet Union and ten other nations signed a treaty unique in the history of nations. "It is in the interest of mankind," declares its preamble, "that Antarctica shall continue forever to be used exclusively for peaceful purposes and shall not become the scene or object of international discord." Some thirty nations, including Canada, have now adhered to the Antarctica Treaty. Canada should urge the treaty's renewal, when it expires in 1989.

The threat—one facing all circumpolar countries—is obvious. Yet they cannot be made to see that their common interests are at stake. An environmental catastrophe in the Arctic is as great a threat to humankind as that represented by accidental nuclear war. How can national interests prevail faced with such obvious facts? A look at the map—or better still a globe—indicates where the trouble starts. The North disappears over the top of the map. The eye is drawn to the temperate zones. The Arctic Ocean might as well be on the bottom of the world, like Antarctica; it was, until recently, hardly better known. Yet the North—the Arctic and the sub-Arctic—is a world of its own. Look at the Arctic from a point above the North Pole. The Canadian North merges with the circumpolar basin, which is the joint responsibility of the circumpolar powers. You have the Canadian, American, Greenlandic and Scandinavian coastlines on the one side, the Soviet coastline on the other. Viewed from the North Pole, the Arctic Ocean is an international lake.

In *Northern Frontier, Northern Homeland* I urged that Canada should call for an international program of research, to be undertaken by the circumpolar countries, to enable us to understand the environmental implications of oil and gas exploration and production in arctic waters. I still believe that there should be an international program of research; it should include not only the impact of oil and gas exploration and production, but also the impact of Soviet water diversion projects on arctic waters and arctic weather, the impact of acid haze in the Arctic, indeed the whole spectrum of arctic environmental concerns. All the circumpolar countries have an interest in seeing such a program established.

As a northern nation, Canada is advancing claims embracing the waters of the arctic archipelago and extending as far as the continental shelf lying beyond. Any such nation has an obligation to promote an international regime to protect arctic waters, arctic weather systems, arctic marine life and the subsistence economies of native peoples of the circumpolar basin.

In a world where men and women still claim to act rationally, it should be possible to undertake an international program of research into the impact of industrial activity on arctic marine life and arctic ice and weather systems. In any such program, there should be a place for the indigenous peoples of the circumpolar countries, for the Arctic is their homeland, and the resources of arctic waters essential to their livelihood. In fact, any such program should be founded on the proposition that the indigenous peoples of the Arctic are the primary guardians of the arctic environment. Certainly, they have acted with a greater sense of responsibility than the nation-states have done.

It is not only we in the industrial democracies who are being urged to reconsider. Before he was expelled from the Soviet Union, Alexander Solzhenitsyn, in his *Letter to the Soviet Leaders,* reminded them

> of what any village graybeard in the Ukraine or Russia had understood from time immemorial and could have explained to the progressive commentators ages ago, had the commentators ever found the time in that dizzy fever of theirs to consult him; that a dozen earthworms can't go on and on gnawing at the same apple forever, that if the earth is a finite object, then its expanses and resources are finite also, and the endless infinite progress dinned into our heads by the dreamers of the enlightenment cannot be accomplished on it.

Solzhenitsyn went on:

> We have squandered our resources foolishly without so much as a backward glance, sapped our soil, mutilated our vast expanses with idiotic "inland seas" and contaminated belts of wasteland around our industrial centres—but for the moment, at least, far more remains untainted by us, which we haven't had time to touch. So let us come to our senses in time, let us change our course.

I know that in urging a circumpolar treaty for international research in arctic waters I run the risk of being misunderstood. Our notions of progress have acquired a technological and industrial definition. For many, the advance of industry and technology to the margins of the globe represents a kind of manifest destiny for industrial man. For others, it represents an unacceptable threat to the future of the biosphere itself. I wish to avoid being thought of as a partisan of either view. But I do urge such a treaty so that a complete examination of the impact of industrial activity on circumpolar waters can take place and so that the advance of industry and technology in the arctic and subarctic seas will take place in a rational and orderly fashion, so that the circumpolar basin—the heritage of all mankind—will be protected.

It is in the North that the survival of the native subsistence economy is essential; it is there that the place of native peoples within our political system will be determined; it is there that our commitment to environmental goals and international co-operation will be tested. In the North lies the future of Canada.

MACKENZIE VALLEY PIPELINE INQUIRY

COMMISSIONER
Mr. Justice Thomas R. Berger

10th Floor
One Nicholas Street
Ottawa, Ontario K1N 7B7

April 15, 1977

The Honourable Warren Allmand
Minister of Indian Affairs and Northern Development
House of Commons
Ottawa, Ontario

Dear Mr. Allmand:
We are now at our last frontier. It is a frontier that all of us have read about, but few of us have seen. Profound issues, touching our deepest concerns as a nation, await us there.

The North is a frontier, but it is a homeland too, the homeland of the Dene, Inuit and Metis, as it is also the home of the white people who live there. And it is a heritage, a unique environment that we are called upon to preserve for all Canadians.

The decisions we have to make are not, therefore, simply about northern pipelines. They are decisions about the protection of the northern environment and the future of northern peoples.

At the formal hearings of the Inquiry in Yellowknife, I heard the evidence of 300 experts on northern conditions, northern environment and northern peoples. But, sitting in a hearing room in Yellowknife, it is easy to forget the real extent of the North. The Mackenzie Valley and the Western Arctic is a vast land where people of four races live, speaking seven different languages. To hear what they had to say, I took the Inquiry to 35 communities—from Sachs Harbour to Fort Smith, from Old Crow to Fort Franklin—to every city and town, village and settlement in the Mackenzie Valley and the Western Arctic. I listened to the evidence of almost one thousand northerners.

I discovered that people in the North have strong feelings about the pipeline and large-scale frontier development. I listened to a brief by northern businessmen in Yellowknife who favour a pipeline through the North. Later, in a native village far away, I heard virtually the whole community express vehement opposition to such a pipeline. Both were talking about the same pipeline; both were talking about the same region—but for one group it is a frontier, for the other a homeland.

All those who had something to say—white or native—were given an opportunity to speak. The native organizations claim to speak for the native people. They oppose the pipeline without a settlement of native claims. The Territorial Council claims to speak for all northerners. It supports the pipeline. Wally Firth, Member of Parliament for the Northwest Territories, opposes the pipeline. I decided that I should give northerners an opportunity to speak for themselves. That is why I held hearings in all northern communities, where the people could speak directly to the Inquiry. I held hearings in the white centres of populations, and in the native villages. I heard from municipal councillors, from band chiefs and band councils and from the people themselves. This report reflects what they told me.

The North is a region of conflicting goals, preferences and aspirations. The conflict focuses on the pipeline. The pipeline represents the advance of the industrial system to the Arctic. The impact of the industrial system upon the native people has been the special concern of the Inquiry, for one thing is certain: the impact of a pipeline will bear especially upon the native people. That is why I have been concerned that the native people should have an opportunity to speak to the Inquiry in their own villages, in their own languages, and in their own way.

I have proceeded on the assumption that, in due course, the industrial system will require the gas and oil of the Western Arctic, and that they will have to be transported along the Mackenzie Valley to markets in the South. I have also proceeded on the assumption that we intend to protect and preserve Canada's northern environment, and that, above all else, we intend to honour the legitimate claims and aspirations of the native people. All of these assumptions are embedded in the federal government's expressed northern policy for the 1970s.

THE CORRIDOR CONCEPT AND CUMULATIVE IMPACT

The proposed natural gas pipeline is not to be considered in isolation. The Expanded Guidelines for Northern Pipelines, tabled in the House of Commons on June 28, 1972, assume that, if a gas pipeline is built, an oil pipeline will follow, and they call for examination of the proposed gas pipeline from the point of view of cumulative impact. We must consider, then, the impact of a transportation corridor for two energy systems, a corridor that may eventually include roads and other transportation systems.

The construction of a gas pipeline and the establishment of an energy corridor will intensify oil and gas exploration activity all along the corridor. The cumulative impact of all these developments will bring immense and irreversible changes to the Mackenzie Valley and the Western Arctic. And we must bear in mind that we have two corridors under consideration: a corridor from Alaska across the Northern Yukon to the Mackenzie Delta, and a corridor along the Mackenzie Valley from the Delta to the Alberta border.

THE PROJECT:
ITS SCOPE AND SCALE

A gas pipeline will entail much more than a right-of-way. It will be a major construction project across our northern territories, across a land that is cold and dark in winter, a land largely inaccessible by rail or road, where it will be necessary to construct wharves, warehouses, storage sites, airstrips—a huge infrastructure—just to build the pipeline. There will be a network of hundreds of miles of roads built over the snow and ice. Take the Arctic Gas project: the capacity of the fleet of tugs and barges on the Mackenzie River will have to be doubled. There will be 6,000 construction workers required North of 60 to build the pipeline, and 1,200 more to build gas plants and gathering systems in the Mackenzie Delta. There will be about 130 gravel mining operations. There will be 600 river and stream crossings. There will be innumerable aircraft, tractors, earth-movers, trucks and trailers. Indeed, the Arctic Gas project has been described as the greatest construction project, in terms of capital expenditure, ever contemplated by private enterprise.

ENGINEERING AND CONSTRUCTION

The gas pipeline across the North from Prudhoe Bay and from the Mackenzie Delta will confront designers and builders with major challenges of engineering and logistics. These relate not only to the size and complexity of the project but also to its remote setting, the arctic climate and terrain, and those components of the project and its design that are innovative or lack precedent.

The question of frost heave is basic to the engineering design of the gas pipeline. Arctic Gas proposes to bury its pipe throughout its length, and to refrigerate the gas to avoid the engineering and environmental problems resulting from thawing permafrost. But where unfrozen ground is encountered, in the zone of discontinuous permafrost or at river crossings, the chilled gas will freeze the ground around the pipe, and may produce frost heave and potential damage to the pipe.

The pipeline companies are obviously having trouble in designing their proposal to deal with frost heave. They are making fundamental changes in the methods proposed for heave control; the methods seem to be getting more complex, and the conditions for success more restrictive. It is likely that the companies will make yet further changes in their proposals, changes that are likely to increase costs and to alter substantially the environmental impact of the project.

Another issue is construction scheduling. The pipeline companies propose to construct the pipeline in winter. But we have limited experience of pipelining in far northern latitudes and in permafrost. There are uncertainties about scheduling, so far as logistics, the construction of snow roads, and productivity are concerned. In this respect, the greatest challenges will be encountered in the Northern Yukon, which is also the most environmentally sensitive area along the route. I am not persuaded that Arctic Gas can meet its construction schedule across the Northern Yukon. Should this occur, there is a likelihood of cost overruns, of construction being extended into the summer, or even of a permanent road being built to permit summer construction. The environmental impact of a change to summer construction would be very severe. The project would then have to be completely reassessed.

I recognize, of course, that the proposals of the pipeline companies are in a preliminary, conceptual stage, not in their final design stage. I recognize, too, that improvements will appear in the final design. But my responsibility is to assess the project proposals as they now stand.

Given the uncertainties relating to design and construction, illustrated by the foregoing comments on frost heave and scheduling, and given the bearing they have on environmental impact and the enforcement of environmental standards, it seems to me unreasonable that the Government of Canada should give unqualified approval to a right-of-way or provide financial guarantees to the project without a convincing resolution of these concerns.

THE NORTHERN ENVIRONMENT

There is a myth that terms and conditions that will protect the environment can be imposed, no matter how large a project is proposed. There is a feeling that, with enough studies and reports, and once enough evidence is accumulated, somehow all will be well. It is an assumption that implies the choice we intend to make. It is an assumption that does not hold in the North.

It is often thought that, because of the immense geographic area of the North, construction of a gas pipeline or establishment of a corridor could not cause major damage to the land, the water or the wildlife. But

within this vast area are tracts of land and water of limited size that are
vital to the survival of whole populations of certain species of mammals,
birds and fish at certain times of the year. Disturbance of such areas by
industrial activities can have adverse biological effects that go far beyond
the areas of impact. This concern with critical habitat and with critical
life stages lies at the heart of my consideration of environmental issues.

We should recognize that in the North, land use regulations, based on
the concept of multiple use, will not always protect environmental
values, and they will never fully protect wilderness values. Withdrawal of
land from any industrial use will be necessary in some instances to preserve wilderness, wildlife species and critical habitat.

THE NORTHERN YUKON

The Northern Yukon is an arctic and sub-arctic wilderness of incredible
beauty, a rich and varied ecosystem inhabited by thriving populations of
wildlife. The Porcupine caribou herd, comprising 110,000 animals or
more, ranges throughout the Northern Yukon and into Alaska. It is one
of the last great caribou herds in North America. The Yukon Coastal
Plain and the Old Crow Flats provide essential habitat for hundreds of
thousands of migratory waterfowl each summer and fall. This unique
ecosystem—the caribou, the birds, other wildlife, and the wilderness
itself—has survived until now because of the inaccessibility of the area.
But it is vulnerable to the kind of disturbance that industrial development would bring.

The Arctic Gas pipeline, to carry gas from Prudhoe Bay, Alaska, to
markets in the Lower 48, would cross this region, along the Coastal
Route. Once a gas pipeline is approved, exploration and development in
the promising oil and gas areas of Northern Alaska will accelerate, and it
is inevitable that the gas pipeline will be looped and that an oil pipeline,
a road and other developments will follow.

Gas pipeline and corridor development along the Coastal Route, passing through the restricted calving range of the Porcupine caribou herd,
would have highly adverse effects on the animals during the critical calving and post-calving phases of their life cycle. The preservation of the
herd is incompatible with the building of a gas pipeline and the establishment of an energy corridor through its calving grounds. If a pipeline
is built along the Coastal Plain, there will be serious losses to the herd.
With the establishment of the corridor I foresee that, within our lifetime,
this herd will be reduced to a remnant. Similarly, some of the large populations of migratory waterfowl and sea birds along the Coastal Route,
particularly the fall staging snow geese, would likely decline in the face of
pipeline and corridor development.

Thus, I have concluded that there are sound environmental reasons for not building a pipeline or establishing an energy corridor along the Coastal Route.

I recommend that no pipeline be built and no energy corridor be established across the Northern Yukon. Moreover, if we are to protect the wilderness, the caribou, birds and other wildlife, we must designate the Northern Yukon, north of the Porcupine River, as a National Wilderness Park. Oil and gas exploration, pipeline construction and industrial activity must be prohibited within the Park. The native people must continue to have the right to hunt, fish and trap within the Park. The Park must indeed be the means for protecting their renewable resource base.

You and your colleagues will have to consider whether Canada ought to provide a corridor across the Yukon for the delivery of Alaskan gas and oil to the Lower 48. I recommend that no such route be approved across the Northern Yukon. An alternate route has been proposed across the Southern Yukon, along the Alaska Highway. Some of the concerns about wildlife, wilderness, and engineering and construction that led me to reject the corridor across the Northern Yukon do not appear to apply in the case of the Alaska Highway Route. It is a route with an established infrastructure. In my view, the construction of a pipeline along this route would not threaten any substantial populations of any species in the Yukon or in Alaska. But I am in no position to endorse such a route: an assessment of social and economic impact must still be made, and native claims have not been settled.

THE MACKENZIE DELTA AND THE BEAUFORT SEA

The Mackenzie Delta and Beaufort Sea region supports a unique and vulnerable arctic ecosystem. Its wildlife has been a mainstay of the native people of the region for a long time, and still is today.

In my opinion, unlike the Northern Yukon, oil and gas development in the Mackenzie Delta–Beaufort Sea region is inevitable. Notwithstanding the disappointing level of discoveries so far, the Delta-Beaufort region has been rated by the Department of Energy, Mines and Resources as one of three frontier areas in Canada that potentially contain major undeveloped reserves of oil and gas.

A decision to build the pipeline now would act as a spur to oil and gas exploration and development in the Mackenzie Delta and the Beaufort Sea. Future discoveries will probably lead to offshore production. It is the impact of this whole range of oil and gas exploration and development activity that must concern us.

In order to protect the Delta ecosystem, the birds and the whales, I recommend that no corridor should cross the outer Delta. Also, strict limitations will have to be placed on other oil and gas facilities on the Delta, particularly the outer Delta. Special measures will be needed to avoid disturbance to fish populations within the Delta. I also propose that a bird sanctuary should extend across the outer part of the Delta to protect migratory waterfowl, giving the Canadian Wildlife Service jurisdiction to regulate industrial activity in the sanctuary.

The white whales of the Beaufort Sea—5,000 in number—come to the warm waters bordering the Mackenzie Delta each summer to have their young. To preserve this population from declining in the face of pipeline construction and the cumulative stresses imposed by ongoing oil and gas exploration, production and transportation, I recommend that a whale sanctuary be established in west Mackenzie Bay covering the principal calving area. If the herd is driven from its calving area, it will die out. Unlike the bird sanctuary, the whale sanctuary will be an area in which oil and gas exploration and development would be forbidden at any time of the year.

Much of the oil and gas potential of the region is believed to lie offshore beneath the Beaufort Sea. You and your colleagues have decided that the risk entailed in the Dome exploratory drilling program in the Beaufort Sea is acceptable, on the ground that it is in the national interest to begin delineating the extent of these reserves. I am not offering any opinion on that decision. I am, however, urging that, once the Dome program is completed, careful consideration be given to the timing and extent of the drilling and development that may take place thereafter. A proliferation of oil and gas exploration and development wells in the Beaufort Sea will pose an environmental risk of a different order of magnitude than the risk entailed in drilling 16 exploration wells to see if oil and gas are to be found there.

The matter is not, however, simply one of Canadian drilling activity in arctic waters. We have preceded all of the other circumpolar countries —the United States, the Soviet Union, Denmark and Norway—across this geographic and technological frontier. We are pioneering on this frontier and establishing the standards that may well guide other circumpolar countries in future arctic drilling and production programs.

The greatest concern in the Beaufort Sea is the threat of oil spills. In my opinion, the techniques presently available will not be successful in controlling or cleaning up a major spill in this remote area, particularly under conditions involving floating ice or rough water. Therefore, I urge the Government of Canada to ensure that improvements in technology for prevention of spills and development of effective technology for containment and clean-up of spills precede further advance of industry in the Beaufort Sea. I further urge that advances in knowledge of the environmental consequences of oil spills should likewise keep ahead of offshore development. Here I am referring not only to impacts on mammals, birds and fish in the Beaufort Sea area but also to the possibility that accumulation of oil in the Arctic Ocean could affect climate. In this I am referring to the possibility that oil spills from offshore petroleum development by all the circumpolar powers could diminish the albedo (the reflective capacity of ice), causing a decrease in the sea ice cover and hence changes in climate. Canada should propose that research be undertaken jointly by the circumpolar powers into the risks and consequences of oil and gas exploration, development and transportation activities around the Arctic Ocean.

THE MACKENZIE VALLEY

The Mackenzie Valley is a natural transportation route that has already seen several decades of industrial development. It is the longest river system in Canada, one of the ten longest rivers in the world, and one of the last great rivers that is not polluted.

I have concluded that it is feasible, from an environmental point of view, to build a pipeline and to establish an energy corridor along the Mackenzie Valley, running south from the Mackenzie Delta to the Alberta border. Unlike the Northern Yukon, no major wildlife populations would be threatened and no wilderness areas would be violated. I believe that we can devise terms and conditions that will allow a pipeline to be built and an energy corridor established along the Mackenzie Valley without significant losses to the populations of birds, furbearers, large mammals and fish. A pipeline along the Mackenzie Valley would impinge on the outer limits of the winter ranges of the Bluenose and the Bathurst caribou herds, but would not cross their calving grounds or disturb their main migration routes. These herds are not threatened.

However, to keep the environmental impacts of a pipeline to an acceptable level, its construction and operation should proceed only under careful planning and strict regulation. The corridor should be based on a comprehensive plan that takes into account the many land use conflicts apparent in the region even today.

Comprehensive land use planning in the Mackenzie Valley can emerge only from a settlement of native claims, but, on purely environmental grounds, there are several areas of land that warrant immediate protection. I recommend sanctuaries to protect migratory waterfowl and the already endangered falcons. These sites have been identified under the International Biological Programme, namely: the Campbell Hills–Dolomite Lake site, which is important to nesting falcons, and the Willow Lake and Mills Lake sites, which are of importance to migratory waterfowl.

NORTHERN SCIENCE
AND RESEARCH

Throughout the Inquiry, we found that there are critical gaps in the information available about the northern environment, about environmental impact, and about engineering design and construction on permafrost terrain and under arctic conditions. I have already referred to the inadequate state of knowledge about frost heave. This is a very practical question. Others, such as the albedo question, that seem to be less definite or to lie far in the future also demand our attention now. There is a whole range of issues that fall between, many of which are discussed in this report.

We are entering an era in the North when the government, its departments and agencies, will have to be in a position to assess—and to judge —the feasibility, desirability and impact of a whole series of proposals for northern oil and gas exploration and development. Industry proposes: government disposes. But for government to make an intelligent disposition of industry's proposals—whether they be for pipelining in permafrost, for drilling in the Beaufort Sea, for under the sea transportation systems, or for tankering in arctic waters—it must have an independent body of knowledge. A continuing and comprehensive program of northern science and research is called for.

CULTURAL IMPACT

It is, however, the people who live in the North that we ought to be most concerned about, especially the native people. Euro-Canadian society has refused to take native culture seriously. European institutions, values and use of land were seen as the basis of culture. Native institutions, values and language were rejected, ignored or misunderstood and— given the native people's use of land—the Europeans had no difficulty in supposing that native people possessed no real culture at all. Education was perceived as the most effective instrument of cultural change: so, educational systems were introduced that were intended to provide the native people with a useful and meaningful cultural inheritance, since their own ancestors had left them none.

The culture, values and traditions of the native people amount to a great deal more than crafts and carvings. Their respect for the wisdom of the elders, their concept of family responsibilities, their willingness to share, their special relationship with the land—all of these values persist today, although native people have been under almost unremitting pressure to abandon them.

Native society is not static. The things the native people have said to this Inquiry should not be regarded as a lament for a lost way of life, but as a plea for an opportunity to shape their own future, out of their own past. They are not seeking to entrench the past, but to build on it.

Today white and native populations in the Mackenzie Valley and Western Arctic are about equal in number. But it is the native people who constitute the permanent population of the North. There they were born, and there they will die. A large part of the white population consists of public servants, employees of the mining industry and of the oil and gas industry and their families. Most of them do not regard the North as their permanent home, and usually return to the South. There are, of course, white people in the North who have lived there all their lives, and some others who intend to make the North their permanent home, but their numbers are small in comparison to the native population.

So the future of the North ought not to be determined only by our own southern ideas of frontier development. It should also reflect the ideas of the people who call it their homeland.

ECONOMIC IMPACT

The pipeline companies see the pipeline as an unqualified gain to the North; northern businessmen perceive it as the impetus for growth and expansion. But all along, the construction of the pipeline has been justified mainly on the ground that it would provide jobs for thousands of native people.

We have been committed to the view that the economic future of the North lay in large-scale industrial development. We have generated, especially in northern business, an atmosphere of expectancy about industrial development. Although there has always been a native economy in the North, based on the bush and the barrens, we have for a decade or more followed policies by which it could only be weakened and depreciated. We have assumed that the native economy is moribund and that the native people should therefore be induced to enter industrial wage employment. But I have found that income in kind from hunting, fishing and trapping is a far more important element in the northern economy than we had thought.

The fact is that large-scale projects based on non-renewable resources have rarely provided permanent employment for any significant number of native people. There is abundant reason to doubt that a pipeline would provide meaningful and ongoing employment to many native people. The pipeline contractors and unions have made it plain that native northerners are not qualified to hold down skilled positions in pipeline construction, and that they will be employed largely in unskilled and semi-skilled jobs. Once the pipeline is built, only about 250 people will be needed to operate it. Most of these jobs are of a technical nature and will have to be filled by qualified personnel from the South.

I have no doubt that terms and conditions could be imposed that would enable northern businesses to expand during the construction of the pipeline. But there are hazards for northern businessmen. Construction of the Mackenzie Valley pipeline could produce a serious distortion of the small business sector of the Northwest Territories. This would raise problems for the orderly development of regional economic and commercial activity in the long run.

If communities in the Mackenzie Valley and Western Arctic are made to depend exclusively on industrial wage employment and if the production of country food for local consumption ceases to be an important component in the economy, then the self-employed will certainly become the unemployed. The point is simple enough: the extension of the industrial system creates unemployment as well as employment. In an industrial economy there is virtually no alternative to a livelihood based on wage employment. Those who are unable or unprepared to work for wages become unemployed and then dependent on welfare. To the extent that the development of the northern frontier undermines the possibilities of self-employment provided by hunting, fishing and trapping, employment and unemployment will go hand-in-hand.

I do not mean to suggest that native people will not want to participate in the opportunities for employment that industrial development will create. Some native people already work alongside workers from the South. Many native people have taken advantage of opportunities for wage employment—particularly in the Delta—on a seasonal basis to obtain the cash they need to equip or re-equip themselves for traditional pursuits. But when the native people are made to feel they have no choice other than the industrial system, when they have no control over entering it or leaving it, when wage labour becomes the strongest, the most compelling and finally the only option, then the disruptive effects of large-scale, rapid development can only proliferate.

It is an illusion to believe that the pipeline will solve the economic problems of the North. Its whole purpose is to deliver northern gas to homes and industries in the South. Indeed, rather than solving the North's economic problems, it may accentuate them.

The native people, both young and old, see clearly the short-term character of pipeline construction. They see the need to build an economic future for themselves on a surer foundation. The real economic problems in the North will be solved only when we accept the view the native people themselves expressed so often to the Inquiry: that is, the strengthening of the native economy. We must look at forms of economic development that really do accord with native values and preferences. If the kinds of things that native people now want are taken seriously, we must cease to regard large-scale industrial development as a panacea for the economic ills of the North.

SOCIAL IMPACT

I am convinced that the native people of the North told the Inquiry of their innermost concerns and their deepest fears. Although they had been told—and some indeed had agreed—that the proposed pipeline would offer them unprecedented opportunities for wage employment, the great majority of them expressed their fears of what a pipeline would bring: an influx of construction workers, more alcoholism, tearing of the social fabric, injury to the land, and the loss of their identity as a people. They said that wage employment on the pipeline would count for little or nothing when set against the social costs. I am persuaded that these fears are well-founded.

The alarming rise in the incidence of alcoholism, crime, violence and welfare dependence in the North in the last decade is closely bound up with the rapid extension of the industrial system and with its intrusion into every part of the native people's lives. The process affects the close link between native people and their past, their own economy, their values and self-respect. The evidence is clear: the more the industrial frontier displaces the homeland in the North, the greater the incidence of social pathology will be. Superimposed on problems that already exist in the Mackenzie Valley and the Western Arctic, the social consequences of the pipeline will not only be serious—they will be devastating.

The social costs of building a pipeline now will be enormous, and no remedial programs are likely to ameliorate them. The expenditure of money, the hiring of social workers, doctors, nurses, even police—these things will not begin to solve the problem. This will mean an advance of the industrial system to the frontier that will not be orderly and beneficial, but sudden, massive and overwhelming.

NATIVE CLAIMS

Native people desire a settlement of native claims before a pipeline is built. They do not want a settlement—in the tradition of the treaties—that will extinguish their rights to the land. They want a settlement that will entrench their rights to the land and that will lay the foundations of native self-determination under the Constitution of Canada.

The native people of the North now insist that the settlement of native claims must be seen as a fundamental re-ordering of their relationship with the rest of us. Their claims must be seen as the means to establishing a social contract based on a clear understanding that they are distinct peoples in history. They insist upon the right to determine their own future, to ensure their place, but not their assimilation, in Canadian life.

The federal government is now prepared to negotiate with the native people on a comprehensive basis, and the native people of the North are prepared to articulate their interests over a broad range of concerns. These concerns begin with the land, but are not limited to it: they include land and land use, renewable and non-renewable resources, schools, health and social services, public order and, overarching all of these, the future shape and composition of political institutions in the North.

The concept of native self-determination must be understood in the context of native claims. When the Dene refer to themselves as a nation, as many of them have, they are not renouncing Canada or Confederation. Rather, they are proclaiming that they are a distinct people, who share a common historical experience, a common set of values, and a common world view. They want their children and their children's children to be secure in that same knowledge of who they are and where they came from. They want their own experience, traditions and values to occupy an honourable place in the contemporary life of our country. Seen in this light, they say their claims will lead to the enhancement of Confederation—not to its renunciation.

It will·be for you and your colleagues, in negotiations with the native people, to determine the extent to which native claims can be acceded to, and to work out the way in which self-determination might be effected in the North, whether by the establishment of native institutions on a geographical basis or by the transfer of certain functions of the Government of Canada and the Government of the Northwest Territories to native institutions.

The idea of new institutions that give meaning to native self-determination should not frighten us. Special status for native people is an element of our constitutional tradition, one that is recognized by the *Constitution Act, 1867,* by the treaties, by the Indian Act, and by the statement of policy approved by Cabinet in July 1976. It is an ethnic thread in our constitutional fabric. In the past, special status has meant Indian reserves. Now the native people wish to substitute self-determination for enforced dependency.

The attainment of native goals implies one thing: the native people must be allowed a choice about their own future. If the pipeline is approved before a settlement of claims takes place, the future of the North —and the place of the native people in the North—will, in effect, have been decided for them.

The construction of the pipeline now will entail a commitment by the

Government of Canada and the Government of the Northwest Territories to a program of large-scale frontier development, which, once begun, cannot be diverted from its course. Once construction begins, the concentration on the non-renewable resource sector and the movement away from the renewable resource sector will become inexorable. The goal of strengthening the native economy will be frustrated.

An increase in the white population in the wake of pipeline construction will entrench southern patterns of political, social and industrial development, will reduce the native people to a minority position, and will undermine their claim to self-determination.

The settlement of native claims is not a mere transaction. Intrinsic to settlement is the establishment of new institutions and programs that will form the basis for native self-determination. It would be wrong, therefore, to think that signing a piece of paper would put the whole question behind us, as if all that were involved was the removal of a legal impediment to industrial development. The native people insist that the settlement of native claims should be a beginning rather than an end of the recognition of native rights and native aspirations. In my opinion, a period of ten years will be required in the Mackenzie Valley and Western Arctic to settle native claims, and to establish the new institutions and new programs that a settlement will entail. No pipeline should be built until these things have been achieved.

It would therefore be dishonest to try to impose an immediate settlement that we know now—and that the native people will know before the ink is dry—will not achieve their goals. They will soon realize—just as the native people on the prairies realized a century ago as the settlers poured in—that the actual course of events on the ground will deny the promises that appear on paper. The advance of the industrial system would determine the course of events, no matter what Parliament, the courts, this Inquiry or anyone else may say.

In recent years in the North we have witnessed a growing sense of native awareness and native identity. The same phenomenon can be observed throughout the country. It is not going to go away. To establish political institutions in the North that ignore this fact of life would be unwise and unjust. Special status can be—and ought to be—a constructive and creative means by which native people, through the development of institutions of their own, can thrive in a new partnership of interests.

IF THERE IS NO PIPELINE NOW

If the native people are to achieve their goals, no pipeline can be built now. Some will say this decision must mean that there will be no economic development in the North. If a pipeline is not built now, so the argument goes, the northern economy will come to a halt. But this view misconstrues the nature of the northern economy and northern development.

If there is no pipeline, the native economy based on hunting, fishing and trapping will scarcely be affected. The mining industry, which is the largest component of the private sector of the economy of both the Yukon Territory and the Northwest Territories, will not be greatly affected. Government, the largest employer and the main source of income for white northerners, and the federal and territorial bureaucracies are not likely to decrease in size simply because a pipeline is not built now.

A decision not to build a pipeline now would not necessarily bring an end to oil and gas exploration. There will be a setback to Inuvik and, to a lesser extent, to other Delta communities. If exploratory drilling in the Delta and the Beaufort Sea ought to continue in the national interest, the Government of Canada has the means to see that it does.

I am convinced that non-renewable resources need not necessarily be the sole basis of the northern economy in the future. We should not place absolute faith in any model of development requiring large-scale technology. The development of the whole renewable resource sector—including the strengthening of the native economy—would enable native people to enter the industrial system without becoming completely dependent on it.

An economy based on modernization of hunting, fishing and trapping, on efficient game and fisheries management, on small-scale enterprise, and on the orderly development of gas and oil resources over a period of years—this is no retreat into the past; rather, it is a rational program for northern development based on the ideals and aspirations of northern native peoples.

To develop a diversified economy will take time. It will be tedious, not glamorous, work. No quick and easy fortunes will be made. There will be failures. The economy will not necessarily attract the interest of the multinational corporations. It will be regarded by many as a step backward. But the evidence I have heard has led me to the conclusion that such a program is the only one that makes sense.

IMPLICATIONS

There should be no pipeline across the Northern Yukon. It would entail irreparable environmental losses of national and international importance. And a Mackenzie Valley pipeline should be postponed for ten years. If it were built now, it would bring limited economic benefits, its social impact would be devastating, and it would frustrate the goals of native claims. Postponement will allow sufficient time for native claims to be settled, and for new programs and new institutions to be established. This does not mean that we must renounce our northern gas and oil. But it does mean that we must allow sufficient time for an orderly, not hasty, program of exploration to determine the full extent of our oil and gas reserves in the Mackenzie Delta and the Beaufort Sea. Postponement will offer time for you and your colleagues to make a rational determination regarding the priorities to be adopted in relation to the exploitation of all our frontier oil and gas resources, at a time when the full extent of our frontier reserves has been ascertained.

I believe that, if you and your colleagues accept the recommendations I am making, we can build a Mackenzie Valley pipeline at a time of our own choosing, along a route of our own choice. With time, it may, after all, be possible to reconcile the urgent claims of northern native people with the future requirements of all Canadians for gas and oil.

Yours truly,

Thos R. Berger

I

THE NORTH

NORTHERN FRONTIER, NORTHERN HOMELAND

THIS INQUIRY WAS APPOINTED TO CONSIDER THE SOCIAL, ENVIRON-
mental and economic impact of a gas pipeline and an energy corridor
across our northern territories, across a land where four races of
people—Indian, Inuit, Metis and white—live, and where seven languages are spoken. The Inquiry was also empowered to recommend
terms and conditions that ought to be imposed to protect the people of
the North, their environment, and their economy, if the pipeline were to
be built.

Today, we realize more fully what was always implicit in the Inquiry's
mandate: this is not simply a debate about a gas pipeline and an energy
corridor, it is a debate about the future of the North and its peoples.

There are two distinct views of the North: one as frontier, the other
as homeland.

We look upon the North as our last frontier. It is natural for us to
think of developing it, of subduing the land and extracting its resources
to fuel Canada's industry and heat our homes. Our whole inclination is
to think of expanding our industrial machine to the limit of our country's
frontiers. In this view, the construction of a gas pipeline is seen as the
next advance in a series of frontier advances that have been intimately
bound up with Canadian history. But the native people say the North is
their homeland. They have lived there for thousands of years. They claim
it is their land, and they believe they have a right to say what its future
ought to be.

The question whether a pipeline shall be built has become the occasion for the joining of these issues.

In the past, Canada has been defined by its frontiers. In the words of Kenneth McNaught:

> From the time of the earliest records Canada has been part of a frontier, just as in her own growth she has fostered frontiers. The struggle of men and of metropolitan centres to extend and control those frontiers, as well as to improve life behind them, lies at the heart of Canadian history—and geography determined many of the conditions of that struggle. [*The Pelican History of Canada,* p. 7]

H. A. Innis insisted that it was Canadian geography and Canadian frontiers that made possible and defined the existence of the country. The nation's lines of transportation and communications were based on the St. Lawrence River, the Great Lakes and western waterways. French and British dependence on fish, fur, timber and wheat influenced the course of Canadian history, one staple after another drawing the nation from one frontier to the next. Innis refuted the notion that Canada's economy is simply a series of projections northward from the economic heartland of North America.

The French, the fur trade, British institutions—these have all played a part from the earliest times in the development of a separate community in the northern half of the continent. But it is a northern tradition that in large measure makes Canada distinct from the United States today. We share a mass culture with the United States, but it is Canada that has—and always has had—a distinct northern geography and a special concern with the North.

What happens in the North, moreover, will be of great importance to the future of our country; it will tell us what kind of a country Canada is; it will tell us what kind of a people we are. In the past, we have thought of the history of our country as a progression from one frontier to the next. Such, in the main, has been the story of white occupation and settlement of North America. But as the retreating frontier has been occupied and settled, the native people living there have become subservient, their lives moulded to the patterns of another culture.

We think of ourselves as a northern people. We may at last have begun to realize that we have something to learn from the people who for centuries have lived in the North, the people who never sought to alter their environment, but rather to live in harmony with it. This Inquiry has given all Canadians an opportunity to listen to the voices on the frontier.

In the past at each frontier we have encountered the native people. The St. Lawrence Valley was the homeland of the Huron and the Iroquois—they were overwhelmed; the West was the homeland of the Cree —they were displaced; the Pacific Coast was the homeland of the

Salish —they were dispossessed. Now, we are told that the North is the homeland of the Dene, the Inuit and the Metis. Today in the North we confront the questions that have confronted Canadians before— questions from which we must not now turn away.

Should the future of the North be determined by the South? The question can, of course, be answered by saying that since 1867 the Government of Canada has had responsibility for the welfare of the native people, and that since 1870 it has had jurisdiction over the Northwest. This is to say that Ottawa is sovereign, and has the power to dispose of the North as it wills. But the Government of Canada has not been satisfied to make such an answer, and has established this Inquiry to make it plain that the goals, aspirations and preferences of the northern peoples should be fully explored before any decision is taken.

The choice we make will decide whether the North is to be primarily a frontier for industry or a homeland for its peoples. We shall have the choice only once. Any attempt to beg the question that now faces us, to suggest that a choice has already been made or need never be made will be an inexcusable evasion of responsibility.

The issues we face are profound ones, going beyond the ideological conflicts that have occupied the world for so long, conflicts over who should run the industrial machine, and who should reap the benefits. Now we are being asked: How much energy does it take to run the industrial machine? Where must the energy come from? Where is the machine going? And what happens to the people who live in the path of the machine?

It may be that, in the national interest, the gas pipeline and the energy corridor should be built. It may be that they should not. But we owe to the peoples of the North, and to future generations, a careful consideration of the consequences before we go ahead with such projects. This report is an attempt to set out what those consequences will be.

THE NORTHERN BIOME

To most Canadians, "the North" is the immense hinterland of Canada that lies beyond the narrow southern strip of our country in which we live and work. Throughout this report, my view of the North is confined largely to Canada's northern territories—the Yukon Territory and the Northwest Territories—and my attention is addressed principally to that part of Canada, including the adjoining sea and islands, that lies to the north of the provinces of British Columbia and Alberta.

In the course of this Inquiry, I have travelled throughout this region. I have learned how remarkably different the land is in winter and in summer. I have seen the great differences between the forest and the tundra.

I have admired the vastness of the land, its variety, its beauty, and the abundance of its wildlife.

I have travelled throughout the Mackenzie Valley, and I have seen the great river in its varied moods. I have crossed the swampy and forested plains and the "great" lakes that extend eastward from the Valley to the edge of the Canadian Shield. I have seen the myriad lakes and ponds and the complex of river channels that form the Mackenzie Delta. I have flown over the Beaufort Sea—in winter covered by ice and snow, in summer by fields of ice floating in the blue water. I have seen the beaches, bars and islands of the Arctic coast, the pingos and lakes around Tuktoyaktuk, the rocky hills at Holman, and the clear rivers of the Yukon Coastal Plain.

On the Old Crow Flats, in the Mackenzie Delta, and along the Beaufort Sea coast I have seen the immense flocks of birds that migrate in their thousands to this arctic area each summer. I have seen the white whales swimming in the shallow coastal waters of the Beaufort Sea around the Mackenzie Delta. I have seen the Porcupine caribou herd in early summer at its calving grounds in the Northern Yukon, and the Bathurst herd at its wintering grounds north of Great Slave Lake. And in every native village I have seen the meat and fish, the fur and hides that the people have harvested from the land and water.

THE BOREAL FOREST AND THE TUNDRA

Biologists divide the North into two great regions called "biomes": the boreal forest and the tundra. The boreal forest is characterized in the minds of most people by spruce trees and muskeg. It is the broad band of coniferous forest that extends right across Canada from Newfoundland to Alaska. The tundra, extending from the boreal forest northward to the Arctic Ocean, comprises one-fifth of the land mass of Canada, but most of us who have never seen it, and know of it simply as a land without trees, sometimes call it "the barrens." Yet the tundra biome includes landscapes as varied and as beautiful as any in Canada—plains and mountains, hills and valleys, rivers, lakes and sea coasts. In winter, land and water merge into a white and grey desert, but the summer brings running water, explosively rapid plant growth, and a remarkable influx of migratory birds.

The two northern biomes—the tundra and the boreal forest—meet along the tree line. The tree line is not really a line, but a transitional zone that is commonly many miles in width. This biologically important boundary, which separates forest and tundra, also separates the traditional lands of the Indians and the Inuit. The tree line may also be viewed as the southern limit of the Arctic, the boundary between the Arctic and the sub-Arctic; this is the distinction I shall adopt in this report. Thus, the entire Mackenzie Valley and most of the Mackenzie Delta lie south of the tree line and are described as sub-arctic. In contrast, the land along the coast of the Beaufort Sea and the islands to the north lie beyond the tree line and are described as arctic.

I have learned from experience that, arctic or sub-arctic, this region is one of great climatic contrasts. In mid-summer, it is never dark, but in mid-winter the only daylight is a combined sunset and sunrise. Summer weather can be pleasantly warm, and in the Mackenzie Valley temperatures in excess of 80°F are not uncommon. But summer weather can also be raw and damp, particularly near the coast where a switch from an offshore to an onshore wind will cause temperatures to drop rapidly almost to freezing, accompanied by fog and drizzle.

Both rainfall and snowfall are light. In the Mackenzie Valley, the amount of precipitation is similar to that at Saskatoon or Regina, but in the true Arctic, including the lands bordering the Beaufort Sea, precipitation is as low as that in the driest parts of the Canadian prairies. For this reason, the Arctic may be described as desert and semi-desert, and it is remarkable, therefore, that the land surface in summer is predominantly wet and swampy, and dotted with innumerable shallow ponds. This apparent anomaly is caused, in large part, by permafrost, perennially frozen ground, which prevents water from draining downward into the ground. The seasonally thawed active layer of the soil holds the water from rain and melting snow like a sponge.

PERMAFROST

In much of Southern Canada, the ground freezes downward from the surface every winter and thaws completely again in the spring. But in the northern half of our country, in the sub-arctic and arctic regions, frost has penetrated below the maximum depth of summer thaw, and a layer of frozen ground persists beneath the surface from year to year. This perennially frozen ground, called permafrost, modifies the character of the landscape in the North and profoundly affects the works of man on and beneath the surface of the land.

In the southern part of the permafrost region, the perennially frozen layer beneath the seasonally thawed "active" layer is only a few feet thick and occurs as patches or islands surrounded by unfrozen ground. Northward, permafrost is more extensive, the layer of frozen ground becomes thicker, and areas of unfrozen ground are smaller and fewer. Farther north still, the permafrost is relatively continuous and may be several hundred to more than a thousand feet thick; but there are areas without permafrost beneath rivers and lakes. To describe the main differences in its distribution, we speak of the continuous and the discontinuous permafrost zones. The proposed pipeline route north of Fort Good Hope lies within the continuous permafrost zone, whereas the route south of Fort Good Hope to around the Alberta border lies in the discontinuous permafrost zone.

Permafrost also occurs offshore beneath the Beaufort Sea, but little is yet known about it there. We believe most of the undersea permafrost was formed on land and has since been inundated by a rising sea level and shoreline erosion.

All of this, of course, is not obvious, but has been learned through a great deal of study. But what is obvious in travelling in the North is the presence of surface features that accompany permafrost. In the discontinuous permafrost zone, there are peat mounds or palsas, speckled and string bogs, and drunken forests with trees tilted in various directions. Farther north, there are pingos, frost-crack patterns, exposed masses of ice, thermokarst depressions caused by the melting of underground ice, as well as characteristic slump features and other signs of thawing soil along the sea coast and river banks, and around lakes and ponds. In summer, there is the all-pervading wetness of the ground surface. In a region that, under warmer conditions, would be desert or semi-desert, ponds, swamps, fens and water-filled frost cracks all bear witness to the inability of water to drain downward through the frozen ground. Permafrost keeps the ground in the North moist, and it profoundly affects the vegetation, insects, birds and other forms of life.

Tundra has been described as land floating on ice. This conception aptly emphasizes the fact that frozen water within the ground gives the terrain unique qualities and creates problems for engineers. Thus, in the permafrost region, rock (which contains little water) is normally no different from rock in temperate regions, but the unconsolidated earth material—the soil—changes radically when the water in it freezes to form ice. The frozen soil will not absorb more water nor can water pass through it: water must therefore remain on the ground surface. Soil cemented together by ice is not easy to dig or to use in construction projects, because it has taken on rock-like properties. True, so long as it is frozen, it provides a solid foundation. But, not uncommonly, when frozen soil thaws, particularly if it is a fine-grained soil, it loses its strength: the soil may flow under its own weight, and the ground surface may subside as water escapes. In ice-rich soils, the effect may be compared with the melting of ice cream. This drastic change in properties occurs whenever the melting of ice in the soil releases more water than the soil can absorb. Such soil is described as containing excess ice.

Thawing of permafrost is only one cause of frost-induced engineering problems in the Arctic and sub-Arctic. Seasonal frost action in the active layer above the perennially frozen ground also causes problems. In winter, moisture in the active layer freezes, producing an upward displacement of the ground, called frost heave; in summer, there is a loss of bearing strength as the active layer thaws and the excess water is released. In some situations, engineering projects can lead to perennial freezing of areas where the ground is unfrozen or to the thickening of (existing) permafrost. When such changes take place in fine soil with abundant water, ice can build up and may cause frost heave. As we shall see later in this report, frost heave represents a serious problem for the proposed buried, chilled pipeline.

When roads, buildings or pipelines must be built where permafrost occurs, the engineers usually try to avoid disturbing the natural temperature regime in the ground. Disturbance of the ground surface is, therefore, kept to a minimum, particularly where peat or other organic material serves as a natural insulating blanket over the frozen ground. Frequently, where the thawing of permafrost would cause engineering or environmental difficulties, the structures are built above the ground on piles to permit air to circulate under them. The trans-Alaska oil pipeline is built on piles for this purpose. A common alternative is to place the structure on a pad of gravel, or of gravel plus insulation, thick enough to prevent heat from reaching the frozen ground. Compressor stations for the proposed Mackenzie Valley gas pipeline would be built on such pads. On the other hand, if a structure must disturb the ground or must be placed underground, then more complex techniques are required to avoid frost problems. The proposal to refrigerate the buried Mackenzie Valley gas pipeline is an example of such techniques.

THE NORTHERN ECOSYSTEM

I have heard hundreds of hours of evidence from experts and laymen alike on the nature of the northern environment. Soil scientists and geotechnical engineers have explained the environmental problems associated with permafrost. Experts on vegetation have described the flora and the measures that can be taken to reestablish plant cover on disturbed areas. Biologists, hunters, trappers and fishermen have told me about the northern animals and fishes—their life cycles, habitat requirements and susceptibilities to disturbance. Throughout all this evidence, I have heard detailed expressions of concern for the northern ecosystem and of the measures that might be used to preserve it in the face of industrial development.

To understand the impact of industrial development on the northern ecosystem and the appropriateness of mitigative measures, it is essential first to understand its general nature and the features that set it apart from more familiar ecosystems in the South. Merely to characterize the North as sensitive, vulnerable or even fragile will not help. Granted, certain species are sensitive: falcons, for example, cannot tolerate disturbances near their nesting sites. The massing of some species such as caribou, white whales and snow geese in certain areas at certain times will make whole populations of them vulnerable. And the response of permafrost to disturbance suggests that its very existence is fragile. But anyone who has visited the North during the long winters and the short mosquito-infested summers will know that northern species must be hardy to survive.

Every ecosystem is built on both living and non-living elements. The two are inextricably linked, and the characteristics of the one are reflected in those of the other. It is not surprising that the combinations of climate and topography in the northern biomes have produced plant and animal populations unique to the North. The relations within the northern ecosystems are not well understood, but at least three characteristics appear to distinguish them: the simplicity of the food chains, the wide oscillations in populations, and the slow growth rates. Dr. Max Dunbar, a marine biologist of international repute, provides an overview of these features in his book *Environment and Common Sense:*

> Arctic ecosystems are simple compared with those in temperate and tropical regions; that is to say, they consist of a comparatively small number of species. There are about 8,600 species of birds in the world; of these only some 56 breed in Greenland, and perhaps a little over 80 in Labrador-Ungava. Colombia, on the other hand, has 1,395, Venezuela 1,150. Of the 3,200 species of mammals known in the world, only 9 are found in the high Arctic, on land, and only 23 in the Cape Thompson area of Alaska. The world is full of fish; well over 23,000 are known. But only about 25 live in arctic waters. The same proportions, approximately, are shown in other groups of animals and plants.
>
> As an example of such simple systems: the lemmings (there are two species in the North, but with fairly separate distributions, so that they are seldom found together) form the herbivore link between the mosses and grasses (the primary producers) and the foxes, snowy owls, and weasels. Here we have only one dominant herbivore, three common predators, and a few species of plants: so far only four species of mammals and birds in any one region. In certain areas, add two more predators: the rough-legged hawk and the gyrfalcon; elsewhere, add caribou and ground squirrels, two other herbivores; here and there, a wolf. In more southerly regions of the North another fox, the red fox, is also found; and a few herbivorous and insectivorous birds, perhaps five species. This gives only 15 species of homotherms or warm-blooded animals, and it is rare to find all of them in one "system" or restricted region. To these must be added the invertebrates and the plants, but this is enough to show how simple the pattern is when compared with the variety of birds and mammals found together in temperate parklands, or, even more so, in the tropical rain forest. In arctic lakes the number of species is very small indeed, and in the sea the same general proportion of species numbers is maintained in

comparison with lower latitudes. Other similar examples could be given for coastal communities and for islands.

The cause of this simplicity is not the low temperatures themselves, contrary to common belief. Living organisms can adapt very easily to low temperatures as such; this is true not only of the warm-blooded forms but of the poikilotherms ("cold-blooded" species) as well. The limiting factor is the ability of the system to produce life in abundance. In the sea, at least, and in lakes, this means that the limiting factor is the supply of inorganic nutrients. . . . On land the limiting factors may be both this lack of nutrients and the long frozen winter when the food supply is very greatly, though not entirely, reduced. In either instance it is food supply rather than low temperature. . . .

One important result of the simplicity of arctic systems is that the component species oscillate in abundance over periods of time. In the example given above, the period of oscillation is controlled by the length of life and reproductive capacity of the lemming, and is maintained at from three to five years with quite remarkable regularity. These oscillations are severe in amplitude, so that they give rise frequently to what amounts to local extinction of species; the populations then have to be built up again by immigration from adjacent areas. The upsetting of this already rather shaky equilibrium by man's activity is probably very easy to do, and hence one must suppose that the North is more, rather than less, sensitive to pollutants and other environmental dislocations. This is the sort of thing upon which we need more precise information than we have at present, and which we need time to obtain.

One important ecological factor that may well be dependent both upon food supply and temperature is growth, the rate at which animals reach maturity. This is especially true of the poikilothermal animals and of plants. This means that damage done to populations of animals and plants takes a long time to repair. One may, for instance, come upon a remote lake full of arctic char, or lake trout, and thrill at the prospect of such excellent fishing. This has happened not infrequently in the North. After two years of fishing by Eskimos, or by visitors, the lake appears to be devoid of fish; the reproductive rate and the growth rate of the fish have not come near to making up for the fishing take, and it may in fact require a rest of many decades before the fish population is restored. The arctic char of the Sylvia Grinnell River, at Frobisher Bay in Baffin Island, take twelve years' growth in the female before ripe eggs are produced, and even then each female spawns only every second or third year. Small wonder that such resources are soon fished out and destroyed. . . .

The factors of population oscillation, then, and of slow growth rates, appear to give the northern ecosystems a quality of sensitivity, a knife-edge balance. A third factor is the simplicity of the system itself, for where so few species are involved the extinction of just one must be a serious matter. Yet one cannot at the moment be dogmatic on this point, because the situation has not been experimentally tested; we do not know how much stress the systems will bear and still survive. [p. 56ff.]

In the North, a certain number of species thrive. They are tough—they have to be to survive—but at the same time they are vulnerable. And in the North, man has the capability to cause irreparable injury to the environment.

Francis Bacon wrote, "Nature to be commanded must be obeyed." The northern environment requires us to obey its rules. Where necessary, we must establish and follow new approaches. That is why we must on this, our last frontier, proceed only with the most complete knowledge of and concern for the flora and fauna of the North, for the biomes of the forest and the tundra.

NORTHERN PEOPLES

The North is the homeland of a complex of indigenous cultures. We in the South may speak airily of "native people," and thereby convey the impression that there is a single culture, a single social system that occupies the vast arctic and sub-arctic terrain. But the term "native" is an inheritance from the European colonists, who usually regarded the original inhabitants of the lands they sought to subdue and settle, as a single group unified by "primitive" customs, and by their political relationship to the colonial powers themselves. In this way, the term "native" obscures essential differences between the cultures encountered in the course of European expansion.

The landscapes of the North have been shaped only marginally by the activities of man. The northern peoples have always been hunters and gatherers, and most have lived with a high degree of mobility. Small groups travelled over large areas, hunting and gathering what they needed, but without altering the environment itself. It is not always easy to remember, as one flies over the unbroken boreal forest, the tundra, or the sea ice, that the Canadian North has been inhabited for many thousands of years. The populations that have used this great area were never large by European standards, but their skills as travellers and hunters made it possible for them to occupy virtually all of the land. Extremely slow rates of northern plant growth and of decay mean that it is possible to see almost everywhere in the North signs of ancient occupation—old house remains, tent rings, fire-cracked rocks—and for archaeologists to find, on or close to the surface, a wealth of artifacts and other evidence to show the richness, diversity and wide extent of northern aboriginal society.

In the North, there are not just "native peoples," but a network of social systems. The Indians of the Mackenzie Valley and Western Arctic are part of the Athabascan language and culture group. They are separated into the Kutchin (or Loucheux), Hare, Slavey, Dogrib and Chipewyan. The Athabascan people are one of the most widely dispersed groups of Indians in North America. In addition to the Indians of the Northwest Territories and the Northern Yukon, they include the Koyukon and Tanana of Alaska, the Tutchone of the Southern Yukon, the Beaver and Carrier of British Columbia, the Navaho and Apache of the Southwest United States, and still others in California and Oregon. All these Indians, with whatever dialectical variation in their languages, regard themselves as *the people.* To the Slavey they are the *Dene,* to the Navaho *Dine;* in Kutchin the word is *Dindjie;* in Apache it is *Nde.* Today, in the North, the Indian people collectively call themselves the *Dene.*

The native peoples of the Western Arctic also include the Eskimos or, as they are now widely known, the Inuit; they occupy part of the Mackenzie Delta and the shores of the Beaufort Sea. Although all of the Inuit, from Siberia to eastern Greenland, speak closely related dialects of the same language, regionally there are differences in technology and social organization that even today complicate anthropological generalizations about them. Certainly the Inuit themselves perceive major differences between their various groups: the Inuvialuit of the Delta see themselves as distinct from the Copper Eskimos, who are their neighbours to the east; and the Copper Eskimos—or Qurdlurturmiut—emphasize that they are unlike the Netsilik, the Aivilik or the Igloolik people, who live still farther east. And, within each of these broad groups, there are yet finer divisions and distinctions that reflect different patterns of land use and are represented by changes in dialect and in hunting techniques.

This brief elaboration of social systems may seem to lie at the periphery of this Inquiry, but it indicates that the Dene and the Inuit—as well as the Metis, to whom I shall return—are distinct peoples in history. They have common interests in relation to the proposed Mackenzie Valley pipeline, and they therefore share many concerns. But the intensity of their feelings, no less than the vigour with which they are now expressing their hopes and fears, reflect historical and cultural depths that cannot be comprehended by the term "native." The North has become our frontier during the past few decades; it has been a homeland of the Dene and Inuit peoples for many thousands of years.

EARLIEST KNOWN MIGRATIONS

The last glaciation affected occupation of the arctic regions of North America in two ways. Covered by a vast ice-sheet, much of the area was

uninhabitable, but the lowered sea level exposed the continental shelf
and provided a land-bridge for migrants across what is now the Bering
Strait, and the interior of Alaska and parts of the Yukon remained free of
ice. The earliest of these migrations occurred probably between 25,000
and 30,000 years ago. Some of the people who crossed the land-bridge at
that time seem to have continued south, giving rise to many early Indian
cultures. A later migration from eastern Asia, perhaps 10,000 to 14,000
years ago, is believed to have taken place just before the final melting of
the ice-sheets. These were the ancestors of the Athabascan Indians, and
their later arrival is evidenced by their occupation of large blocks of land
in northwestern North America. Yet a third migration, around 5,000
years ago, is thought to have brought the predecessors of the Eskimo
peoples to the New World.

The people of the Thule culture, famous for their skills as whale hunters, are probably the descendants of these earlier Palaeo-Eskimo people.
About a thousand years ago, they spread throughout the Arctic, displac-
ing the Dorset culture, which had developed in Northern Canada in
about 1,000 B.C. Superbly equipped for life on the barrens and on the
sea ice, the range of the Thule people in what is now Canada eventually
included all the coastal areas, practically all of the islands of the Arctic
Archipelago, and reached as far east as the Gulf of St. Lawrence and
Newfoundland. The Inuit of today are their direct descendants.

It must, of course, be recognized that all models of early Arctic
occupation remain speculative, and that the full historical extent of occupation of Northern Canada is only beginning to be documented. As archaeological work advances, however, so we will more and more realize
the cultural heritage of which the Inuit and Dene are a part. But it is
already evident that Indians were established in the forestlands of Western and Northern Canada, and Palaeo-Eskimos inhabited the northern
rim of the "New World" some 5,000 years before Alexander Mackenzie
reached the Arctic coast.

DISTINCTIVE MATERIAL
AND INTELLECTUAL CULTURES

The specialized skills and knowledge of the Dene and Inuit corre-
sponded, of course, to the different terrains that each people has so long
inhabited. The dog team, for example, was the principal means of travel,
although the sledge styles and hitches varied regionally. The relationship
between these variations and the kinds of terrain in which they were
used can be illustrated by a comparison between the fan-hitch of the Inuit of the Central and Eastern Arctic and the tandem- or line-hitch used
by the Dene and the Inuit of the Western Arctic. The former was ideal

for travel on rough ice and the barrens; the latter was suited for travel over snowy lakes and through trees. The range of each broadly corresponds to the two kinds of landscape.

Both Inuit and Dene societies used caribou skin for clothing. The density of the fur and the fact that the hairs are hollow make the skin both light and extremely effective insulation, so it is ideal for arctic garments. Despite many conventions of style and varieties of sewing, differences that have given each group or society its distinctive clothing, both the Dene and Inuit regarded the caribou as their most important source of winter clothing.

Inuit and Dene cultures are not merely a response to environmental conditions. Each society, armed with its own skills and perceptions, found and used the North in its own distinctive way. One example of a distinctive and essential element of material culture is the Inuit harpoon. This brilliantly successful device, with its detachable head and turning blade, is found throughout Inuit territory, and it evidently came with them from Asia.

The Inuit and Dene also speak different languages. Some thousands of years separate their ancestors' departures from Asia, and it is not surprising, therefore, that the Eskimoan and Athabascan languages have no more in common than do English and Hungarian. Indeed, the linguistic contact between them even today is so limited that virtually no words have been borrowed from one by the other, despite the fact that the hunting grounds of some Athabascan groups overlapped with those of some Inuit. Because there are no longer any Asiatic peoples (with the exception of some 1,500 Siberian Inuit, who represent a back-migration across the Bering Strait), who speak versions of either of the two language families, it is not possible to establish a link between the two even in ancient times.

The various Athabascan languages spoken in Northern Canada bear the same kind of relation to one another that exists among the Romance languages of Europe. The structure of Athabascan grammer is noted for its use of prefixes, and its vocabulary is finely tuned to descriptions of the environment. Moreover, the nature of its word-forming system equips it well for the task of inventing new terms.

The Inuit language is agglutinative and very regular. Each word-like expression is composed of several items, and a word can be as intricate as a whole sentence in English. This agglutination is found in all of the Inuit dialects and, although the dialects most remote from one another are not readily mutually intelligible, the single language, with comparatively minor variations, reaches from Siberia to eastern Greenland—a spread of some 5,000 miles.

The specialized material and intellectual culture of the Inuit and the Dene obviously cannot be elaborated in this report, but I wish to emphasize that each of these peoples had its own way of hunting, of making clothes, of raising children, of dealing with one another, and of regarding the environment and the spiritual powers they saw as integral to their world. Their knowledge of the land and its life constitute distinctive ethno-scientific traditions.

THE METIS

During the past 150 years, the Metis have joined the Dene and Inuit of the Mackenzie Valley as one of the groups now included in the category of "northern native people." The first Metis who moved into the North in the early 19th century settled around Great Slave Lake, and they trace their ancestry to the unions between *coureurs de bois* and Indian women in the early days of the fur trade. Richard Slobodin, in *Metis of the Mackenzie District,* has described their heritage:

> The Metis nationality or ethnic group . . . evolved in Quebec and Ontario during a period from the late 17th to the early 19th centuries, through the activities of *coureurs de bois* and other fur trade functionaries who, with their offspring by Indian women, developed a way of life partly Indian, partly marginal European, but in time distinct from both. . . . On the prairies and the high plains, the Metis way of life underwent a further ecological adaptation. It was here, among Metis centering on the Red and Saskatchewan River Valleys, that consciousness of kind was heightened to the level of incipient nationality, a tendency culminating in the declaration of Metis nationhood and the consequent insurrections of 1870 and 1885. [p. 12]

In the aftermath of the Northwest Rebellion of 1885, many Metis moved North and settled in what is now the Northwest Territories.

Other Metis are the descendants of unions between Hudson's Bay Company men—mainly of Scottish origin—and Dene women. The children of these unions usually intermarried with the original Dene inhabitants, so that in most native communities in the North there are close family ties between the Metis and the Dene.

The Metis culture has been patterned after that of the Dene. In *Our Metis Heritage . . . A Portrayal,* produced by the Metis Association of the Northwest Territories, we are given this account of the location of the Metis between the Dene and white worlds:

> For most Metis families in the present Northwest Territories, it would appear that the woman passed on to her children all that she knew of her own culture, which was the Indian culture, and the man's influence

though significant, played a secondary role in the emergent Metis way of life. This may account in part for the fact that the Metis lifestyle was very closely patterned after the Indian.

The Metis were equipped with survival mechanisms to operate in both worlds; they could hunt, trap and live off the land like their Indian ancestors, or they could take advantage of their white ancestors' technology through education.

Although the N.W.T. Metis seem to have chosen to maintain the traditional relationship with the Indian, they have creatively succeeded in building and sustaining a unique way of life. [p. 95]

Discussion of the Metis brings us to changes that have occurred in recent times. These are matters to which I shall return, and they need not be more than adumbrated here. I have tried to indicate the depth and richness of aboriginal cultures; I urge that we not lose sight of their historical reality, their values, and their right to command our respect. The North has been a homeland to the native people for thousands of years; it has been a frontier only since the fur trade, and a major oil and gas frontier only since the 1960s.

II

ENGINEERING

AND CONSTRUCTION

TRANSPORTATION AND CONSTRUCTION
IN THE NORTHWEST

THE EARLY YEARS Fur-traders of the Montreal-based North
West Company followed the water routes explored by the French to the
western plains, then extended them north to Lake Athabasca, where
they built Fort Chipewyan in 1788. A year later, Alexander Mackenzie
set out across Great Slave Lake and down the long northern river that
now bears his name. It proved to extend just over a thousand miles
through rich new fur territory, and soon the North West Company had
established trading posts along its banks at Trout River in 1796, and at
sites near the present settlements of Fort Simpson, Fort Norman and
Fort Good Hope in the following decade.

In the last century, the traders travelled by York boat from Methy
Portage to the 16-mile stretch of rapids on Slave River above present-day
Fort Smith, around which they had to portage. (This river route was
shortened by the extension of rail from Edmonton to Waterways early in
this century, and York boats were replaced by steamboats.) They then
continued down the Slave River to Fort Resolution, across Great Slave
Lake to the head of the Mackenzie, and down the Mackenzie as far as the
Delta. Today, the Mackenzie River is still the principal means of trans-
porting supplies to settlements along the Mackenzie Valley and in the
Western Arctic. And it is this fleet of tugs and barges on the Mackenzie
River that will have to be expanded to carry the equipment, material and
supplies for the proposed pipeline.

In 1888, a Select Committee of the Senate was appointed "to inquire
into the resources of the Great Mackenzie Basin and the country eastward to Hudson's Bay," but Northern Canada first came to international

notice in the late 1890s, when gold was discovered in the Yukon Territory. An estimated 100,000 men and women sought the gold fields, and almost overnight Dawson City became the largest city in Canada west of Winnipeg, with a population of over 30,000.

The city was built on difficult permafrost soils. Most of its early foundations were simple mud sills of local timbers laid in gravel or sand and levelled with the same material. Wood was the primary building material for the banks, post office, hotels and dance halls and the many homes that were built. The city acquired such urban services as running water, electric lighting and telephones. On the gold fields themselves, the Yukon Gold Company built a 70-mile ditch system to provide water for a large-scale dredging operation on the Klondike River and its tributaries. This project, which included 13 miles of 42- to 54-inch-diameter wood-stave and steel pipe, was a remarkable engineering feat on an isolated frontier.

The 1920s witnessed the development of the petroleum reserves at Norman Wells. Mackenzie himself had reported oil seepages on the river bank, but it was only in 1914 that a geologist, T. O. Bosworth, staked three claims near these seepages. Imperial Oil acquired these claims in 1919, and by 1924 six wells had been drilled, three of which were producers. A small refinery was built, but the market was so small that in the same year the wells were capped and the refinery shut down. During the development of the petroleum reserves at Norman Wells, the detrimental results of thawing perennially frozen water-bearing silts and clays soon made themselves evident, and experimentation began with the installation of foundation on gravel pads.

In the early 1930s, after rich mineral deposits had been discovered at Yellowknife and at Port Radium on Great Bear Lake, the refinery at Norman Wells was reopened to supply gasoline and fuel oil for riverboats and mine machinery. Between 1937 and 1972, heavy fuel oil was barged from Norman Wells to the rapids on Great Bear River, transported by a 2-inch 8.5-mile pipeline around the rapids, then barged the remainder of the way to the Eldorado uranium mine on Great Bear Lake.

DEFENCE PROJECTS DURING AND AFTER THE SECOND WORLD WAR During the Second World War the United States Army undertook two major construction projects in the Canadian North: the Northwest Staging Route and an associated highway, now called the Alaska Highway; and the Canol Project to transport men, materials, equipment and oil to defend Alaska against the Japanese.

The Alaska Highway connected Dawson Creek, B.C., to Fairbanks, Alaska, following the Northwest Staging Route airports at Fort St. John and Fort Nelson, B.C., Watson Lake and Whitehorse, Y.T., and Big

Delta, Alaska. The construction began in March 1942, and it involved a force that totalled some 11,000 officers and men over the construction period. By the end of October 1942, a passable pioneer road, 1,428 miles long and 26 feet wide, linked Dawson Creek to Big Delta. Permafrost conditions were ignored during construction, which resulted in road failures and severe icings at many locations. During most of 1943, 81 contractors under the United States Public Roads Administration worked on an all-weather gravel road with a civilian force that totalled some 15,950 men over the construction period. The total cost of the project was $147 million. When the war ended, the United States handed over the Canadian section of the Alaska Highway to Canada.

In 1942, also, the United States Army undertook the Canol project to transport oil from Norman Wells across the Mackenzie Mountains to Whitehorse. The oil was to be refined there, then delivered to Alaska to aid the war effort. The labour force over the construction period of the pipeline involved 2,500 military personnel and approximately 22,550 civilians. A pioneer road preceded pipelaying and the building of pumping stations. Except at its southern end, the road was laid entirely over permafrost. The road performed satisfactorily during its short period of use, April 1944 to May 1945, except for icings on some stretches. The pipeline, consisting of 100 miles of 6-inch pipe and 500 miles of 4-inch pipe, was laid on the ground beside the road, and pumping stations were spaced about 50 miles apart. This project was completed in 1944 and cost $134 million. Very little oil reached Whitehorse by the pipeline, and when the war ended, the Canol road was closed and the pipeline dismantled.

Between 1955 and 1957, Canada and the United States built the Distant Early Warning Line (DEW Line), a chain of radar stations intended to detect foreign aircraft in polar regions and to relay the warning to North American Air Defence Command units. The line stretches 5,000 miles along the Arctic coast from Point Barrow, Alaska, to Cape Dyer, Baffin Island. The construction of the DEW Line involved airlifting a total of about 25,000 men and one-half million tons of equipment by commercial aircraft. Approximately 45,000 flights averaging 720 miles each were made.

POST-WAR PERIOD   In 1954, construction began on Inuvik, a new regional administrative centre for the Western Arctic at a site on the east side of the Mackenzie Delta. All major buildings, including serviced housing, are elevated on piles. The air space between the buildings and the ground dissipates heat losses from the buildings, thus reducing the possibility of permafrost degradation and associated shifting of foundations. These buildings have performed satisfactorily; only a few of the

14,000 piles installed have shown any significant movement owing to thaw settlement.

Other new towns have been built farther south, but they did not encounter the same formidable permafrost problems. In the 1960s, Cominco's development of the rich lead-zinc deposits on the south shore of Great Slave Lake led to the construction of a large mill and the associated mining town of Pine Point. Edzo, another new town, was built at the head of the North Arm of Great Slave Lake in 1971. At Yellowknife and Hay River, there are suburbs and high-rises that would have been difficult to imagine in such settings only a few years ago. The development of the Northern Transportation Company Limited (NTCL) drydock and trans-shipment facilities at Hay River is representative of the recent growth in transportation.

TRANSPORTATION Barge and boat transportation on the Athabasca, Slave and Mackenzie Rivers has served the transportation needs of the Northwest for more than a century. Today, water transport northward from Hay River continues to be important, particularly for construction materials, heavy equipment and fuels. Although freight traffic on the Mackenzie River has had intermittent periods of rapid growth, its long-term annual growth rate is about nine percent. This growth peaked in 1972 at 477,000 tons; since then annual traffic has averaged around 400,000 tons.

Northern Transportation Company Limited, a crown corporation, is the largest common carrier in the Mackenzie River system, and it also serves the Arctic coast from Alaska to Spence Bay. KAPS Transport Limited, the second largest operator, is licensed to transport goods to and from exploration and drilling sites, and building and construction sites in the Mackenzie watershed.

In recent years, there have also been major air, rail and road developments in the Western Arctic. Northern air services began in the region in 1920, with float-equipped aircraft. During and shortly after the Second World War, airfields were built at several settlements on Great Slave Lake and along the Mackenzie River, including Hay River, Yellowknife, Fort Resolution, Fort Providence, Fort Simpson and Norman Wells, and both scheduled and charter flights in the Western Arctic increased steadily.

Today, there is air service to all of the Mackenzie River settlements, although its frequency varies. Pacific Western Airlines, the largest carrier operating in the Northwest Territories, has the most extensive network of routes; and chartered aircraft serve the smaller and remoter settlements. These carriers, commercial and private, are essential to the communities in the Mackenzie Valley and the Western Arctic, the territorial and federal governments, tourist lodges, and construction companies, and they play a vital role in the activities related to oil and gas exploration.

The Great Slave Lake Railway, built in the early 1960s, extends from Grimshaw, Alberta, to Hay River, Northwest Territories. The railway, which closely parallels the Mackenzie Highway, was constructed primarily to ship concentrates from Cominco's mine at Pine Point, to which it is connected by a branch line. Heavy goods are shipped by rail to Hay River, then trans-shipped to barges for the voyage down the Mackenzie River.

The Mackenzie Highway between Grimshaw and Hay River was built between 1946 and 1948. In 1960, as part of the federal Roads to Resources program, it was extended 280 miles around the north end of Great Slave Lake to Yellowknife; in 1970, the highway reached Fort Simpson, and it is planned to reach Wrigley by 1979. There has been road construction between Arctic Red River and Inuvik, but it is not complete.

A second major highway project, the Dempster Highway, was begun in 1959 and is scheduled for completion in the late 1970s. It will link Dawson City to Inuvik and will connect with the Mackenzie Highway.

Recent gas and oil exploration activity in the Mackenzie Valley and Western Arctic used existing transportation systems in the region, which has helped these systems to expand to their present capacities. The nature and level of future petroleum development will clearly have an important influence on the future development of these transportation systems. Implementation of the pipeline proposal will involve major expansion in existing transportation capabilities.

THE PIPELINE PROJECT: ITS SCOPE AND SCALE

The pipeline that Canadian Arctic Gas Pipeline Limited proposes to build presents quite novel problems of science, engineering and logistics. The pipeline will be very long, and will carry enormous volumes of gas. But these are not unique characteristics: what makes the pipeline unique from an engineering point of view is that it will be buried in ice-rich, permanently frozen soil—permafrost—and the gas transported in the pipe will be refrigerated. The pipeline is to be built across our northern territories, a land that is cold and dark throughout the long winter, a land that is at present largely inaccessible by road or rail, and through which a large infrastructure of roads, wharves, airstrips and other work sites must be built. The pipeline's impact will not, therefore, be confined to its right-of-way.

UNIQUE ASPECTS OF THE PROJECT

The pipeline that Arctic Gas proposes to build would be longer than any pipeline in the world: it is 2,400 miles from Prudhoe Bay to the Lower 48. Pipelines have, of course, been built over great distances in the past. The 31-inch trans-Arabian pipeline (now abandoned) from Abaiq Field in Arabia to Sidon in Lebanon is 1,047 miles long; the 36-inch Colonial pipeline from Houston to New Jersey is 1,531 miles long. And pipelines have been built and are being built today across difficult terrain and in northern latitudes. The trans-Andean pipeline crosses one of the most rugged mountain ranges in the world, and the trans-Alaska pipeline crosses three mountain ranges. Some of the biggest pipelines in the world have been built in Siberia, and both these and the trans-Alpine pipelines were constructed in severe climatic conditions. But there is not a great deal we can learn from the experience of the Soviet Union, the United States and other nations that is directly relevant to the design and operation of a buried refrigerated pipeline.

Normally, gas flows through a pipeline at temperatures above freezing. Compressors drive the gas through the pipe, and the process of compressing gas makes it hot. If the pipeline is buried in permafrost, heat from the gas will thaw the ground around the pipe. Such thawing could lead to severe and costly engineering and environmental problems where the soil contains any appreciable quantity of ice. Problems arising from progressive sinking of the ground, blocking of drainage, erosion or slope failure could damage or rupture the pipe. To avoid these problems, Arctic Gas proposes to chill the gas passing through the pipeline so there will be no heat loss to melt the permafrost. Chillers will, therefore, be needed to extract the heat generated by compression before the gas goes into the pipeline and through the permafrost.

A pipeline running south from the Mackenzie Delta along the Mackenzie Valley must cross about 250 miles of continuous and about 550 miles of discontinuous permafrost. It cannot avoid long stretches of ice-rich soil in both zones of permafrost. A pipeline across the Northern Yukon would lie entirely within the zone of continuous permafrost. Thus, the Arctic Gas proposal cannot avoid the problem. Arctic Gas must either refrigerate a pipeline through the permafrost or, at much greater cost, lay a pipeline on the ground or elevated above it. Now, if a chilled and buried pipeline passes through ground that is not frozen, it will freeze the ground around it. This change may lead to a build-up of ice in the ground around the pipe and may cause the pipe to move upward. This is known as frost heave.

MAGNITUDE OF THE PROJECT

A pipeline through the Canadian North has been likened to a string across a football field. This simile is misleading and is indicative of a utopian view of pipeline construction. Of course, the area required for the right-of-way, compressor stations, and ancillary facilities is miniscule when measured against the great mass of the Canadian North. Although Arctic Gas proposes to lay 1,100 miles of pipeline across the Yukon and Northwest Territories, its total land requirement for the right-of-way and related facilities is only about 40 square miles. Such a figure gives a mistaken impression of the magnitude of the construction project. It is not just a 120-foot right-of-way.

The estimated cost of the Arctic Gas project within Canada now stands at about $8 billion. A network of roads largely of snow and ice must be built. The capacity of the fleet of tugs and barges on the Mackenzie River must be greatly increased. Nine construction spreads and 6,000 construction workers will be required North of 60 to build the pipeline. Imperial, Gulf and Shell will need 1,200 more workers to build the gas plants and gas gathering systems in the Mackenzie Delta. There will be about 130 gravel mining and borrow operations, and about 600 water crossings. There will be about 700 crawler tractors, 400 earth movers, 350 tractor trucks, 350 trailers and 1,500 trucks. There will be almost one million tons of pipe. There will be aircraft, helicopters, and airstrips. Arctic Gas proposes to use about 20 wharf sites; and plans to build about 15 STOL airstrips of 2,900 feet each and five airstrips of 6,000 feet each. Carson Templeton, Chairman of the Environment Protection Board, has likened the building of a pipeline in the North in winter to the logistics of landing the Allied forces on the beaches of Normandy. The pipeline's effects will be felt far beyond the area of land across which it is built.

THE NORTHERN ENVIRONMENT

ENVIRONMENTAL ATTITUDES AND ENVIRONMENTAL VALUES

THE HISTORY OF NORTH AMERICA IS THE HISTORY OF THE FRON-
tier: of pushing back the wilderness, cultivating the soil, populating the
land, and then building an industrial way of life. The conquest of the
frontier in North America is a remarkable episode in human history, and
it altered the face of the continent. The achievement was prodigious, and
there is no need here to tell how transportation networks were evolved,
cities founded, industries established, commerce expanded, and unpar-
alleled agricultural productivity developed. The superabundance of land
and resources gave rise to a conviction that the continent's resources
were inexhaustible. Land on the eastern seaboard was abandoned almost
as rapidly as it had been cleared. Thomas Jefferson wrote, "We can buy
an acre of new land cheaper than we can manure an old one."

Cultivation of agriculturally unsuitable soils left a legacy of abandoned
farms, rural poverty, ruined landscapes and silt-choked streams. Soil erosion and pollution by countless sources of domestic and industrial wastes
choked many of our rivers, reducing a once bountiful fishery. The buffalo herds, estimated to number about 75 million, were reduced in only a
few decades to a few hundred survivors. The prairies were ploughed and
overgrazed, setting the stage for the disastrous dust-bowl conditions of
this century. In *Democracy in America,* Alexis de Tocqueville wrote of
the United States he visited in 1831:

The Americans themselves never think about [the wilds], they are in-
sensible to the wonders of inanimate nature . . . their eyes are fixed upon

another sight, [they] march across these wilds, draining swamps, turning the course of rivers, peopling solitudes, and subduing nature. [p. 47]

We should recognize the links between attitudes to environment and attitudes to native peoples. The assault upon the environment was also an assault on their way of life. To be sure, it was often an assault carried out under the banners of benevolence and enlightened progress, but it was nonetheless an assault. The native peoples and their land were, and to some extent continue to be, under siege.

We have observed the passage of the white man from the eastern seaboard of North America into the great plains and yet farther west. He has penetrated the North, but his occupation of the North is not yet complete. There are those with an abiding faith in technology, who believe that technology can overcome all environmental problems. They believe there is no point at which the imperatives of industrial development cannot be reconciled with environmental values. But there are others who believe that industrial development must be slowed or halted if we are to preserve the environment.

Different views of the North can be distinguished by the emphasis placed either on the achievement of industrial development at the frontier or on its cost. A particular idea of progress is firmly embedded in our economic system and in the national consciousness; but there is also in Canada a strong identification with the values of the wilderness and of the land itself. No account of environmental attitudes would be complete that did not recognize this deeply felt, and perhaps deeply Canadian, concern with the environment for its own sake. The judgment of this Inquiry must, therefore, recognize at least two sets of powerful, historically entrenched—but conflicting—attitudes and values.

In recent years, we have seen the growth of ecological awareness, and a growing concern for wilderness, wildlife resources and environmental legislation that parallels—although it does not match—the increasing power of our technology, the consumption of natural resources, and the impacts of rapid change. There are situations in which the two sets of attitudes and values simply cannot be reconciled. The question then turns on the depth of our commitment to environmental values when they stand in the way of technological and industrial advance.

This opposition of views is particularly clear in the North. The northern native people, along with many other witnesses at the Inquiry, insisted that the land they have long depended upon will be injured by the construction of a pipeline and the establishment of an energy corridor. Environmentalists pointed out that the North, the last great wilderness area of Canada, is slow to recover from environmental degradation; its protection against penetration by industry is, therefore, of vital importance to all Canadians. It is not easy to measure that concern against the more precisely calculated interests of industry. But we must accept the reality of this opposition, and we must try and face the questions that are posed in the North of today: Should we open up the North as we opened up the West? Should the values that conditioned our attitudes toward the environment in the past prevail in the North today and tomorrow? Perhaps we can see the force of, and even some answers to, these questions by examining the concept, as it has developed, of preserving the wilderness on this continent.

WILDERNESS

Wilderness is a non-renewable resource. If we are to preserve wilderness areas in the North, we must do so now. The available areas will diminish with each new industrial development on the frontier. We have not yet in Canada developed a legislative framework for the protection of wilderness, but a model exists in the United States.

A century ago, for the first time in history, a tract of land in its natural state was set aside for its own sake, for its intrinsic values, not for the resources it might later provide. That was Yellowstone National Park, and it marked the beginning of the national park system. This idea of preserving unexploited and superb examples of nature was adopted within 15 years in Canada, and it rapidly spread to other nations.

Initially, Canadian and American parks seemed to be designated to preserve natural geological features found in magnificent settings, such as geysers (Yellowstone, 1872) and hot springs (Banff, 1885). In a few years, concern for the giant trees of the Sierra Nevada led to the establishment of Sequoia National Park, and plant life came to be regarded as a valuable component of land in its natural state. Then wildlife was accorded recognition. The idea of preserving wilderness itself continued to develop, culminating in the passage by the United States in 1964 of the Wilderness Act. This Act, in defining wilderness, called it a place:

> where the earth and its community of life are untrammeled by man, where man himself is a visitor who does not remain. [p. 1]

I rely here on American experience because I see no difference between the United States and Canada in the perception of environmental values. I have heard witnesses from Alaska and the Lower 48. What they said about wildlife and wilderness did not distinguish them from Canadians, but rather reinforced my impressions of the values that Canadian society now embraces.

Let me be clear about the importance that is hereby accorded to wilderness. No one seeks to turn back the clock, to return in some way to nature, or even to deplore, in a high-minded and sentimental manner, the real achievements of modern-day life. Rather, the suggestion here is that wilderness constitutes an important—perhaps an invaluable—part of modern-day life; its preservation is a contribution to, not a repudiation of, the civilization upon which we depend.

Wallace Stegner wrote in 1960:

> Without any remaining wilderness we are committed . . . to a headlong drive into our technological termite-life, the Brave New World of a completely man-controlled environment. . . . We simply need that wild country . . . [as] part of the geography of hope. [cited in W. Schwartz, *Voices for the Wilderness,* p. 284ff.]

The difficulty in describing the importance of wilderness is that you cannot attach a dollar value to it or to its use and enjoyment, any more than you can to the rare and endangered species, or to archaeological finds. The value of wilderness cannot be weighed in the scale of market values. It is a national heritage. Many who sense change everywhere, recognize that our northern wilderness is irreplaceable.

Sigurd F. Olson, an American naturalist, writing of the Canadian North in *The Lonely Land,* said:

> There are few places left on the North American continent where men can still see the country as it was before Europeans came and know some of the challenges and freedoms of those who saw it first, but in the Canadian Northwest it can still be done. [p. 5]

Wilderness implies to all of us a remote landscape and the presence of wildlife. I think there are three kinds of wilderness species. The first are species that, because of their intolerance of man or their need for large areas of land, can survive only in the wilderness. Such are caribou, wolf and grizzly bear. These species require large areas of wilderness to protect the integrity of their populations and preserve their habitat. Second are the species that conjure up visions of wilderness for every Canadian, although they are often seen in other areas, too. I do not believe there can be a Canadian anywhere who does not think of wilderness on hearing the call of a loon or of migrating geese. Third are the rare and endangered species that do not inherently require a wilderness habitat, but, because they are tolerant of man, have been driven close to extinction. The peregrine falcon, trumpeter swan and whooping crane are well-known examples of species that are abundant (if abundant at all) only in wilderness areas. Our concern is that the process of adaptation and evolution through millennia of each of these species should not be ended. We cannot allow the extinction of these species, if it can be prevented. These species, like wilderness itself, need protection in the North today.

Wilderness is a resource that can be used by both public and private interests, in both a consuming and a non-consuming way. A consuming use of the wilderness destroys or degrades it, and so decreases its value for other users. Industrial and commercial interests are almost invariably consumers; they do not use the wilderness itself, but some aspect of it. Non-consuming use is represented by the traditional pursuits of the native people, and by certain recreational activities.

To some people, the notion of preserving a wilderness area inviolate from industry is anathema—as though we were on the brink of starvation and could not survive without exploiting the resources of every last piece of ground in our country. They would argue that the urge to develop, to build, to consume, is fundamental to man's very nature and that this urge ought not to be checked; even if, were we to follow this urge, it would produce no more than a marginal—perhaps even an illusory—increment to our material well-being. But this argument would apply to northern wilderness areas only if there were no other way in which, and no other area where, man could satisfy this urge. This manifestly is not the case.

IV

THE NORTHERN YUKON

A UNIQUE HERITAGE

MY FIRST VIEW OF THE NORTHERN YUKON WAS FROM A HELICOP-
ter, flying along the Arctic coast in June 1975. The ice had not yet left the
shore, and two tugs were still frozen in at Herschel Island. Seals were
everywhere on the ice. As we turned away from the ocean, I could see
three grizzlies on the tundra. Then, as we left the coast and headed
across the British Mountains, I saw hundreds of caribou, part of the Porcupine herd. They had already been to the coast to calve, but they had
not yet come together in their magnificent annual aggregation, when tens
of thousands of animals move together across the land. Caribou were
scattered on the coastal plain, in the foothills and in the mountains.

At the coast, the tundra was still brown but as we went up the Firth
River we began to see trees. At first there were just a few, then more and
more until, by the time we reached Old Crow Flats, there were trees
everywhere and the earth was green.

Old Crow Flats lie on an alluvial plain with mountains in the far distance on all sides. The Flats comprise a multitude of lakes, through
which the Old Crow River meanders. I saw caribou, moose and thousands of waterfowl on the Flats, and there, too, I met the people of Old
Crow.

I visited a dozen camps on the Flats, where people from Old Crow
were out hunting muskrats. They go out "ratting" in the middle of May,
when the ice still covers the lakes, and come back in mid-June, when the
ice has gone. They trap muskrats on the ice until it thaws; after that they
hunt them with rifles along the shore, travelling by canoe. At each camp
there were two or three tents, and there were muskrats everywhere. The
people hunt at night under the midnight sun, and during the day they

skin their catch. The pelts are put on stretchers to dry, and the meat is hung on racks.

The native people came here long ago from the Old World, across the Bering Strait. A fleshing tool, made from a caribou leg bone and notched by man, has been found by archaeologists on Old Crow Flats. This implement, used to scrape the flesh from hides, is estimated to be about 30,000 years old, and it may be the oldest evidence we have of the entry of man into the western hemisphere.

The Yukon interior is the only substantial region of Canada that was not overrun by glaciers during the Pleistocene Epoch. Only here in the Yukon and in adjoining parts of Alaska can we obtain a relatively complete and continuous record of human occupation of the tundra and the boreal forest.

Like Columbus thousands of years later, the people who came from Asia to the western hemisphere did not realize they had set foot upon a new continent. In small family or kinship groups, they crossed the land-bridge that once linked Asia with North America. They lived by hunting large mammals—mammoth, bison, horse and caribou; of these, only the caribou has survived in this region.

The caribou have been the mainstay of the native people of Old Crow for thousands of years. Today these people are apprehensive, because they fear that the caribou, and thus they themselves, are threatened. They know the power of the white man. They know that elsewhere the great animal herds have died off with the advance of agriculture and industry. They have seen the white man come and dominate them and their land. Exploration crews, bulldozers and the airstrip that crowds their village against the Porcupine River are continuing reminders of this encroachment. These people fear that the white man may destroy their land and the caribou. They and the caribou have made a long journey together across time and the continents. Is this journey to end now?

The caribou go to the Arctic Coastal Plain of the Yukon in summer to have their young. Many factors combine to create a uniquely favourable habitat for their calving grounds there. Good forage provides the high levels of energy that the caribou need to bear and nourish their young, then to migrate southward, and to survive the winter. In summer, when the sun never sets, the coastal plain seems never to sleep. It is a place of growth and productivity, of movement and sound. But the summer lasts for only a short time. Winter, which lasts some eight months of the year, is bitterly cold and, but for the wind, silent.

Once fed and fattened, the caribou gather in their tens of thousands and travel in a great herd through the foothills and the mountains far southward into the boreal forest. The native people of Old Crow have always taken caribou as they migrate southward, and the energy that the animals stored up while grazing on the coastal plain nourishes the people through the winter. These animals are the last link in a food chain that transfers energy from the sun, through plants, then through the caribou, to man. And the people of Old Crow need only a very small proportion of the herd for their food.

In the old days, but still within living memory, the Old Crow people intercepted the caribou on their migration in late summer and fall by driving them into huge corrals, the outlines of which can still be seen. They consisted of poles lashed together with willow roots to form a fence and were placed along the herd's main migration routes. Because they stood among the trees, they were not readily visible. Some fences had wings up to three miles long, and an inner pocket one-quarter to one-half mile deep. Once inside the fences, the caribou were caught with snares and speared. The corrals illustrate the technological ingenuity of the native people.

About the turn of the century, the people began to obtain rifles and, within a year or two, the caribou fences were abandoned. Today only their outlines can be seen: so quickly may one technology displace another. The native people welcomed that change, for it enabled them to harvest caribou more effectively. But they do not see the technology that Arctic Gas proposes to introduce into the Northern Yukon in the same way. They see it as a threat, and they are deeply concerned about what its effects may be on their environment, their way of life and their community.

The Northern Yukon is an arctic and sub-arctic wilderness of incredible beauty, a rich and varied ecosystem: nine million acres of land in its natural state, inhabited by thriving populations of plants and animals. This wilderness has come down through the ages, and it is a heritage that future generations, living in an industrial world even more complex than ours, will surely cherish.

In late August, thousands of snow geese gather on the Arctic Coastal Plain to feed on the tundra grasses, sedges and berries, before embarking on the flight to their wintering grounds. Just as the caribou must build up an energy surplus to sustain them, so must the geese and, indeed, all other arctic waterfowl and shorebirds store up energy for their long southward migration to California, the Gulf Coast, or Central and South America.

The peregrine falcon, golden eagle and other birds of prey nest in the Northern Yukon. These species are dwindling in numbers because of the loss of their former ranges on the North American continent and because of toxic materials in their food. Here in these remote mountains they still nest and rear their young, undisturbed by man.

One-fifth of the world's whistling swans nest along the Arctic coast of the Yukon and in the Mackenzie Delta region. The Old Crow Flats, the

Delta and the Arctic coast provide critical habitat for other waterfowl, including canvasback, scaup, scoter, wigeon, old squaw and mallard. These northern wetlands are particularly important during years of drought on the prairies. Then the waterfowl flock North in much larger numbers than usual, and are thus able to survive to breed again in the South in more favourable years.

You will find polar bear on the ice along the coast, the barren-ground grizzly on the open tundra, and the black bear around Old Crow Flats. You will find moose and Dall sheep, wolf, fox, beaver, wolverine, lynx and, of course, muskrat.

But of all the species of the Northern Yukon, the barren-ground caribou is the most important to the people of Old Crow. On this animal they have always depended for a living. The Porcupine herd, which now stands at about 110,000 animals, is one of the last great herds of North America.

The Northern Yukon is a place of contrasts: of an explosively productive but brief summer and of a long, hard winter; of rugged mountains and stark plains. Its teeming marshes and shorelands give it a beauty equalled by few other places on earth. The ecosystem is unique and vulnerable.

This is why the proposal by Arctic Gas to build a pipeline across the Northern Yukon, to open up this wilderness, poses a threat. This ecosystem, with its magnificent wildlife and scenic beauty, has always been protected by its inaccessibility. With pipeline construction, the development of supply and service roads, the intensification of the search for oil and gas, the establishment of an energy corridor, and the increasing occupation of the Northern Yukon, it will no longer be inaccessible to man and his machines.

The proposal by Arctic Gas to build a pipeline across the Northern Yukon confronts us with a fundamental choice. It is a choice that depends not simply upon the impact of a pipeline across the Northern Yukon, but upon the impact of the establishment of a corridor across it. Opening up this country to industrial development will have lasting effects on the great wilderness and on the native people who live there.

In this chapter, I shall try to outline the full nature and consequences of that choice. Arctic Gas has proposed two possible routes through the Northern Yukon: the Coastal Route and the Interior Route. I have concluded that there are sound environmental grounds for not building the pipeline on the Coastal Route. There are also sound environmental grounds for not building it on the Interior Route, but they are not as compelling as they are in the case of the Coastal Route. However, the social impact of a pipeline along the Interior Route would be devastating to the people of Old Crow. I recommend, therefore, that no pipeline be built across the Northern Yukon along either of the proposed routes. If a pipeline must be built to carry Alaskan gas through Canada to markets in the Lower 48, then it should follow a more southern route.

MAN AND THE LAND: OLD CROW

The people of Old Crow are the only people who live permanently in the Northern Yukon. What does the land mean to them? When I took the Inquiry to their village, they told me that, in their view, the construction of a pipeline across the Northern Yukon would change their homeland and their way of life forever.

The Arctic Gas pipeline on the proposed Interior Route would pass between the village of Old Crow and Old Crow Flats. If this route were followed, a construction camp of 800 workers would be established near the village. The people of Old Crow do not look forward to that prospect, but, at the same time, they oppose a pipeline along the Coastal Route, because of the threat it represents to the calving grounds of the Porcupine herd on the coastal plain: they believe that the decline of the herd would undermine their way of life. Whichever route the gas pipeline takes, it may be followed by an oil pipeline, and by increased gas and oil exploration and development along the route. The people of Old Crow realize the implications of this.

The whole village told me they were opposed to the pipeline. I heard 81 people testify; virtually everyone, man and woman, young and old, spoke and they spoke with one voice. Here are the words of 21-year-old Louise Frost, who expressed the feelings of her people:

> I can see our country being destroyed and my people pushed on reservations, and the white men taking over as they please. . . . The pipeline is only the beginning of all this. If it ever does come through, there will be a time when other companies will want to join in on this. Any major development that has taken place in the North has been of a rapid nature. Their only purpose in coming here is to extract the non-renewable resources, not to the benefit of northerners, but of . . . southern Canadians and Americans. To really bring the whole picture into focus, you can describe it as the rape of the northland to satisfy the greed and the needs of southern consumers, and when development of this nature happens, it only destroys; it does not leave any permanent jobs for people who make the North their home. The whole process does not leave very much for us to be proud of, and along with their equipment and technology, they also impose on the northern people their white culture and all its value systems, which leaves nothing to the people who have been living off the land for

thousands of years. So to put it bluntly, the process of the white man is destroying the Indian ways of life. [C1569ff.]

To assess the environmental and social impact of a pipeline across the Northern Yukon, we must understand the relation between the people of Old Crow and the land and animals.

The fall caribou hunt, when the animals migrate southward to their winter range, after they have fed and fattened on the coastal plain and the nearby mountains, has always been the most important event in the yearly cycle of the Old Crow people. They believe the pipeline will interfere with the caribou migration and break what they see is the essential link between their past and their future. Peter Charlie told the Inquiry about the caribou migration:

> People used to travel back and forth . . . and in the fall after the freeze-up, the caribou would migrate up around Driftwood River, and they crossed the river there, and when the caribou does that, that means that there's going to be caribou amongst the timber country. And when they hear that, it makes the people very happy that the caribou have migrated into the timber country. Now, this migration that I am telling you about happened many, many years ago. Now today, the caribou still migrate the same way. Every fall, my children go up the river, and they get the meat from where these caribou migrate. Now today, I hear about the pipeline that is going through, it's going to spoil all these routes where the caribou migrate. It really makes me sad to hear about the pipeline. [C1390ff.]

The Old Crow people fear that the proposed pipeline would adversely affect the Porcupine caribou herd and therefore their way of life. A pipeline on the Coastal Route would disturb the caribou on their calving range and could reduce the size of the herd.

The people of Old Crow are also concerned about the impact of the Interior Route on the Old Crow Flats. The spring muskrat hunt on the Flats is an event of cultural and economic significance to the people of the village. It provides meat, cash from the sale of fur, and an opportunity for the whole family to get out onto the land.

The threat is obvious and immediate. Alfred Charlie, speaking through an interpreter, put it this way:

> One time he went to Whitehorse to a meeting about this Crow Flats, and there were a lot of people in that meeting from different places. . . . He told those people that if people start to come to Crow Flats to drill for oil and do their seismic in Crow Flats, they will probably mess up the place, and then probably if they strike oil under Crow Flats, everything will be

messed up. . . . He told those people, some of you are working, some of you are government people; you make money, you put money in the bank. He said [Old Crow] people don't do that; they don't put money in the bank, but when they want to make money, they use Crow Flats for a bank, they go back there to trap and hunt muskrat so they use it as a bank. . . .

He heard lots of good things about the pipeline from different people from the oil companies . . . but we don't hear no bad things, everything is going to be perfect. But there's going to be trucks, there's going to be bulldozers and other vehicles that travel over the land, and all these travel by power, oil power and gas power, and they will be refuelling different places and they are going to spill a lot of oil on the ground. . . . They will pollute the water with it. Perhaps fish will get sick from this, too. Suppose we eat fish like that and people don't expect to live healthy with that kind of food. Our main food in Crow Flats is muskrat . . . and supposing we eat sick muskrat from this polluted water. [C1358ff.]

These concerns are shared by all generations at Old Crow. Lorraine Netro, 19 years old, testified:

I was born and raised in Old Crow. . . . The proposed pipeline route is supposed to be put through the most important piece of land to the Old Crow people, the Old Crow Flats. I do not agree with this pipeline route at all. . . . The young people, my generation now, will need this land for our future, and also for the future of our children. We depend on this land as much as our parents do. . . . If the pipeline comes through, what will become of our future? . . . Are we going to look forward to dead or sick muskrats floating around in the polluted lakes, or forests with no birds singing? I do not think any . . . person will even go out into this kind of country to try to hunt in that kind of hunting ground. All that they could do is to remember how beautiful and rich this land used to be. I do not want to see this happen to our land, and to our people. . . . I hope we can keep on living the way we are today, for tomorrow and forever, developing in our own way for generations to come. I do not want the proposed pipeline route through our country. [C1560ff.]

The Old Crow people expressed deep concern about the impact the construction of the pipeline would have on the social fabric of the village. They feel that new people and new influences will come to undermine the traditional values of the village. When the development cycle has run its course, the Old Crow they know today will no longer exist. Marie Bruce testified:

Meaningful existence means a lot to the people of Old Crow. It is probably the most important thing in a person's life. I [would] like Old Crow to be the way it is today. . . . Old Crow will end up deserted like Dawson City . . . in 1898, there was a gold rush in Dawson and people from all over the world went there. When it was over, everyone left Dawson City. This also will happen to Old Crow. It will be very hard to go back to your own way of life after this happens. . . . It is a good feeling when you have nothing or no one to fear in Old Crow. Everyone knows each other here, and they all help make it a better place to live. . . . You can still go to bed here without locking your doors, and you can still walk alone at night without any fear. [C1529ff.]

James Allen is an Indian employed at Old Crow by the Yukon Lands and Forest Service. He had this to say:

If the pipeline moved a camp of 800 men near Old Crow, I think it would be disastrous for the community as a whole. Many of the social diseases which have destroyed many Indian communities in the South would move in, such as alcoholism, child abuse, mental and physical health, broken homes, broken marriages, and many other points that break down a healthy society. Also, where there are 800 men, some sort of liquor outlet soon follows. Liquor would become easily obtainable in the village. The white people say money is the root of all evil, but in our Indian communities today, liquor is the root of all evil. [C1559ff.]

The white people who live in Old Crow feel the same way. The Anglican minister, the Reverend Mr. John Watts, told the Inquiry that, although the church is still important in the lives of the villagers, he feared the situation would change with pipeline construction and the presence of many outsiders. The serious impact of the Alaska Highway on native communities in the Southern Yukon, a generation ago, undermined native values and community life there; he feared that this history may be repeated in Old Crow.

Father Jean-Marie Mouchet, the Roman Catholic priest at Old Crow, told the Inquiry of the code that governs life in Old Crow: it is a complex web of shared understanding and experience within which people carry on their lives. Father Mouchet expressed the fear that outsiders, attracted to the region by the pipeline, would neither understand nor respect this code.

Herta Richter, a nurse in Old Crow, opposed the pipeline:

. . . the pipeline will certainly be a great disaster to this area, and I'm not sure if I could tolerate to stay here after it comes. It would be too painful to see the change in these people and in the surroundings. [C1579]

The people of Old Crow know that a pipeline along the Coastal Route would threaten the calving grounds of the Porcupine caribou herd, and, if a pipeline along the Coastal Route were to lead to the loss of the herd, the impact of its loss on their village and on their way of life would be great.

To the people of Old Crow, the pipeline is symbolic of the white man's ways and his values. Their opposition to the pipeline is so strongly and deeply felt that a decision to proceed with it in the face of their opposition will be to them the clearest affirmation that their way of life and everything they cherish as valuable is, in the eyes of the white society, worthless. It would mean the end of Old Crow as the people know it.

The people of Old Crow have summed up the situation for themselves. Indeed, there is as much wisdom in Old Crow as there is in Ottawa. In the words of Alice Frost:

> Do [the white people] have a right to ask us to give up this beautiful land of ours? Do they have a right to spoil our land and to destroy our wild game for their benefit? Do they have any right to ask us to change our way of life, that we have lived for centuries? Do they have any right . . . to decide our future? We live peacefully . . . in harmony with nature, here in Old Crow. You won't find very many places like this left in this world. [C1566]

PORCUPINE CARIBOU HERD

SENSITIVITIES AND CONCERNS

The Porcupine caribou herd, comprising 110,000 animals or more, ranges throughout the Northern Yukon and into Alaska. It is one of the last great caribou herds, and it accounts for about 20 percent of the caribou in North America. The Porcupine herd has flourished until now because of the isolation of its range. The only communities within it are Old Crow in the Yukon and Kaktovik and Arctic Village in Alaska. The herd is vulnerable to the changes that will accompany industrial development and increased contact with man.

A caribou "herd" is defined as a group of animals that calve in a traditional area different from that used by other groups. The calving grounds of the Porcupine herd are on the Arctic Coast Plain—on the tundra near the shore of the Beaufort Sea in Northwestern Yukon and Northeastern Alaska. Every spring the Porcupine herd leaves the spruce forests of the interior of the Yukon—the Ogilvie Mountains, the Eagle Plains and the Richardson Mountains—where they have wintered, to travel hundreds of miles north to calve. They begin their journey, which may cover 800 miles, in March. At first they move slowly, and they usually reach the Porcupine River late in April. We still do not know how the caribou learn to follow their migration routes, but we do know that in their migration to the coast they leave behind most of the wolf population—a major predator—which dens during April and May. The arrival of the herd at the calving grounds in late May or early June, before the blood-sucking insects emerge, is predictable.

Calving takes place between late May and mid-June on the sedge meadows and the ridges of the coastal plain and the foothills from Babbage River in the Yukon to Camden Bay in Alaska. After the calves are born, the animals come together to escape the impact of the mosquitoes and botflies and begin to move eastward along the coast. This post-calving aggregation of a large part of the Porcupine herd within a few square miles is one of the last remaining marvels of the natural world in North America. It may be compared to the massing of buffalo, a sight that will never be seen again.

The herd continues its post-calving migration eastward along the coastal plain through July, but by August it begins to migrate southward towards the fall and winter range. In September large numbers of caribou pass through Old Crow Flats, crossing the Porcupine River later in the same month. The rut occurs in mid-October in the mountains.

Most of the Porcupine caribou herd spends nine months of the year in the interior of the Yukon and Alaska. This country offers both open habitat and forest, and in it caribou can move from low areas to higher ground to locate favourable plant or snow conditions, or relief from insects. This herd may be in a better position than other Canadian herds to avoid sudden losses by the failure of a given plant food, or unfavourable weather.

Most of the biologists who gave evidence at the Inquiry regard continued use of the calving grounds as essential to the survival of the herd: any interference with them or with the post-calving aggregation could be critical. They argued, therefore, against building the pipeline along the Coastal Route through the calving grounds.

I think the calving grounds are absolutely vital to the herd during the calving season, and interference with the herd at that time and at that place must be avoided. Caribou are more sensitive to disturbance when they are calving and immediately afterward than they are at other times of the year. Disturbance could prevent or delay movement of pregnant cows to the calving grounds, forcing them to calve in unsuitable areas where predation or other factors may cause a very high loss of newborn calves. The first 24 hours of the calf's life are crucial: it is then the cow and the calf learn to know one another, so that when they join the herd of thousands of animals they will be able to find each other. The females seem to require a short sedentary period to learn to recognize their calves. When the herds are disturbed, females and young are frequently separated. For example, a helicopter forced by fog to fly low across the calving grounds would be a serious disturbance to the caribou—and fog is common along the north coast. A single such flight could cause the loss of many calves.

Once the calves begin to nurse, the cows join together in small groups and, when the mosquito season arrives, the herd gathers to limit the impact of these insects. The animals are thin when they arrive on the coast in June, but they are sleek and fat by the end of August. The herd is under great stress after calving, for mosquitoes and other insects attack them relentlessly. At this time, also, the animals' energy demands for nursing and for antler growth are at their maximum. The greatest loss of calves occurs at this season, and the herd may go for several years before enough calves survive to replace the natural losses among the adults, but over the years the delicate balance of the herd is maintained.

The Porcupine herd has not been subjected to any great slaughter since the days of whaling at the turn of the century, when significant numbers of caribou were killed every year to feed the crews overwintering on the Arctic coast. Today animals from this land are taken principally by native people from Old Crow, Aklavik and Fort McPherson in Canada and Kaktovik and Arctic Village in Alaska. Each of these communities takes some 500 animals each year, and the total annual kill is about 4,000 animals, a tolerable level given the present condition and size of the herd. But this picture is changing. The Dempster Highway now crosses part of the winter range of the herd, and already hunters on it may be taking 500 caribou annually. Obviously this new harvest will have to be watched with care.

Caribou are disturbed by any unfamiliar sight or noise. Low-flying aircraft may cause the herd to run and even to stampede, frights that use up great amounts of energy. The animals are disturbed by people, machinery and sudden noises, such as blasting, and when these annoyances are repeated, they can be driven from their ranges. Dr. Peter Lent, a biologist from the University of Alaska, explained that the migratory barren-ground caribou is a wilderness species that can survive only in a wilderness where it has virtually untrammelled access to a vast range. Lent said that when other caribou populations have shrunk, they retreated from peripheral ranges, but they persisted in returning to the same calving grounds. He therefore urged the protection of the calving grounds and the post-calving area on the coast.

Dr. George Calef presented to the Inquiry an analysis of recorded changes in the size of various caribou herds during their contact with industrial man. The Fortymile herd used to roam the Yukon Territory and east central Alaska. In 1920, Olaus J. Murie estimated this herd to be 568,000 animals, but its population stands today at something like 6,000 animals. The Nelchina herd of Southeast Alaska consisted of 70,000 animals in 1962; by 1973, it had been reduced to only 8,000 animals. The

Kaminuriak herd used to winter in Northern Manitoba. Although the Hudson Bay Railway, built in the late 1920s, crossed their winter range, the herd continued to use it for many years. By the early 1960s, however, the caribou had stopped crossing the railway, and they no longer foraged south of the Churchill River. The herd stood at 149,000 in 1955 and at 63,000 in 1967. Dr. David Klein has written about the gradual abandonment of ranges in Scandinavia by reindeer, after their migration routes had been interrupted by rail or highway traffic.

In my judgment the evidence, though circumstantial, is compelling. Increased access to the Porcupine herd and increased human and industrial activity can be expected to have major adverse impacts on the herd.

DEMPSTER HIGHWAY IMPACTS ON CARIBOU

Upon completion, the Dempster Highway will connect Mackenzie Delta and Dawson City in the Yukon. It crosses the wintering grounds and migration routes of the Porcupine caribou, and this, it is said, represents a great threat to the herd. In determining the impact of a pipeline along either route, and in recommending terms and conditions to ameliorate its impact, we must consider the impact of the Dempster Highway as well.

The highway passes through more than 250 miles of caribou winter range. During migration, the highway and its traffic could deflect the animals from their normal migration routes or disrupt their normal migration schedule. Migrating caribou are subject to disturbance by men and machines. To a degree, they can tolerate the close presence of men, if they have not learned to associate men with harassment and injury. We know from experience at Prudhoe Bay and elsewhere that caribou in small groups can become used to vehicular traffic. In general, however, any road along which vehicles pass frequently is almost impassable for herds of caribou. The Dempster Highway will form a barrier to passage of the herd and, much more important, it will increase the access to the herd by hunters. With regard to the Dempster Highway, Ronald Jakimchuk, a wildlife consultant retained by Arctic Gas, said:

> I feel that there is a distinct threat to the Porcupine herd. This threat constitutes human access through their winter range and through one of their major spring migration routes. [F14326ff.]

At present, only about 4,000 animals are taken by hunting each year from the Porcupine caribou herd in the Yukon and Alaska. This is a tolerable level. But unrestricted access for other hunters via the Dempster Highway would lead to intolerable pressure on the herd. Jakimchuk and other biologists highlighted the need to develop and implement controls over hunting along the highway to avoid this threat to the herd.

Such controls are needed, not only along the highway itself, but also on hunting from winter roads, seismic lines and other access routes that have been and will be open to people travelling along the highway. The impact of the Dempster Highway can, I think, be limited, if appropriate measures are taken. These measures include restrictions on hunting along and near the highway.

The Dempster Highway is near completion, but Jakimchuk and Arctic Gas have estimated the impact of the gas pipeline on caribou without taking into account the impact of the completed highway. In my opinion, this is not realistic. The completed highway and its traffic, as well as hunting from it, will have placed the herd under stress before any pipeline is built. Therefore, a pipeline and an energy corridor along either the Coastal or the Interior Route would affect the herd already under pressure from the highway, not the herd as it exists now.

But the Dempster Highway's impact on the herd will be nothing like as great as that of a pipeline along the Coastal Route because the highway does not go near the calving grounds. It impinges on the winter range, but not in a way that is likely to deprive the animals of significant habitat. The herd can survive the loss of part of its wintering range, but it could not survive the loss of its calving grounds.

BIRDS

Among the many species of birds that summer along the pipeline route in the Northern Yukon, two groups are of particular concern. The first group includes species that are rare and relatively rare, especially birds of prey such as the peregrine falcon and the golden eagle.

The second group includes populations of waterfowl, which congregate in large flocks in relatively confined areas or within limited ranges during some critical parts of their life cycle. Such concentrated populations are found along the full length of the Coastal Route in the Yukon and Alaska.

The coastal plain of the Yukon and Alaska is an important nesting and moulting area for ducks, geese, swans, loons and various shorebirds. It is the fall staging area for snow geese, which in some years number in the hundreds of thousands. The nearshore waters are used for moulting by thousands of ducks, and the coastal area in general serves as a migration corridor, both eastward and westward, for millions of waterfowl and shorebirds.

Although Arctic Gas proposes to carry out its main construction activities along the Coastal Route in winter, when there are few birds in the area, it cannot eliminate all concern for the project's impact on birds. During summer, in the construction period, there will be aircraft and barge movements; activities at the coastal stockpile sites, compressor sites and airfields; and perhaps gravel operations and other activities along the pipeline route. During operation of the pipeline, there will be noise from compressors and from blow-down, aircraft and barge movement, vehicles, and probably repair and maintenance work. During both construction and operation, fuel could be spilled into coastal waters from onshore storage tanks or from barges or barge-unloading. The birds could be adversely affected if the lakes they use for nesting and feeding are contaminated or made turbid, or if the removal of water from them during winter for snow roads or pipe testing caused lower water levels to persist into the summer. Finally, there could be physical disturbance of the coastal beaches, bars and spits that are of critical importance to the birds.

Arctic Gas has proposed various measures to reduce or to avoid adverse impacts on birds. Nonetheless, adverse effects on them would be an inevitable complement to a gas pipeline on the Coastal Route. Our basic concern for these birds, and our objective in protecting them, is to permit these international migratory populations to continue to use this region year after year without having their numbers progressively diminished. I have heard various opinions on whether or not the gas pipeline by itself would cause an unavoidable or substantial reduction in the bird populations that use the coast, but it is significant that all of the bird specialists would prefer that the pipeline should not follow the Coastal Route. And, if we consider the gas pipeline, not in isolation but as the first step in the development of an energy corridor along the Coastal Route, then it appears that the cumulative effect of these developments would inevitably lead to progressive decline in some bird populations.

SNOW GEESE

In late August, great flocks of snow geese gather on the Yukon Coastal Plain, the adjacent coastal plain in Alaska, and the outer parts of the Mackenzie Delta. For about a month, they graze near the proposed Coastal Route, building up energy for their long southward flight. Disturbance of the birds during this highly critical period of energy build-up could mean that some of them, both juveniles and adults, might not have the stamina to complete their southward migration. In the long term, pipeline and corridor development could lead to decline of this internationally important goose population.

The lesser snow geese of the Pacific Flyway winter primarily in the Central Valley of California. In spring, they fly north to nest in large colonies in the western Canadian Arctic and on Wrangel Island off the coast of northeastern Siberia. The Pipeline Application Assessment Group has described the Canadian population of these geese as follows:

Each spring, thousands of birds return from their wintering areas in the southern United States by way of the Mackenzie River Valley. They require open water, and they rest, feed and mate on the partly flooded river islands and on nearby lakes after the break-up of the river ice. Their destinations are the few suitable nesting areas at the mouths of the Anderson and Smoke Rivers (Northwest Territories), Banks Island, and a few small scattered sites near the marine interface of the Mackenzie Delta. Snow geese are colonial nesters, returning each year to the same areas. Such areas have extensive brood-raising capabilities.

By mid-August the geese gather on the islands of the Delta in flocks of some 20,000 to 50,000 birds, totalling 500,000 in some years. They then fly westward to the North Slope of the Yukon Territory and Northeast Alaska. Here they feed intensively on berries and sedges for four to six weeks to prepare themselves for the long migration to the wheat fields of southern Alberta and beyond. They usually fly non-stop the 800 miles between the North Slope and Hay Lake in northern Alberta. [*Mackenzie Valley Pipeline Assessment,* p. 296]

During their stay on the staging grounds, snow geese are highly sensitive to human presence, noise, and aircraft. Dr. William Gunn, an ornithological consultant to Arctic Gas, described to the Inquiry experiments to test the sensitivity of snow geese. In one such experiment, the geese would not feed any closer than 1.5 miles from a device simulating the noise made by a compressor station, and birds flying over it diverted their course by 90 degrees or more. Gunn also reported that snow geese are sensitive to the presence of aircraft and they show evidence of being disturbed by flushing at a mean distance of 1.6 miles from small aircraft, 2.5 miles from large aircraft, and 2.3 miles from small helicopters. They also flushed in response to aircraft flying at altitudes of 8,000 to 10,000 feet, the maximum height at which the test flights were conducted. Deliberate harassing of flocks of geese in an area approximately five miles by ten miles cleared them out of the area in 15 minutes.

On the basis of data on the rates of disturbance at a time when the birds, especially the juveniles, needed to build up their energy reserves for migration, Gunn concluded that a potentially severe problem could arise if the present frequency of aircraft flights in the region were to double.

Jerald Jacobson, in Volume 4 of the *Environmental Impact Assessment* published in 1974 by the Environment Protection Board, generalized the available information on the response of snow geese to various human and industrial activities, and he inferred that geese may avoid an area as large as 20 square miles around an operating drill rig, 28 square miles around an operating compressor station, and 250 square miles around an airstrip during takeoff and landing of aircraft. He also drew the following conclusions regarding the effect of aircraft:

The use of airstrips and general operation of aircraft for construction and operation activities from 15 August to 15 October on the Yukon coast is a major conflict, and could seriously degrade or even destroy the integrity of the area for fall staging snow geese. . . .

Because "There is no practical flight altitude that does not frighten snow geese" (Salter and Davis 1974*b*), unrestricted aircraft traffic on the Yukon coast from 15 August to 15 October could be expected to disturb snow geese on 100 percent of the staging area. Any increase in aircraft traffic will result in increased disturbance to snow geese and reduce the suitability of the area up to some unknown threshold level, when it may become unacceptable to fall staging snow geese. There are no data available on the cumulative and long-term effects of aircraft disturbance to snow geese, or on their accommodation to aircraft disturbance during this stage of their life cycle. [p. 139]

Of course, Arctic Gas proposes to schedule its principal construction activities in winter after the geese have flown south, and to restrict noisy activities during both construction and operation of the pipeline when the geese are feeding before going south. Nevertheless, aircraft flights, shipping, activities at wharf and storage sites and construction at camp and compressor sites appear to be inevitable during the construction phase even when the geese are on their staging grounds. Similar potentially disturbing activities at this season would take place throughout the operating life of the pipeline.

The gas pipeline's impact on the fall staging snow geese would not be limited to the Yukon and Alaska Coastal Plain. If the Arctic Gas Cross-Delta Route is followed, the impact would spread to the outer parts of the Mackenzie Delta that are used by fall staging snow geese. Particular concern has been expressed before the Inquiry over construction activities at the Shallow Bay and other Delta channel crossings during this season. They include the effects of shipping, aircraft and especially hovercraft noise, the effects of waterborne fuel spills on the wetlands in the Delta, and the effects of a compressor station or other long-term facilities on the outer Delta.

What would be the effect on the snow geese of the pipeline, the energy corridor, and related industrial development throughout their fall staging grounds? These disturbances would inevitably involve a progressive increase in the numbers of people, of aircraft, barge and vehicle movement, and machinery noise. From the evidence before me, it appears that this population of snow geese would certainly dwindle, and it could decline drastically if the stresses imposed by industrial development on their fall staging grounds were continued through a succession of years when spring was late or snow came early.

A NATIONAL WILDERNESS PARK
FOR THE NORTHERN YUKON

The Northern Yukon has been described by Dr. George Calef as:

> . . . a land richer in wildlife, in variety of landscape and vegetation, and in archaeological value than any other in the Canadian Arctic. Here high mountains, spruce forests, tundra, wide "flats" of lakes and ponds, majestic valleys, . . . and the arctic seacoast come together to form the living fabric of the arctic wilderness. Altogether there are nine million acres of spectacular land in its natural state, inhabited by thriving populations of northern plants and animals including some species which are in serious danger elsewhere. [*The Urgent Need for a Canadian Arctic Wildlife Range*, p. 1]

If this unique area of wilderness and its wildlife are to be protected, the Arctic Gas pipeline should not be built across the Northern Yukon. The region should not be open to any other future proposal to transport energy across it, or to oil and gas exploration and development in general. This summarizes my approach in the earlier parts of this chapter. But now we must go further. It seems to me that, if this kind of protection of the land, the environment and the people is to be effective, the Northern Yukon must be formally designated as an area in which industrial development of any kind is to be totally and permanently excluded. I therefore urge the Government of Canada to reserve the Northern Yukon as a wilderness park.

The park that I propose for the Northern Yukon should be set up under the National Parks system, but it would be a new kind of park—a wilderness park. It would afford absolute protection to wilderness and the environment by excluding all industrial activity within it. Of course there would have to be guarantees permitting the native people to continue to live and to carry on their traditional activities within the park without interference. In my opinion, there should be an immediate withdrawal of the land and water areas needed for this park, which could be effected by designating it as a land reserve under Section 19(c) of the Territorial Lands Act. This action would serve as a clear indication of intent and as the starting point for the planning of the park and negotiations with the United States regarding its relationship to the Arctic National Wildlife Range in Alaska.

The wilderness park that I am proposing would comprise all land between the Alaska–Yukon border and the Yukon–Northwest Territories border from the Porcupine River northward to the coast, including Herschel Island and all other islands adjoining the coast. Its northern boundary would be three miles offshore. This park would cover approximately the same area as the Canadian part of the proposed International Wildlife Range, and would adjoin the Arctic National Wildlife Range in Alaska.

The size and boundaries of the proposed park would protect important habitats of migrating birds, the Porcupine caribou herd, and various other mammals; they would also protect the most important hunting and trapping areas of the Old Crow people and the unique wilderness area of the Northern Yukon. The park would include the Yukon Coastal Plain and the Old Crow Flats. The Canadian sector of the Porcupine caribou herd's spring and summer range and the critically important calving range of the herd would lie within it. But the area represents a compromise: the main wintering range of the caribou herd lies south of the Porcupine River and south of the proposed wilderness park. The Dempster Highway and extensive oil and gas exploration on the Eagle Plains render this part of their winter range unsuitable for reservation as a wilderness area.

WILDLIFE RANGE IN ALASKA

The wilderness does not stop, of course, at the boundary between Alaska and the Yukon. The northeast part of Alaska, contiguous to the Northern Yukon, is a part of the same wilderness. In fact, the calving grounds of the Porcupine caribou herd extend well into Alaska, along the coastal plain as far as Camden Bay, 100 miles to the west of the international boundary; the area of concentrated use by staging snow geese, by nesting and moulting waterfowl and by seabirds also extends far into Alaska.

So a wilderness park in the Northern Yukon would not, by itself, altogether protect the caribou herd and the migratory birds. We shall need the cooperation of the United States to ensure complete protection for the herd.

Dr. Robert Weeden, a biologist from Alaska, says that if no pipeline is built, and no oil and gas development occurs, the Arctic National Wildlife Range will serve as an ecological reserve and as an ecological base from which to monitor changes brought about by future developments in Alaska. But the existing Arctic National Wildlife Range is not inviolate to oil and gas exploration and development. If the wilderness, the caribou herd and the snow geese on the Alaskan side of the border are to be protected, the Range must be elevated to wilderness status.

INTERNATIONAL WILDLIFE RANGE

The international movements of caribou, waterfowl, bears and other animals have led, of course, to consideration of a wildlife range in the Northern Yukon to adjoin and complement the wildlife range in Alaska.

A pipeline across the Northern Yukon would not only destroy the possibility of establishing a true wilderness park there, but it would undermine efforts in the United States to convert the Arctic National Wildlife Range to wilderness status. Weeden, speaking for the State of Alaska, said:

> The State has taken the position that such an intrusion upon an untouched area is irreversible and tragic, whatever steps are taken to mitigate its effects. [F7545]

The largest wildlife refuge in the United States would be in jeopardy and the possibility of combining it with a Canadian range to form one of the largest wildlife refuges in the world would be thwarted.

OIL AND GAS POTENTIAL

If we create a wilderness park in the Northern Yukon, shall we be denying ourselves indispensable supplies of gas and oil? Will it become necessary, in any event, to invade this wilderness? No one can say for sure, but no evidence brought before me indicated or even suggested that the Northern Yukon is a first-priority oil-and-gas province. There has been extensive exploratory drilling east of it in the Mackenzie Delta area and west of it in Alaska. In these areas, the coastal plain and the offshore continental shelf are considerably wider than they are in the Yukon. The zone of potential oil and gas exploration along the north coast of the Yukon is narrow, and the area has not achieved any prominence in exploration strategy so far. It is also noteworthy that the three deep exploratory test wells drilled near the Yukon coast were dry.

NATIVE PEOPLE AND THE WILDERNESS PARK

My proposal for a wilderness park is specifically designed to benefit the native people by protecting their renewable resources and by preserving the land in its natural state, thus ensuring the physical basis for their way of life. This benefit extends to the Old Crow people, who live within the area of the proposed park, the Indians from Fort McPherson and Aklavik, who hunt in the eastern part of the proposed park, and the Inuit, largely from Aklavik, who hunt and fish along the Yukon coast. All of these people depend on the Porcupine caribou herd, the protection of which is one of the principal purposes of the proposed park.

The rights that the native people of Old Crow and the Mackenzie Delta would enjoy throughout the area covered by the park would have to be negotiated between the Government of Canada and themselves as part of a comprehensive settlement of native claims, but I do not think the dedication now of the Northern Yukon as a park would prejudice those claims.

Preservation of the wilderness and of the caribou herd is plainly in keeping with the desires of the native people. But, there are certain essential conditions that would have to be observed: the native people must be guaranteed at the outset their right to live, hunt, trap and fish within the park, and to take caribou within its boundaries; and the people of Old Crow must play an important part in the management of the park and, in particular, of the caribou herd. It is my judgment that the establishment of the park and of a management plan in cooperation with the native people, building both upon their knowledge and experience and that of the scientists who have studied the caribou and the Northern Yukon biota, can be consistent with and complementary to these principles.

We have already some experience in the establishment and management of parks (although not wilderness parks) in the North and have seen their effects on the interests of the native people. At Nahanni Butte the Inquiry was told that the Dene play no part in the management of the South Nahanni National Park. This experience must not be repeated in the wilderness park for the Northern Yukon that I am urging upon the Government of Canada. The conditions I have outlined will, in my judgment, avoid such a repetition and will avoid prejudice to native claims.

It may be said that no one will visit the park because it is too remote. Only the wealthy, it may be argued, will have the opportunity to see the caribou and to enjoy the solitude and the scenery. But Canadians of ordinary means and less are there now, enjoying these wonders of nature. I speak, of course, of the native people. Is that not enough? Canadians from the provinces do not have to visit the wilderness or see the herd of caribou to confirm its existence or to justify its retention. The point I am making here is that the preservation of the wilderness and its wildlife can be justified on the grounds of its importance to the native people. But the preservation of wilderness can also be justified because it is there, an Arctic ecosystem, in which life forms are limited in number, and where, if we exterminate them, we impoverish the frontier, our knowledge of the frontier, and the variety and beauty of the earth's creatures.

AN ALTERNATIVE ROUTE ACROSS THE YUKON

I have recommended that no pipeline be built and no energy corridor be established across the Northern Yukon along either of the routes proposed by Arctic Gas. This means that, if gas from Prudhoe Bay and, subsequently, gas and oil from other sources in Alaska must pass overland to the Lower 48, the pipeline will have to be routed through the southern part of the Yukon Territory. The only overland route that has been seriously advanced as an alternative to the routes proposed by Arctic Gas is the Alaska Highway Route (also known as the Fairbanks Route) which is the route proposed for the Alcan Pipeline. This route would follow the trans-Alaska pipeline from Prudhoe Bay to Fairbanks, the Alaska Highway to the eastern border of Alaska and then cross the Southern Yukon into British Columbia and Alberta.

At Whitehorse, I heard evidence from Arctic Gas and from other participants in the Inquiry, comparing this route with the Coastal and Interior Routes. On the basis of that evidence, many of the concerns that led me to reject the pipeline routes across the Northern Yukon do not appear to apply to the Alaska Highway Route.

No major populations of any wildlife species appear to be threatened by the construction of a pipeline paralleling the Alaska Highway, either in the Yukon or in Alaska. The route follows an existing corridor along the trans-Alaska pipeline north of Fairbanks and along the Alaska Highway south and east of Fairbanks. Like the trans-Alaska pipeline, this route would come into contact with only small numbers of caribou south of Prudhoe Bay. Elsewhere, although there are important wildlife populations in the area traversed by the proposed route, they apparently would not have major contact with the corridor.

The concerns that I have expressed about the scheduling and logistics of building a pipeline across the Northern Yukon would not apply (or would be much less important) if a pipeline were built along the Alaska Highway Route. The Arctic Gas pipeline would have to be built in the cold and darkness of winter north of the Arctic Circle, from a snow working surface. It would depend upon a limited shipping season, and a whole infrastructure would have to be established to bring in material, equipment and supplies. In contrast, a pipeline following the Alaska Highway Route in Canada could probably be built in either winter or summer, and it would cross an area with less extreme winter weather, and follow a main highway that has a short connection to the Pacific coast.

Within Canada, only short sections of the Alaska Highway Route would encounter permafrost, and the problems of pipeline construction and operation across permafrost and of controlling frost heave would be of little concern. Of course, permafrost does exist throughout most of the Alaska portion of this proposed route.

I have not examined the social and economic impact of a pipeline along the Alaska Highway Route. Neither have I considered the question of native claims in the Southern Yukon. The Council of Yukon Indians have advised that native claims must be settled in the Southern Yukon before any pipeline is built. These matters would be of fundamental importance in any decision to build a pipeline across the Southern Yukon and they must be assessed carefully before any recommendation is made for a pipeline along the Alaska Highway. Certainly, I am in no position to make such a recommendation.

If a decision should be made in favour of a pipeline along the Alaska Highway Route, or over any other southerly route across the Yukon Territory, I recommend that any agreement in this regard between Canada and the United States should include provisions to protect the Porcupine caribou herd and the wilderness of the Northern Yukon and Northeastern Alaska. By this agreement, Canada should undertake to establish a wilderness park in the Northern Yukon and the United States should agree to accord wilderness status to its Arctic National Wildlife Range, thus creating a unique international wilderness park in the Arctic. It would be an important symbol of the dedication of our two countries to environmental as well as industrial goals.

THE MACKENZIE DELTA –
BEAUFORT SEA REGION

THE MACKENZIE DELTA AND THE BEAUFORT SEA TOGETHER CON-
stitute an area of great importance and sensitivity for wildlife, birds and
fish, an area where the land, the water and their renewable resources are
still necessary to the life and culture of many native people. The impact
of the construction of the pipeline across the Delta will be significant,
but even more significant will be the oil and gas exploration and development that will be associated with, and that will follow, the pipeline.
There appears to be a major petroleum province in the Delta–Beaufort
area. What we do now will largely determine the impact that the development of this province will have on the environment of the region.

I intend, therefore, to discuss at some length the impact that the
pipeline and related activities will have on the Delta-Beaufort region, because here the exploration and development activity generated by the
pipeline will be most intense.

Arctic Gas proposes to lay the pipeline from Alaska across the outer
part of the Mackenzie Delta. Arctic Gas also proposes to build a pipeline
southward from the Richards Island area. Whatever route the pipeline
follows will cause major environmental concerns in the Mackenzie Delta
region.

The gas plants and the gas gathering lines associated with them will be
built in the Delta area by the producer companies, Imperial, Gulf and
Shell, not by the pipeline companies, but these plants and gathering lines
are so obviously part of the pipeline system that any consideration of the
impact of the pipeline must include them as well. After all, if the right-of-
way for the gas pipeline is not granted, the gas plants and gas gathering
systems will not be built.

The Pipeline Guidelines foresee a whole group of activities within a corridor. If there are pipelines running along an energy corridor from the Arctic to the mid-continent, then there will be a further extension of oil and gas exploration and development into the Beaufort Sea.

It is up to the National Energy Board to determine the extent of the reserves of oil and gas in the Delta and the Beaufort Sea. But this Inquiry, if it is to do its job, must assess the impact of exploration and development that would follow approval of a pipeline, and explore the penumbra of environmental and social issues that surround such activities. It is from this perspective that the Inquiry must determine the impact that a gas pipeline would have and recommend the terms and conditions under which a right-of-way should be granted, if a pipeline is to be built.

The pipeline cannot be considered in isolation. The environment of the North, the ecosystems of the North, are continuous and interdependent. They cannot be divided. Similarly, we cannot understand the consequences industrial development would have by hiving off a convenient component of it, and examining it in detail, while ignoring the broader implications of the whole range of its effects.

Canada has chosen to pioneer offshore oil and gas exploration in the Arctic. We are in advance of other circumpolar nations on this geographical and technological frontier. The pipeline, once built, will stimulate yet more oil and gas exploration offshore and it will lead toward full-scale development and production in the Beaufort Sea itself.

Canadians have a grave responsibility in this matter. There can be no doubt that the other circumpolar powers—the United States, the Soviet Union, Denmark and Norway—will follow us offshore. What we do there—the standards we set and our performance—will be closely watched.

MAN AND THE LAND

The Inquiry held its first community hearing in Aklavik. We went there in early spring, when the nights were still dark and the days were crisp and clear with cold.

While we were at Aklavik, I visited Archie Headpoint's camp, six or seven miles out of town. To get there we drove along the West Channel of the Mackenzie River. (Once the channels have frozen, one pass with a bulldozer will clear an ice road.) Headpoint's cabin was just above the bank of the Mackenzie. Out on the ice, in the middle of the channel, we could see one of Shell's seismic exploration camps, a series of trailers on runners.

Archie Headpoint's camp is a collection of small, cluttered buildings.

In his log cabin, where he and his family have lived for a long time, the skins of muskrats hung to dry. We sat there for a while, talking and drinking tea.

The contrast between the old Arctic and the new, between the northern homeland and the northern frontier, could be seen in the few acres around that cabin. There, the landscape is crisscrossed by seismic trails and vehicle tracks that seem to come from nowhere and to go nowhere—all this right alongside the ponds where the Headpoints have always hunted muskrats in the past. The Headpoints complained that the land was no longer as productive as it had been, that the seismic trails extending from the West Channel up into the foothills of the Richardson Mountains had blocked the streams and polluted the ponds.

Following our visit to Headpoint's camp, we had lunch at the seismic exploration camp. There we met engineers and technicians, men devoted to the task of finding oil and gas—men seeking to make the northern frontier productive for the South. The camp was laid out in neat rows. Its colour—bright orange—contrasted sharply with the cold blue-white of the landscape.

There, above the Arctic Circle, just half a mile from each other, were the two Norths side by side—the North of Shell Canada, with its links to the South and the markets of the world, and the North of Archie Headpoint, with its links to the land and to a past shared by the people who have always lived there.

Can these two Norths coexist in the Mackenzie Delta and the Beaufort Sea? Or must one recede into the past, while the other commands the future? This issue confronted us in the Delta communities—Aklavik, Inuvik and Tuktoyaktuk—and at Fort McPherson and Arctic Red River. And the same issue confronted us at the Inuit settlements on the shores of the Beaufort Sea. I held hearings in all of these places, too: Sachs Harbour, Holman, Paulatuk and North Star Harbour. These settlements are far from the route of the proposed pipeline, but oil and gas exploration in and around the Beaufort Sea concerns the people who live there, because they depend on the fish, seals, whales and polar bears for which the Beaufort Sea is vital habitat.

We may sometimes think that the history of the Delta began with Mackenzie's arrival in 1789, or with the establishment of Inuvik in 1955, or even with the coming of oil and gas exploration in the 1960s. But there were native people in the Delta region when Mackenzie arrived—and they had been there for thousands of years.

Mackenzie's expedition extended the fur trade down the whole length of the Mackenzie River, but the fur trade was conducted on a regular basis in the Delta region only after the establishment of Fort McPherson, on the Peel River in 1840. First the Dene and later the Inuit traded there.

The Dene of the region hunted and trapped during the winter in the

Richardson and Ogilvie Mountains, then brought their furs to Fort McPherson in June. They spent the summer at fish camps in the Delta, then returned to Fort McPherson in the fall to trade their dried fish; after that they went back to the mountains for the winter.

It is estimated that there were about 2,000 bowhead whales in the Beaufort Sea before the turn of the century. In 1889 the American whaling fleet, sailing from San Francisco, entered the Beaufort Sea, and they returned each year until 1912. During those 23 years, about 1,500 bowhead whales were killed in Canadian waters. The stock of whales in the Beaufort Sea was virtually exterminated and today only 100 or 200 bowheads summer there.

The Eskimos supplied the whalers with meat, which brought very great pressure to bear on the caribou. Dr. Arthur Martell of the Canadian Wildlife Service believes this pressure drove the Bluenose caribou herd away from the Delta. According to Knut Lang, after the whaling period the native people of the Delta had to travel far inland to hunt caribou. In the late 1920s, caribou began to reappear in the foothills west of the Mackenzie Delta. Until about 10 years ago, the Bluenose herd used to stay east of the Anderson River, but now it appears to be returning to the range it used to inhabit in the Delta region. Since the 1960s, the herd has been expanding westward toward the Mackenzie River.

Not only the caribou of the Delta were affected by the Eskimos, hunting for the whalers. By the early 1900s, the muskoxen were extirpated from the Delta region, and the western boundary of their range lay to the east of the Anderson River.

With the collapse of the whaling industry—and with the disappearance of the bowhead, muskox and Delta caribou—the fur trade resumed its role as a vital part of the Inuit economy and the source of guns, ammunition and other trade goods on which they had come to rely. With the rising prices for fur, particularly for white fox, and the emergence of muskrat as an important commercial fur, the Mackenzie Delta became an important centre of the fur trade. In 1911, Aklavik was established at a natural camping place in the Delta, which further encouraged the harvesting of muskrats. By the early 1920s, the prices of both muskrat and white fox had increased 20-fold over what they had been at the turn of the century. The Delta trappers, harvesting muskrats by the hundred thousands, attained unprecedented prosperity. Many families bought their own schooners. But in the mid-twenties, high fur prices and an increasing number of both white and Alaskan Inuit immigrant trappers led to overharvesting in the Delta and an expansion of the Inuit trapping areas. Some Inuit moved to Banks Island, where white fox were abundant, and established what has since become the thriving trapping community of Sachs Harbour.

The Delta people remember the 1920s as a period of good times, when the relationship between man and the land was productive. We must remember that, although trapping fur for sale was important, it was, and is, only a part of the native economy. Then, as now, country food—caribou, seal, whale, polar bear, fish, goose—constituted a vital part of the native people's diet.

Land use patterns have changed in the last 20 years, as the people moved from their camps into settlements, but there is a clear continuity between past and present native land use. Muskrats are still important. At Fort McPherson and Arctic Red River, the spring "ratting" season pulls everyone down to the Delta or the Travaillant Lake area. In spring, Aklavik is nearly abandoned because its people are out hunting muskrats, and many wage-earners in Inuvik leave their regular jobs to participate in the hunt. As Annie C. Gordon said at Aklavik:

> At this time of the year [April], the people go out trapping muskrats, and in May and June the people go out to their spring camps. Some stay until June 15 and some come back early. At this time when they are out, they hunt muskrats. It's a good thing, it is a good living, it is good living out there. Every year we go out with the children. We always say that we are going to stay in town for the spring, but when spring comes we always end up going out. We take the whole family out, and sometimes we take other children to enjoy it with our family. It's fun out there. Sometimes we take the whole family out on a hunt, just to go out for fun, and they enjoy doing it. The country is so nice in the spring, it's so quiet. It's hard work when the hunters come back, when you're skinning muskrats. But I enjoy doing that kind of work, and it's fun when you go out and shoot muskrats all night. [C122ff.]

Native families have fishing camps throughout the Delta, especially around Aklavik. I visited many of these camps, where families spend the summer, catching fish and drying them for winter use.

I visited Whitefish Station, where native families, many of them from Inuvik, spend the summers harvesting the white whales and preparing the meat for the winter. I visited Holman in winter and watched some recently killed caribou being divided up. At Paulatuk I saw frozen char and caribou stored on the roof of every house.

The Inuit of Tuktoyaktuk, Paulatuk, Sachs Harbour, Holman and Coppermine hunt ringed and bearded seals in the Beaufort Sea, Amundsen Gulf and Coronation Gulf. At Holman—which alone takes as many as 8,000 seals a year—Jimmy Memorana spoke of the importance of the seals to the Inuit:

> . . . they are the food of the people and they are the income of the people, and they use [those] seals all year around, for food and for cash. [C3986]

Frank Elanik of Aklavik spoke of the importance of the caribou to the native people, Inuit, Dene and Metis:

> My family eat about 30 caribou a year. . . . If I had to buy from the Bay, I don't know how I would live. [C24]

Mark Noksana of Tuktoyaktuk spoke of the importance of the whales in the Inuit diet:

> . . the muktuk we [have] eating whales, we can't go without it. If we go without it . . . we can't feel good. [C4398]

There is, then, in the Delta, a concentration of concerns, a compression of the social, environmental and economic forces at work elsewhere along the route of the pipeline and the corridor. There in the Delta, and extending into the Beaufort Sea, is a uniquely productive ecological system, a system that is vital to the native people.

REGION AND ENVIRONMENT

To understand the impact of pipelines and of oil and gas exploration and development in the Mackenzie Delta and the Beaufort Sea, we must have some knowledge of the geography of the three areas in the Delta–Beaufort region: the Mackenzie Delta itself, the Delta region, and the Beaufort Sea.

The Mackenzie Delta is a maze of islands, channels, lakes and swamps. It is forested except for tundra areas along the coast. In spring, the flood waters of the Mackenzie River cause break-up in the Delta and around the channel mouths earlier than in adjacent parts of the Beaufort Sea. In summer, the warm, turbid river water flows out beyond the Delta in a layer over the colder and denser sea water. Thus, the Delta region has a warmer summer and longer season of open water than the areas just east and west of it. The Delta itself may be likened to a huge, wet sponge. It is one of the most productive areas for wildlife in the Canadian Arctic, supporting innumerable muskrats and substantial populations of other furbearers, such as beaver, mink and marten, as well as fox, bear, moose, and a variety of small mammals. The channels and lakes of the Delta abound with fish. In summer, many thousands of waterfowl and other birds pass through the Delta or nest there. White whales calve in its warm waters. Because of these natural features, the Delta is of special significance to the native people of Aklavik, Fort McPherson and Inuvik, and even of Arctic Red River and Tuktoyaktuk, for trapping, hunting and fishing. The entire Delta lies within a few feet of river level or sea level, and much of it is subject to periodic flooding. The sponge-like nature of the Delta means that waterborne pollution would have far-reaching effects on the Delta, its wildlife, and its people.

The area described here as the Delta region is a largely treeless lowland extending some 100 miles eastward from the Mackenzie Delta, and it includes the area around Tuktoyaktuk, the Eskimo Lakes and Cape Bathurst. This area, which is used extensively by the people of Tuktoyaktuk, supports Canada's only reindeer herd. The Bluenose caribou herd at the northwestern limit of its present range occupies the southern fringe of the area. Arctic fox is an important furbearer in this area, and the coast of the Delta region, like the Delta itself, supports tens of thousands of migratory waterfowl and shorebirds in summer. There are freshwater fish in coastal bays, and white whales spend the summer in the warm waters that border the Delta region and particularly the Delta itself.

In winter, the Beaufort Sea is completely ice covered. A zone of land-fast ice extends outward from the shore for some tens of miles, and is separated from the moving polar pack ice by a narrow shear zone characterized by rapidly deforming, heavily ridged and irregular ice. This zone contains leads of open water in winter, and in spring becomes a belt of discontinuous open leads hundreds of miles long. In summer, the land-fast ice melts, and the polar pack retreats farther offshore, in some seasons to the general vicinity of the edge of the continental shelf. Within the Beaufort Sea region, the principal area of environmental concern is the shear zone and the open leads at the edge of the land-fast ice. This area provides critical habitat for migrating birds in the spring and for polar bears and seals in both winter and spring.

WILDLIFE

FISH Although fish are present in the streams, lakes and coastal waters throughout the Delta region, they are most abundant and most important for local people in the Delta itself. Native people catch fish for domestic use at many locations within the Delta and in the streams and lakes tributary to it. As some indication of the importance of this resource, the community of Aklavik consumed approximately 294,000 pounds of fish in 1973.

About a dozen species of fish occur in the Delta, including broad and humpback whitefish, inconnu, cisco, pike, chub, burbot, sucker, grayling, lake trout and arctic char. They live in the main river channels, bays at the river mouth, and small channels and lakes throughout the Delta. Some populations of fish simply pass through the Delta on their way to the sea or to locations back upstream. Others spend most of their life cycle in the Delta. Unfortunately, because of the turbidity of the water, the multitude of channels and small waterbodies, the large size of the main channels and the long period of ice cover, there are critical gaps in our information about these fish resources, and we need that information to assess properly the impact of industrial development on the Delta. There are few details available concerning the location and timing of critical life situations, such as spawning, overwintering and migration, in which the fish populations are at greatest risk from industrial activities.

BIRDS The Delta, the coast of the Delta region, the coastal waters and the offshore leads of the Beaufort Sea are of very great importance for migratory birds. Every spring millions of geese, swans, ducks, gulls, terns and many other species converge on the Delta–Beaufort region from wintering grounds in Southern Canada, the United States, South America and even the Antarctic. They are an international renewable resource that nature, political boundaries and treaties have made the responsibility of Canada.

In its ornithological relationship to other regions in the Western Arctic, the Delta has been described as a huge funnel. It attracts birds from literally every point of the compass, from Banks Island, Anderson River, Liverpool Bay, the north slope of the Yukon and Alaska, and by way of the Mackenzie Valley from the prairies and Central and South America. Although the Mackenzie Valley is a major flyway, birds also migrate east and west along the Arctic coast of the Beaufort Sea. For example, there is a spectacular spring migration of ducks from the Pacific Ocean, along the south shore of the Beaufort Sea and past the Delta, following the leads in the ice. These leads of open water are crucial habitat for resting and feeding. The coastal bays and lagoons, barrier beaches and islands offer vital nesting and moulting grounds for the birds arriving from all directions.

Dr. Tom Barry of the Canadian Wildlife Service estimates that two million migrating seabirds and waterfowl, representing about 100 species, frequent the Beaufort Sea and its coastal margins. The Mackenzie Delta itself offers nesting ground for a waterfowl population that ranges from 80,000 to 350,000. As I described in the preceding chapter, several hundred thousand snow geese pass through the area in spring and fall, and in some years they use the outer Delta for staging. Spring leads in the ice of the Beaufort Sea at places like Cape Dalhousie may be occupied by 50,000 or more birds at a time. A week later those birds will have moved on, and tens of thousands more will be occupying the same lead. During one fall migration period, from July 10 to September 17, 1972, 240,000 birds, representing more than 50 species, were recorded passing Nunaluk Spit on the north coast of the Yukon. The vitality of the whole region is obvious.

Another area of critical importance for waterfowl and other birds is the outer, treeless part of the Mackenzie Delta, including its bordering bays, inlets and channel mouths. This area is used extensively by nesting and moulting ducks, swans, cranes and various other species, including a small colony of snow geese. In some years, when there is early snow on the Yukon Coastal Plain, the Delta edge serves as the principal fall staging area for the migrating snow geese. I will recommend that this entire area be protected by bird sanctuaries.

MAMMALS   The variety of habitat in the Delta–Beaufort region supports a broad range of mammals, from lemmings to whales. These varied animals have a correspondingly varied sensitivity to industrial development. Many of the mammals could tolerate industrial intrusion, but for others, such activities would be intolerable, and a serious decline in these populations could be anticipated. Perhaps I can explain this diversity by citing a few examples.

The white whales of the Beaufort Sea depend on the warm, shallow waters of Mackenzie Bay. Every summer the whales concentrate there to give birth to their young. These mammals are wary of man, and if they are disturbed at this time, a year's calves could be endangered or lost. Offshore oil and gas activities within the whale concentration areas during the summer could ultimately lead to a decline in the whale populations. I therefore give special attention to them in this chapter and recommend that a whale sanctuary be established to protect their principal calving area.

Grizzly bears and polar bears are widely distributed in the Delta–Beaufort area. Although their numbers are relatively small, they range over large areas. They are attracted by camps and waste disposal sites, and encounters with man often result in the death of the bear. This kind of encounter, together with the disturbance of denning sites in winter, are threats to the bear populations of this region.

The muskrat is the most important economically of the aquatic furbearers in the Delta region. I have already described the importance of these animals to the native people. The Delta provides abundant habitat for muskrats, so disturbance would have to be widespread before it affected the whole population. Although locally vulnerable, these aquatic furbearers have the potential for relatively rapid recovery and will recolonize disturbed habitats that have not been permanently spoiled. Because of these adaptive features, there appears to be no need for concern over their long-term welfare, so long as short-term damage to habitat is corrected. However, in some areas where they have been traditionally harvested, short-term and local depletion could affect the economic well-being of trappers.

A semi-domesticated reindeer herd ranges east of the Delta. This herd was introduced into the area in 1935, and now its 5,000 animals are managed by local native people as a renewable resource. The herd's range and its seasonal movements have been manipulated by man, so the effects of industrial development may be expected to be less critical to the reindeer than to caribou.

The Bluenose caribou herd ranges east and south of the Delta region. Present oil and gas activity touch only the edge of this herd's range, but successive industrial development, combined with current northwestward expansion of the herd's range, may impose some constraints. But this again is a minor impact, and in marked contrast to the impact that the pipeline and energy corridor would have on the Porcupine caribou herd on its calving grounds in the Northern Yukon.

I think that these few examples indicate that the mammals of the Delta–Beaufort region will respond differently to industrial development. Some, like the white whales, will be very vulnerable at certain times and places. Others, like the muskrats, reindeer and caribou, may be affected but not threatened. This distinction is important because it dictates how impacts should be controlled. In some cases, a species can be protected effectively only by prohibiting industrial activity in critical areas, but in other cases regulation of industrial development may be adequate. The critical consideration in each case is the degree of biological sensitivity.

BIOLOGICAL SENSITIVITY

THE FOOD CHAIN Although arctic ecosystems have been described as sensitive, or even fragile, I think it is more accurate to say that they are vulnerable. At the beginning of this report, I quote Dr. Max Dunbar to explain this idea of vulnerability and how it relates to the small number of species in the Arctic and to simple food chains.

The sensitivity of wildlife in the Delta–Beaufort region is not determined simply by assessing the direct effect of industrial impact on large and conspicuous species like the white whales. Dr. Norman Snow of the Department of Indian Affairs and Northern Development reminded the Inquiry that the highly visible components of the ecosystem —the birds, mammals and fish—represent only about five percent of the animal kingdom. The other 95 percent is composed of invertebrates, some of them microscopic in size but exceedingly numerous. These populations are the crucial links in many food chains, and on them the whole ecosystem, therefore, depends.

Biologists who testified before the Inquiry were careful to explain that, despite the relative simplicity of arctic food chains, their nature is not well understood. We have only begun to study them, but we have learned enough to understand their vulnerability. The native people understand this problem very well, and it is, in fact, their concern for the vulnerability of the food chain that underlies many of their fears about the impact of oil and gas exploration and development. At Holman, Simon Kataoyak told the Inquiry:

> You know, we talk about oil spills and so forth. I'd like to say a little bit about it because, if there's an oil spill, it's going to involve Holman Island and all this part of the area because of the currents. . . .
>
> You see, if an oil spill occurs, it's going to spread. That's for sure, you know that. Well, seals are not going to die right away, we know it. It takes a long time to get rid of [them]. The thing we're going to get rid of first is the shrimps [and] what they eat. . . . Seals are going to live for a little longer time but what the fish and whales eat are the things that are going to be first to be killed. Then the seals are going to be killed. . . .
>
> So you see, they have to study hard to prevent these things first before they ever go ahead because there's little—they call them *amogoak,* you know those shrimps, there's a lot of them in the water. That's what the seals [eat], you find them in their stomach, *amogoaks,* and even whales. . . .
>
> But when you [are] travelling in the ocean, something like that—it's nice, it's calm weather. What happens when you look in the water? You could see those little creatures that are this long, they're just like jelly and they've got a red head and they're moving like this all the time. Well, that's what whales and seals eat. So if an oil spill occurs, if that thing slows up or if it's drifting around, that's the first thing that's going to be killed. So they got to know how to prevent those things. . . .
>
> They tell us they know how to drill. Sure, we agree because they're experts. But do they know how to do the safeties? They haven't tried it. [C3943ff.]

Marine biologists from Environment Canada described the Beaufort Sea marine ecosystem. Although complex by arctic standards, it is nevertheless a simple food chain compared to food chains found farther south where the diversity of species is greater and none of them is dominant. The relation between what eats what in the Beaufort Sea is easily illustrated. A typical sequence is diatom-shrimp-fish-seal; another is flagellate-krill-whale. There are, of course, alternative linkages in arctic marine food chains, such as a bird preying on fish or man killing a whale. Nevertheless, as Kataoyak told the Inquiry, a group of shrimp-like creatures underpins most of the food chains in that cold sea.

These shrimp-like creatures depend on the marine equivalent of pastures. Part of this marine pasture, one that is unique to the arctic seas, is an under-ice flora that appears to be an important component of the diatom-shrimp-fish-seal food chain. In late spring, before the ice is thin enough for the light to penetrate to stimulate the growth of the microscopic plants that float in open water, dense concentrations of diatoms grow under the ice. They flourish briefly on the limited nutrients that are available in the ice and with far lower light intensity than other forms of phytoplankton require. They provide a "pasture" for crustaceans on the bottom of the floating ice, and they form the base of the food chains that include arctic cod, seals and whales. It will be seen at once that these under-ice colonies of diatoms peculiar to the Arctic would be highly vulnerable to oil trapped under the ice. Our present scant knowledge of these food chains makes it difficult to assess the extent of the damage that would occur to them, but it is clear that they are highly vulnerable to pollution or disturbance.

CRITICAL LIFE STAGES The second concept basic to understanding the sensitivity of arctic species is that of critical stages in the life of a species. This is a fundamental aspect of wildlife sensitivity everywhere, but the highly developed winter–summer seasonality of the arctic environment and the relatively simple nature of the arctic food chains combine to make certain life stages critical to the survival of whole populations of certain species.

I have described how the calving grounds of the Porcupine caribou herd and the staging areas of the snow geese in the Northern Yukon are critical to the survival of those two populations because almost all the animals are concentrated in small areas at a time when their vulnerability to disturbance is high, and because there are no suitable alternative areas for calving and staging.

In the Delta–Beaufort region there are critical life stage areas that are essential to the survival of other populations. The nesting, staging and moulting areas of the outer Delta are vital to very large populations of various species of birds. The offshore leads are critical for birds, seals and polar bears. The spawning and overwintering waters and migration routes in the Delta region are critical for various fish populations. The calving grounds in the shallow waters of the Delta are critical for the white whales of the Beaufort Sea. Similarly, other mammals of the region have den sites, calving areas, migration routes and wintering areas that are critical.

The most sensitive species are those that concentrate a major portion of the population on very limited habitat during a critical life stage. If industrial development impinges on that habitat, the species will be very vulnerable to impact, either directly through disturbance or indirectly through alteration of habitat or disruption of the food chain.

THE STATE OF ENVIRONMENTAL KNOWLEDGE
Both physical scientists and biologists have spoken to the Inquiry of our lack of knowledge about various natural processes, about reactions to

changes induced by man, and about the effectiveness of mitigative measures.

Dr. Art Martell, of the Canadian Wildlife Service, listed some of the important gaps in our knowledge of the biology of species that inhabit the coastal areas and the Delta. He included freshwater fish, birds (particularly waterfowl), certain furbearers, caribou, moose, Dall sheep, bears and whales.

There are even greater gaps in our knowledge of the Beaufort Sea. Dr. Allen Milne, head of the Beaufort Sea Project, and James Shearer, who had conducted research under this program described how little we know of aspects of the physical environment, such as sea-bed scour and sea-bed permafrost. Dr. Douglas Pimlott of the Canadian Arctic Resources Committee told the Inquiry that there is a pronounced imbalance between our knowledge of arctic marine ecosystems and the proposed industrial developments. In his view, our present knowledge approximates to a time base of 1890 as compared to other areas that are experiencing similar development. Dr. Jonathon Percy of the Fisheries and Marine Service, Environment Canada, said our knowledge of the effect of oil on the arctic marine environment is meagre and fragmented and that we have little knowledge of even the most basic ecology and physiology of most of the arctic marine species. Percy testified that our ecological ignorance makes it difficult to sustain or to refute predictions of widespread environmental disaster. Although attempts have been made to determine the impact of oil upon marine mammals and waterfowl, little attention has been paid to smaller organisms on which the larger forms of life depend. Where oil spills have occurred in the Arctic, we have learned very little because there was a complete absence of pre-spill baseline data.

We must learn more about the rates of degradation of oil by bacteria under varying circumstances. Assessment of the degradation rates will require greater knowledge of the populations of bacteria and of their natural variations. In laboratory tests, crude oils inhibit productivity and growth of phytoplankton under many, but not all, circumstances. We need to understand these interactions. We must also learn about effects of oil on the algal bloom that forms on and within the lower surface of ice in spring. This ice flora is an important fraction of the total biological production in the Arctic Ocean.

The gaps in environmental knowledge that I have listed here for the Delta–Beaufort region are complemented by a similar need for environmental information in the other areas that are of concern to this Inquiry: the Mackenzie Valley and the Northern Yukon. Together they underline the fact that present scientific knowledge is inadequate to serve the needs of government in assessing the impact of proposed oil and gas developments in the North. If government is to conduct such assessments effectively, it must undertake the scientific research that is required to provide this information.

Dr. Max Dunbar wrote *Environment and Common Sense* in 1971. What he said then about our knowledge of the North is still applicable today:

> We have been caught in a state of scientific near-nudity in the particular respect in which we now so urgently need protective covering: namely, knowledge of what the proposed developments will do to the environment, in precise terms, and knowledge of what should be done to conserve and to protect [it]. [p. 53]

INDUSTRY'S PLANS

Although the oil reserves at Norman Wells have been known to the industry since 1919, it is only within the last two decades that we have seen oil and gas exploration expand into the Northern Yukon, the Mackenzie Delta and the Beaufort Sea. In 1968, the discovery of gas at Prudhoe Bay in Alaska stimulated activity in the Western Arctic and focused national attention on the Delta–Beaufort region as a potential petroleum-producing area.

Drilling in the Delta region began in the mid-1960s, and Imperial made the first discovery of oil at Atkinson Point in 1970. Other discoveries of oil and gas have followed, and more than 100 holes have been drilled in the Delta region. About three-quarters of the region that is of most interest to the industry lies offshore under the Beaufort Sea. The permits granted so far in the Delta–Beaufort region cover the whole continental shelf out to and even beyond the 600-foot water-depth line.

In 1973 exploratory work began in the shallow waters adjacent to the coast. Artificial islands, built as drilling bases, have all been located within the zone of land-fast ice and in water less than 60 feet deep. Imperial and Sun Oil have already built about 15 islands and they expect to build several more.

In the summer of 1976, exploratory drilling began in the deeper water of the Beaufort Sea, when Canadian Marine Drilling Limited (CANMAR), a wholly-owned subsidiary of Dome Petroleum, moved two drill ships into the Beaufort Sea. They began by drilling two holes and made preparations for a further five. The first two holes are in water depths of 85 and 190 feet, and both are in the shear zone between the land-fast ice and the permanent polar pack ice. Moving ice may threaten drilling operations here even in summer.

But exploratory drilling, whether on land or offshore, is only part of the total activity that leads to the delineation of reserves and their eventual production. The Delta–Beaufort region has witnessed more than a decade of all phases of exploratory work. The forested portion of the Delta is a grid of arrow-straight paths bulldozed by seismic crews in their mapping of subsurface geological formations. There is already a major infrastructure of camps, wharves, stockpile sites, airstrips and winter roads to support this exploration. For example, the Gulf base at Swimming Point in the Delta is a self-sufficient distribution centre for men and material. It has a winter airstrip for jet aircraft and crews are rotated in and out directly from Calgary. Imperial and Shell have extensive facilities at Tununuk and Camp Farewell, respectively, and Imperial has a base camp and other facilities at Tuktoyaktuk.

Over the years, the exploration program has produced results; oil and gas have been found. There is a great deal of controversy about the extent of reserves in the Mackenzie Delta and the Beaufort Sea, but they are believed to be large enough to justify the expenditure of millions of dollars.

Exploration has expanded to offshore areas, and discoveries have been made there. Offshore production facilities would involve the creation of islands, and sea-bed pipelines would be needed for production. If a gas pipeline is built, it will probably be looped, and an oil pipeline may follow. Airports, roads, docks, stockpile sites—a whole industrial infrastructure would be needed for production. Tanker terminals and tanker transportation may follow.

These prospects indicate that the Delta–Beaufort region may become one of Canada's major oil and gas producing regions. With this in mind, let me turn to the proposals for a gas pipeline and gas production facilities.

PIPELINE PROPOSALS

In January 1976, Arctic Gas announced that it would seek a right-of-way to transport Alaskan gas across the northern part of the Delta (the Cross-Delta Route) to join the main line from Richards Island near Tununuk Point.

The Cross-Delta Route involves about 52 miles of right-of-way across the northern part of the Mackenzie Delta. Of this, 16 miles would be 48-inch-diameter single pipe, and 36 miles would be 36-inch-diameter twinned pipes. The two pipes would normally be laid 50 feet apart on land, 200 feet apart under Shallow Bay and as much as 4,000 feet apart under some of the main channels of the Delta. In crossing the Mackenzie Delta, some 12 miles of the right-of-way would be under water. This includes the 4.5 miles across Shallow Bay and the major crossings of West Channel, Middle (or Reindeer) Channel and Langley Channel. The four major water crossings would be built in summer, but the rest of the construction, including some 35 separate crossings of small channels and lakes, would be done in winter.

GAS PLANT PROPOSALS

Three gas plants are proposed to process natural gas for pipeline transmission. Clearly the industry has great expectations for the future in the Delta and offshore areas.

Two of the proposed gas plants, those of Imperial at Taglu and Shell at Niglintgak, will be in the Delta. Gulf proposes to build the third plant at Parsons Lake, east of the Delta proper. Gas gathering systems will bring the gas from the fields to each of the plants. The capital cost of these three gas plants and gathering systems will exceed $1 billion.

FUTURE PROSPECTS

The construction of the three plants and the pipeline will greatly increase barge traffic down the Mackenzie River, along the Arctic coast, and in Kugmallit Bay. When the plants and systems are in place, there will be gas plants, pipelines, compressor stations, flow lines, camps, on-site housing, all-weather roads, airfields, docks and regular passage of aircraft and vehicles across the Delta.

The extent of these operations is apparent, but they may well be only a beginning, for we can expect additional developments in the Delta and the Delta region. If there are pipelines running along an energy corridor from the Arctic to the mid-continent, there will be an extension of exploration and development into the Beaufort Sea. Roland Horsfield of Imperial suggested that most of the remaining potential of the Mackenzie Basin lies offshore in the Beaufort Sea. Dan Motyka of Gulf told the Inquiry that the hydrocarbon potential of the area increases farther offshore.

DELTA REGION IMPACTS

If we deal with each project piecemeal, we run the risk of missing the point. We are considering the establishment of a major petroleum province in the Delta–Beaufort region, and our predictions of impact will be sound only if we consider them comprehensively. The Delta supports a unique ecosystem and has been aptly compared to the Everglades. The ecosystem must be protected as a unit. However, to illustrate the impact that the pipeline and related activities will have on the Delta region, I shall concentrate on the principal biological concerns, the fish, birds and white whales. I intend to discuss the whales separately in the next section because of the direct threat that oil and gas developments pose to that population as a whole. Impacts on other species such as muskrat, beaver, reindeer, caribou and bear will be limited in extent and can be ameliorated. Little is said here about oil spills and their impact, because this subject is dealt with in some detail in a subsequent section.

FISH A properly regulated, scheduled and routed gas pipeline project, in itself, will probably have only local and short-term impact on fish, and little or no long-term impact—assuming there are no large spills of toxic materials. But it is not reasonable to consider the pipeline by itself; there will be other projects, and they will pose risks to the fish. The effects will be evident in decreased populations of the most economically important fish species, such as humpback whitefish, broad whitefish, inconnu, arctic char, and arctic and least cisco. Development will also disrupt fishing activities in the area.

When asked about the possibility of establishing an oil pipeline and an energy corridor along the route (in keeping with the government's 1972 Pipeline Guidelines), Dr. Peter McCart, fisheries consultant to Arctic Gas, said that he would be very reticent about a proposal to put an oil pipeline across the Delta. Jeff Stein of Environment Canada told the Inquiry that the Mackenzie Delta has been designated by the federal Fisheries and Marine Service as an area likely to be sensitive to pipeline construction. He concluded:

> ... the Mackenzie River Delta provides essential habitat for the maintenance of the fresh-water, coastal marine and anadromous fish resources in much of the southern Beaufort Sea area and lower Mackenzie River. The inshore zone is an important nursery, feeding and overwintering site for both nearshore and offshore organisms. It is especially important to those anadromous species which form the basis of the domestic and commercial fishery in the Delta; that is, broad whitefish, arctic char, arctic cisco and inconnu. Standing stocks of fish are greatest nearshore, since the anadromous species tend to frequent shallow coastal waters during the summer months rather than moving far offshore. Proposed developments in the Delta region can be expected to adversely affect aquatic resources. [F18436ff.]

Of course, pipelines are not the only kind of development that can adversely affect fish populations in the Delta. The construction and operation of gas plants, drilling and other exploration activities, and dredging or gravel-pit operations could all have impacts. For example, the plan that Imperial Oil described to the Inquiry for dredging sand at Big Horn Point could cause risks to important fish populations, but insufficient information was then available about the site to predict the magnitude of this concern.

BIRDS Dr. William Gunn, ornithological consultant to Arctic Gas, told the Inquiry that the whole of the Delta is important for waterfowl. In June, July and August 1975, he made four aerial surveys along the Arctic Gas Cross–Delta Route and found that the greatest number of nesting waterfowl occurred along the outer Mackenzie Delta section of the route in June. The Cross–Delta Route crosses some prime waterfowl habitats, especially on Ellice Island, where staging geese concentrate and there are important nesting grounds for swans, cranes and ducks. Originally a compressor station was planned for the middle of that area, but Arctic Gas has agreed, on the advice of Gunn, to move the compressor station to the eastern fringe of the Delta. Gunn also found that the Delta habitat may, in a given year, be as vital as the north slope of the Yukon to the snow geese. Normally, the majority of the snow geese stage on the north slope, but in 1975, it was snow-covered in early September when the geese arrived, and most of the geese moved into the Shallow Bay area of the Delta. The peak number of geese there was an estimated 325,000 out of a total of 375,000 in the entire region. These birds are extremely vulnerable to aircraft overflights and to the kind of disturbance that would be associated with the summer construction of the Shallow Bay crossing as well as the ongoing activity associated with an operating pipeline.

That is why Gunn and Dr. Tom Barry of the Canadian Wildlife Service would prefer a crossing farther upstream than that now proposed by Arctic Gas. They are concerned that the route chosen by Arctic Gas will cross vital nesting and staging areas in the Delta.

Both Gunn and Barry spoke at length about the devastating impact of oil spills on birds. Both emphasized the lack of any suitable means of rehabilitating birds that come into contact with oil, even in temperate climates. Oil mats the feathers together so they are no longer able to function for flight, to repel water or for insulation. Once this happens, the birds generally die by drowning or exposure; they are also harmed by the direct toxic effects of oil when ingested through preening their feathers in an attempt to rid themselves of contaminants. When cross-examined about an oil pipeline following a gas pipeline across the Delta, Gunn said:

> My concern is with the possibility of oil leaks or spills along the line, in areas that are of particular importance to birds, since there are numbers of these in the Delta. I feel that it might be difficult to find a suitable route across the Delta on that basis. [F20213]

In his report, *The Need to Preserve the Integrity of the Mackenzie Delta,* Gunn went beyond the pipeline proposals and considered the impact of a broad range of hydro-carbon developments in the Delta. He noted that the pipeline, in itself, and a reasonable number of oil and gas wells would not, in themselves, compromise the integrity of the environment. But he added:

> The problem, however, comes with the establishment of processing plants at or near the wellhead for the purpose of modifying the composition of the gas (or oil) to a form suitable for extended transmission. . . .
>
> Although the environmental effects of any one of these plants might individually be acceptable, we are particularly concerned with the combined and cumulative effects. Because we believe that they would unquestionably result in deterioration of the Delta as a viable ecological unit, we are therefore strongly opposed to processing plants on the Delta. In our view, these plants should be located on the "mainland" to the southeast, where they could be connected to Inuvik by a permanent road. [p. 9ff.]

AMELIORATION OF IMPACTS IN THE DELTA REGION

The first condition for the amelioration of impact in the Delta is a requirement that no pipeline be allowed to cross the Mackenzie Delta. This conclusion is based on the pipeline's impact on birds and fish that I have outlined, the impact on white whales that I will discuss in the next section, and on the overall importance and sensitivity of the outer Delta ecosystem in general.

To protect the fish resources of the Delta, research must keep pace with development activity. It is only by filling in the gaps in our knowledge that effective measures can be instituted to limit impacts to an acceptable level. This can be done on a project-by-project basis.

Such measures will not, however, suffice to protect the birds of the Delta. The migratory birds that use the region are an important international wildlife resource; the whole Delta, and particularly the outer Delta, is critical for them. Gunn has said that the whole Arctic coast from Prudhoe Bay to the Delta is ornithologically sensitive. I have already discussed the importance of the north slope of the Yukon for birds, particularly snow geese. The wilderness park in the Northern Yukon that I have proposed would protect them.

Witnesses before the Inquiry said that the boundaries of the Kendall Island Bird Sanctuary are being redrawn. On the basis of the evidence placed before me, I consider it important to extend the sanctuary westward to cover the entire outer Delta across to the wilderness park that I have recommended for the Northern Yukon.

The establishment of such a bird sanctuary, unlike the wilderness park, will not prohibit oil and gas exploration and development. In fact, there already are proposals for two gas plants within the Kendall Island Bird Sanctuary. But a sanctuary does provide protection to the birds by placing regulatory powers in the hands of the Canadian Wildlife Service, which has a statutory mandate to protect migratory birds. I urge that when the sanctuary is established, the means should be provided at the same time to protect the habitat on which the birds depend.

WHALES AND A WHALE SANCTUARY

In summer the white whales of the Beaufort Sea converge on the Mackenzie Delta to calve. The herd—some 5,000 animals—remains in the vicinity of the Delta throughout the summer, then leaves for the open sea. For these animals, the warm waters around the Mackenzie Delta, especially Mackenzie Bay, are critical habitat, for here they have their young. Nowhere else, so far as we know, can they go for this essential part of their life cycle. We must preserve these waters from any disturbance that would drive the whales from them.

Construction of the gas pipeline across Shallow Bay, as proposed by Arctic Gas, and construction of an oil pipeline along the same corridor, together with associated barge and aircraft activity, would have a definite impact on the whale population; but the long-term threat comprises the whole complex of petroleum activities in the coastal waters bordering the Mackenzie Delta, Richards Island and adjacent areas. These activities would include construction of artificial islands or other drilling platforms, associated dredging and barge movements, drilling of wells, construction of flow lines, and blasting. The cumulative and long-term impact would be great.

It is imperative, if we are to protect the whales, to establish a whale sanctuary in Mackenzie Bay and to forbid oil and gas exploration and development and pipeline construction within it.

Our knowledge of the white whales of the Beaufort Sea is limited. We do not even know whether they winter in the Pacific Ocean or remain in the Arctic Ocean. In spring, they migrate along leads in the pack ice into the Beaufort Sea from the west, arriving in May or June. The whales move into the warm, shallow water around the Delta in late June or early July as soon as there are open leads through the ice, and stay around the channel mouths until mid-August. They are there in large numbers: the population was estimated at 3,500 to 4,000 in 1973, 1974 and 1975. Whales have been sighted throughout the Delta, and even as far south as Point Separation.

The Inuit who spoke to the Inquiry at Tuktoyaktuk testified that whales come from Mackenzie Bay into Kugmallit Bay as soon as the ice north of Kendall Island allows them to get around it, in late June or July. Even though they may go back into Mackenzie Bay, they return to Kugmallit Bay and stay there well into September. If summer is late, the whales may not reach Mackenzie Bay until mid-August, and they will then stay in Kugmallit Bay until late September. By the end of September, they can be seen offshore near the pack ice.

Many Inuit and some Indians regularly go out to hunt whales from camps in the Delta, and the people of Tuktoyaktuk go out from the village daily. Archaeological finds indicate that the Inuit have hunted white whales from Kittigazuit and Radio Creek for at least 500 years. Today, they take about 150 whales a year. It is estimated that they kill about 300, but they are able to recover only about half of that number. This level of hunting does not diminish the herd.

Robert Webb of Slaney and Company conducted a study of white whales for Imperial Oil in the area between Kugmallit Bay and the west side of Mackenzie Bay, and south into Shallow Bay, beyond the proposed pipeline crossing. The purpose of the study was to determine the effect that the construction of offshore islands would have on the distribution of whales in the Delta and on the taking of whales by native people. The study, which began in 1972, continued through the summer of 1975. In two of these four years, apparently few whales entered Shallow Bay; but in the other two years they were observed as far south as the mouth of Reindeer Channel. However, Webb feels that the infrequency of the observations and the turbidity of the Delta water may limit the reliability of these observations. Perhaps whales did enter Shallow Bay in larger numbers, but were simply not observed. It is not known exactly where the whales drop their calves. New-born calves have been sighted in Shallow Bay and Kugmallit Bay, but their dark colour makes them difficult to see in the turbid water. Probably most calves are born in the main whale concentration area in west Mackenzie Bay–Shallow Bay. The warm river water is essential habitat for the new-born young until they develop enough blubber to survive in the colder oceanic water. If they had to move out earlier, the calves would lose body heat and die in the cold water.

THE LONG-TERM THREAT

The construction of a pipeline across the Delta may bar the whales' access to Shallow Bay. If it does keep them from Shallow Bay, the herd probably will be diminished only slightly, if we can assume that the crossing would be built in just one summer, and that the only calves lost would be those that would have been dropped in Shallow Bay. Even if the whales were kept right out of Mackenzie Bay by barge traffic and related activity during the period of pipeline construction, and even if the construction took two or three years, the worst that might happen would be the loss of two or three years' calves. These losses could reduce the size of the herd but would not threaten its survival. But a pipeline across Shallow Bay cannot be considered in isolation. It is only a beginning.

If the pipeline is built, there will be increased oil and gas exploration and development in the Beaufort Sea. This development, both nearshore and offshore, will have a large impact on the whale population, greater in the long run than that of a pipeline crossing the Mackenzie Delta.

Although the whales concentrate in west Mackenzie Bay–Shallow Bay, east Mackenzie Bay and Kugmallit Bay, it is the west Mackenzie Bay–Shallow Bay area that is critical. Dr. David Sergeant of the Department of the Environment, who is Canada's leading authority on white whales, says that if calving were seriously disrupted annually, the population could ultimately die out. He is supported by Dr. Paul Brodie, who is also an authority on the subject. Sergeant's view is that the cumulative impact of oil and gas exploration and development may lead to the gradual expulsion of the calving whales from Mackenzie Bay. Sergeant called our attention to the experience at the mouth of Churchill River, at Churchill, Manitoba, which was once a calving ground for white whales. The port facilities there have driven the whales away to calve elsewhere, and their major calving area now is at the mouth of Seal River, about 20 miles to the north which, fortunately, can accommodate them.

Sergeant cannot see any other river mouths in the neighbourhood of the Mackenzie Delta that could receive a large number of whales for calving. None receive them now. A few whales move into Liverpool Bay and around the mouth of the Anderson River in late July, after they have left the Delta. But these waters become free of ice later than those around the Delta, and to reach them the whales would have to postpone calving. That may or may not be possible. In any event, the warm water available at the mouth of the Anderson River could not support the herd that now calves around the Mackenzie Delta, and the seasonal variation of ice conditions might well close off that estuary in some years. Sergeant, summarizing his evidence, stated:

> . . . the population of white whales which calves in the Mackenzie is virtually the whole of the population in the Beaufort Sea. I postulate that simultaneous oil and gas activities throughout the whole Delta in July each year could so disturb the whale herd that they would be unable to reproduce successfully. In time, the herd would die out. If we wish to maintain the herd, we must initiate measures now [for example, establish a special reserve for calving whales] which we can be certain will allow its successful reproduction annually. [F18496ff.]

A WHALE SANCTUARY

I think a whale sanctuary should be established in west Mackenzie Bay, where the main mass of white whales gather in July, and where the main calving area is located. No oil and gas exploration should be allowed there, no artificial islands built there, no wells drilled there, and no pipelines allowed to cross it.

Sergeant and Webb agree that, of the three areas where the whales are found in concentrations between June 20 and August 15, west Mackenzie Bay is the most important area because it is the main calving area. The sanctuary should be the same size or greater than the area used by the main herd of whales in west Mackenzie Bay in most years.

In recommending a whale sanctuary, I have relied upon the evidence of Sergeant and Brodie. Their views on the long-term threat that oil and gas exploration and development in the Mackenzie Delta hold for the white whales were not challenged by Arctic Gas. Neither were they challenged by Imperial, Gulf and Shell, all of whom were represented by counsel when the evidence was heard. I have relied also on the evidence given by Inuit hunters at the hearings held in the Delta communities.

Is there any alternative to a whale sanctuary? It could be argued that, if oil and gas exploration and development were suspended in the summer, to be resumed again in winter when the whales are out at sea, the sanctuary would not be necessary. I think this idea is impractical. Once you permitted exploration of the waters of the sanctuary, even if you began by restricting such activity to the winter, you would inevitably find that certain activities must go on in summer. If industry is permitted to explore in these waters, there may be a need for summer seismic exploration, artificial islands for drilling platforms, and barge traffic during the short ice-free season. If oil or gas is discovered, then flow lines will be built. There are, in fact, a multitude of activities that can be carried out efficiently and economically only in summer.

Sergeant has proposed a sanctuary in which not only oil and gas exploration and development but also whale hunting by native people would be prohibited. There is an irony here. Many native people in Aklavik, Tuktoyaktuk, Sachs Harbour, Holman, Paulatuk and Inuvik told the Inquiry that they oppose oil and gas exploration and development in the Mackenzie Delta and the Beaufort Sea because of the impact they fear it will have on whales. A sanctuary would offer a measure of protection to the herd, and it would coincide with the wish of the native people to protect the herd. But if, at the same time, they are denied the right to hunt whales, what I regard as one of the main purposes of the sanctuary would be undermined.

I do not advocate a sanctuary in which native people are forbidden to hunt: I think their claim on these animals is fundamental. I think native hunting can be permitted without endangering the herd. Hunting is heaviest in Kugmallit Bay, and east Mackenzie Bay, which are remote from the proposed sanctuary. If hunting pressure appeared to threaten the herd, it could be reduced or even prohibited. But no such check could be imposed upon oil and gas exploration and development in the sanctuary, once a pipeline is built and the corridor established.

Is a whale sanctuary in west Mackenzie Bay a practical proposition? What will its effect be on future oil and gas exploration? Will it impose an unacceptable check on oil and gas exploration and development in the Mackenzie Delta and the Beaufort Sea? These are very difficult questions to answer. However, I note that the areas of intense petroleum exploration, to date, lie east of the proposed whale sanctuary, both offshore and onshore. Moreover, there has been substantially less seismic work in the sanctuary area than in adjoining areas to the east. If this trend continues, and if it reflects a difference in petroleum potential, then a whale sanctuary can be set aside, and oil and gas activity can be forbidden there without impairing industry's ability to tap the principal sources of petroleum beneath the Beaufort Sea.

The proposed sanctuary is itself a compromise. The evidence shows that in past years there have been whale concentrations northeast of the proposed sanctuary, in an area where a number of artificial islands have recently been established. I am not proposing that the sanctuary extend that far: that area has already, in a sense, been given over to industrial use. I should draw the northern boundary of the sanctuary south of the Adgo field, where gas and oil have been found. This seems to me a reasonable compromise between the competing uses. The sanctuary would not then deny industry access to any waters where discoveries have been made, and yet it would retain within its waters the areas where most calving occurs.

The trend of exploration appears to offer us an opportunity to set aside certain offshore waters as a whale sanctuary, but this trend is by no means a certainty. In the final analysis, the Government of Canada will have to decide whether or not to protect this herd of whales. If we decide to protect them, we must establish a sanctuary that will be inviolate regardless of the prospects for oil and gas discoveries. Once a discovery has been made within the sanctuary, it would be difficult to resist the urge to look for other reserves near it. We must decide whether we are going to protect these animals or not. If we are going to protect them, we must establish a whale sanctuary now.

OFFSHORE CONCERNS

THE MOVE OFFSHORE

Exploration has now moved offshore. Permits granted cover the whole continental shelf of the Beaufort Sea. Spokesmen for the industry told the Inquiry that the greatest potential reserves are thought to be there. Ten wells have already been drilled offshore from man-made islands. Dome Petroleum, through its subsidiary CANMAR, has begun a 16-hole deep-water exploratory program from drill ships. Two wells were drilled in the summer of 1976.

Offshore petroleum development in the Beaufort Sea is in its infancy.

But if the pipeline were approved and industry were assured of a transportation system for gas and a corridor for oil, both onshore and offshore exploration would be intensified. Flow lines, pipelines, oil and gas processing facilities, delineation drilling and related logistics and support activities would expand beyond the Delta and the man-made islands already built.

The Beaufort Sea offers one of the world's most hostile marine environments to oil and gas exploration. Much of it is covered by the permanent polar pack ice, which circulates slowly around the Polar Basin. The area between the polar pack and land is seasonally covered by ice. Land-fast ice forms during the fall along the shoreline and shallow water areas, and drilling from man-made islands has taken place in this zone. Between the land-fast ice and the polar pack is the shear zone, where currents and other forces cause the ice to move, forming huge pressure ridges with intermittent leads of open water. It is in this shear zone that Dome Petroleum's wells are located. In summer, when CANMAR drills these wells, ice flows moving across this area are a hazard to the ships and drilling operations.

The industry's ability to do this work under these formidable conditions represents a major achievement, and it has taken us across a technological and geographic frontier that no other nation has yet crossed. It is, nevertheless, a pioneering venture that entails serious short-term and long-term environmental risk. Vince Steen, in speaking to the Inquiry, voiced the concern of many Inuit people:

> Now they want to drill out there. Now they want to build [a] pipeline, and they say they're not going to hurt the country while they do it. . . .
>
> If they drill out there, if they finish off what little whales are left, what little seals are left, what little polar bears are left, with one oil spill of any size big enough to hurt those animals, we're finished. The Eskimo population and culture is finished, because you [will] have to live as a white man and you [will] have nothing left. You have no more seals to feed the foxes. You've got no more fish to feed the seals, and you've got no more seals to feed the polar bears, and the polar bears are going to go looking for some white men then, because they've got nothing left to eat.
>
> Already in the Eastern Arctic there are Eskimos getting seals covered with oil, and there's no oil work there yet, just from ships spilling their used oil; and seals, because they're covered with oil, they've got no more hair on their heads, no more hair on their body, and they're starving. That's on record in Yellowknife the last two weeks or so.
>
> If they get . . . an oil spill out there in that moving ice where they can't control it, that's the end of the seals. I think that not only will this part of the world suffer if the ocean is finished, I think every [Eskimo, from Alaska] all the way to the Eastern Arctic is going to suffer because that oil is

going to finish the seals. It's going to finish the fish, and those fish don't just stay here, they go all over. Same with the seals, same with the polar bears, they go all over the place, and if they come here and get soaked with oil, they're finished.

For the Eskimo to believe now that the white man is not going to do any damage out there with his oil drilling and his oil wells is just about impossible, because he hasn't proven himself, as far as I'm concerned he hasn't proven himself worthy of being believed any more. That includes the federal government because I know I've worked with them, and I've done seismic work for them where they just blew up fish, and they had to be shut down by the federal Fisheries, there were so many fish killed. But he was not going to shut himself down, not as long as there was nobody seeing him doing it. . . . So how can you just blame the oil company or the average white man? It's the government. The government is not running things—they're not even controlling themselves, how can they control anybody else? [C4201ff.]

The move to drill offshore began in 1971, when Imperial Oil applied for permission to build an island to use as a drilling platform in the Beaufort Sea. The Government of Canada granted that permission in 1973, and the artificial island, called Immerk, was built in shallow coastal waters with material dredged from the sea floor.

In the winter of 1973–1974, Panarctic drilled its first well in the high Arctic from reinforced ice in Hecla and Griper Bay, near Melville Island. This and subsequent offshore wells in the high Arctic have been drilled from ice-thickened pads on sea ice. The drilling is done in late winter and early spring, but it must stop while there is still enough time in the season to drill a relief well, should one be required to control a blowout.

The drilling in Hecla and Griper Bay and from Immerk set a precedent of great importance; it marked the transition from land to marine operations in the Arctic and the first move toward a new frontier of exploration. This frontier was extended when, on July 31, 1973, the Cabinet gave approval in principle to Dome's drilling program in the Beaufort Sea.

Because Dome's program is in the shear zone, drilling from the ice is impossible; it must, therefore, take place during the short summer season from ships. Special safety precautions and quick evacuation measures have been developed in case ice threatens the drill sites. But the summer season of open water is very short, and, if there were a blowout, the time available to drill a relief well would be severely limited. If a blowout occurred late in the season, it might not be possible to control it with a relief well until the following summer.

Although drilling from artificial islands poses similar problems, the risks are not of the same order of magnitude. If another island had to be built to control a blowout, that could be done in summer and winter, although break-up and freeze-up might prolong the construction period. Artificial islands in deep water may create further problems because of the long time required to build the island needed for the relief well.

After the Cabinet's approval in principle of offshore drilling, the government initiated the Beaufort Sea Project. This joint government-industry venture was planned as a two-year program, and much of the work took place during the season of open water, which usually lasts about two and one-half months.

If a pipeline is built, the industry will be eager to proceed with a drilling program going far beyond Dome's 16 wells. It is the risks of this expanded program that concern me.

SEA-BED PERMAFROST AND ICE SCOUR

To illustrate the novel technological challenges that lie ahead in petroleum development in the Beaufort Sea and the risks that may lead to oil spills, let me describe briefly some problems created by sea-bed permafrost and ice scour. According to James Shearer, floating ice in the Beaufort Sea scours the sea floor out to about the 100-foot contour, although most recent scouring is thought to be within water depths of up to 60 feet. The depth of scour penetration into the sea floor varies: most are less than 10 feet, but some scours 25 feet deep have been noted. This ice action obviously poses real threats for platforms and sea-bed installations, such as pipelines or flow lines connecting wells to offshore and onshore production facilities.

The native people who live in the Beaufort region are well aware of this problem and are therefore quite anxious about offshore development. Here is what Sandy Wolki told the Inquiry when we visited North Star Harbour:

> I am concerned about the drilling offshore . . . it may be disaster for sure. . . . At one time . . . I was chasing a polar bear along the ridges and I had to jump from one ridge to another because they were like huge mountains . . . I got among those pressure ridges, it's way out and it's very deep, but in the gouges from that pressure it was bringing some mud up and [I] saw some earth on top of the pressure ridge that was almost unbelievable because it was in the deep water. . . .
>
> If they build a pipeline from the Beaufort Sea to the mainland, if that type of pressure starts to build up [it doesn't matter how] much protection or no matter how well you put it in, it will have some effect on the pipeline because of the ice and the gouges that it worked with. Taking mud from the bottom is something that we haven't studied yet.
>
> . . . even the scientists or whoever is studying that area . . . haven't done enough studies or don't know enough about it because when [I] was out

there . . . the pressure ice was so heavy that it was just like mountains . . . that's just the surface part. What about the bottom part? . . . [I] know the large percentage of ice is in the bottom and when [I saw] this mud coming up from the deep water [I am] really concerned because nobody really has studied it or made any true look at it. . . . [I've] seen it with [my] own eyes and if they can do that gouging way out down deep, there must be some . . . heavy or strong pressure . . . somewhere in order to develop this type of mud. Because of the rolling, I guess it starts to build up pressure, the ice starts to build up pressure. [I] saw some thickness of the ice . . . it's not just thin ice, it's all heavy ice.

[I am] concerned about it because nobody really knows anything about that pressure ridge. It's really strange to see it, and if they build a pipeline anywhere in the Beaufort Sea and this type of thing should happen to occur there's bound to be some damage or disaster within that time. [C4151ff.]

There is permafrost in the ground below the Beaufort Sea. In some places the frozen soils seem to be very close to the surface, but we do not know how much ice they contain. If, as appears likely, the offshore flow lines must pass through frozen ground, it will be important not to melt the permafrost, in order to prevent subsidence and damage to the flow lines. The same kinds of problems that we discussed earlier in connection with a buried refrigerated gas pipeline are present here: the melting of permafrost and the possibility of creating frost heave.

Questions relating to offshore permafrost, ice scour and offshore production and transportation of hydrocarbons cannot be left for industry alone to solve. I therefore urge again that the Government of Canada establish a northern research program into these basic problems to provide the knowledge it will require concerning industrial development in the North.

SPILLS AND BLOWOUTS

One of the major risks in an expanded program of offshore exploration and development is an oil spill. I am talking here about a major oil spill, such as from a blowout beneath the sea or the sinking of an oil tanker. The chances of such a spill are difficult to calculate and different estimates of the probability have been quoted. But this much is clear: increased activity increases the possibility of such a spill. The consequences of a major oil spill would be catastrophic.

How much oil might be released from a blowout on the sea bottom? Dr. Allen Milne said that, if an undersea blowout ran wild for a year, the volume of oil discharged under the ice would be comparable to that carried by a supertanker.

There have been blowouts in the Arctic, but fortunately, none has involved oil. Of the two gas wells that have blown out in the high Arctic, one ran wild for nine months, discharging gas into the air. Dome Petroleum had trouble with the two wells drilled in the Beaufort Sea in 1976: one well had a blowout involving fresh water, the other had an underground blowout in which gas escaped from the well into a porous rock formation before it reached the surface. Both were said to be under control by the end of the 1976 drilling season.

When you consider the industry's high hopes and, indeed, their oft-stated expectations of substantial oil and gas reserves under the Beaufort Sea, you see that the chances of an oil blowout in these hazardous waters cannot be discounted. There is much to be said for a very conservative approach in these matters.

We should not forget that the people who are most concerned are the native people. Here is what Sam Raddi, President of the Committee for Original Peoples Entitlement, told me in Inuvik:

> For the people that want to drill on Beaufort Sea, Mr. Berger, I want you to take note of this. I spent a lot of time with my father—he is 74 years old—and his cousin, Phillip Nuviak, who is 84 years old. . . . They tell me in their stories that the old-timers, their great-grandfathers, would tell them that one day, if the ocean, the Beaufort Sea ever loses its fish and wildlife, the whales, the fishes, the seals, the polar bears, if the Beaufort Sea will lose that, the natives—the Eskimos—will have very little chance to survive. They said the main source of food comes from the ocean and they always tell us to respect the whole Beaufort Sea.
>
> So we have been trying all these years to protect the whole Beaufort Sea, and also the animals on the land, respect the land and the animals, not to overkill them. Now, Mr. Berger, it seems like this is the end of a lot of food for us. If they ever drill in the Beaufort Sea, if they ever have an accident, nobody really knows how much damage it will make on the Beaufort Sea. Nobody really knows how many fish it will kill, or whales, polar bears, the little whales and the bowheads.
>
> These people that did research on the Beaufort Sea will never be able to answer these things. When will the fish and the whales come back? They got no answer, and yet they want to go ahead and drill on the Beaufort Sea. It's the Eskimos that will pay for any damage, any oil spills, any damage to wildlife, it will be us that will be paying for it the rest of our lives. God knows if the fish and the whales will ever come back. We don't know.
>
> Mr. Berger, I hope you take note of this and it's unfair to us because there's very little research done on the Beaufort Sea. Two years of research and they feel they have enough information to give a permit to go out and

drill. That's not true because we lived here millions of years, and we know in two years they cannot get all the answers to what they are trying to achieve. [C3458ff.]

SPILL CLEAN-UP

DELTA SPILLS AND CLEAN-UP

A spill within the Delta would quickly spread through its myriad channels, subchannels, swamps, bogs, lakes and mud flats. Although the degree of pollution would vary with the site of the spill and the river level at the time, it is physical conditions such as these that led Dr. Norman Snow, a biologist with the Department of Indian Affairs and Northern Development, to conclude:

> ... the Mackenzie Delta and its immediate adjacent offshore area represents a set of conditions which would tend to maximize the adverse effects of an oil spill if one were to occur there. [F19125ff.]

Spills on land are relatively easy to manage. The main problems arise when a spill reaches water. If there is a major spill in the Delta, it is highly probable that it will get into the water, because of the myriad channels and lakes that make up the Delta and because of the extent of seasonal flooding.

But it is not just a spill within the Delta that would threaten it. A spill anywhere along the lower Mackenzie River could be carried into the Delta. Oil spilled in the Beaufort Sea could be carried along the coast into the waters bordering the Delta and, through the action of storm surges and reversing currents, onto the Delta itself. If an oil spill did spread through the Delta, the possibilities of cleaning it up are minimal. The oil would remain for a long time.

An oil spill in the Delta could seriously impair the productivity of its wildlife resources. Chemical pollutants in the water could alter the food chain. Valuable habitat could be lost. Salt marsh grasses, seaweeds and other aquatic vegetation could be destroyed. If such damage is extensive, sediments normally held stationary by the roots of these plants could be eroded. Vegetation so polluted generally takes two or three years to recover. We know from an oil-spill experiment in Caribou Bar Creek that a small quantity of crude oil reduced the zoobenthic organisms to one-third of their previous abundance. Snow said that successive spills or heavier contamination would produce an even greater decrease, thereby impairing a stream's capacity to sustain fish. He summarized the effects of an oil spill on birds in these words:

Seabirds are probably the most obvious casualties of oil spills. Mortality usually results from the destruction of the water-proofing and heat-insulation ability of their feathers and also from oil ingestion during preening. The Delta and offshore areas are utilized extensively by many bird species . . . [and] apart from the direct mortality from oil spills, [there is] the additional long-term component which may result from the loss of nestlings, the nest sites themselves being rendered useless for future generations, by oil contamination, and the threat of degrading feeding, brood-rearing and staging areas. [F19127ff.]

What response could be made to an oil spill in the Delta? If it were a major spill, there is very little that could be done. If a major spill cannot be efficiently cleaned up—and we know it cannot be—in the more favourable conditions of the temperate latitudes, one certainly could not be cleaned up in the harsher and remoter northern environment.

BEAUFORT SEA SPILLS AND CLEAN-UP

Spills of oil in the Beaufort Sea, whether from a blowout or from another source, may be caught up in the sea ice, dispersed in the water column, absorbed into bottom sediments and spread along the coast. The oil and ice interaction may take many forms. Oil could be encased in growing seasonal ice and could move long distances in that form before being released in the spring melt. Or it might be incorporated into the polar ice pack, where it would be retained for many years. Oil could accumulate under the floating ice or spread along open water leads.

The spread of oil in the vicinity of the Delta would be enhanced by the movement of the river water in rapidly changing patterns over the denser and colder sea water. Our knowledge of these water movements is limited.

In the spring, the higher forms of marine life, such as seal, polar bear and white whale, migrate along the open leads in the ice. Oil would also move along these leads as they open up in the spring. As the band of open water in the shear zone expands, oil will move closer to shore and, finally, when the land-fast ice melts, oil will move freely about and reach the shoreline.

Birds that migrate to the Arctic in spring seek out these areas of open water. Landing on oiled water is likely to be fatal for them. According to Dr. Tom Barry of the Canadian Wildlife Service, a lead of open water in the ice off Cape Dalhousie, at the tip of Tuktoyaktuk Peninsula, may be occupied by 50,000 birds at any one time in the late spring. These birds are replaced in a few days by 50,000 others, who need the open water to feed and rest, and so on through the migration period. The possibilities for enormous losses of bird life are obvious.

A spill of oil could work right through the food chain. I have described the under-ice biota in the Beaufort Sea. If oil reduces the food supply of benthic invertebrates and fish, the seals will be affected, and through them the polar bear is threatened. Even though the polar bears might not be threatened directly by an oil spill, they might well be threatened indirectly.

Dr. Allen Milne, head of the Beaufort Sea Project, testified that the consequences would be very serious if a major oil spill occurred in the Beaufort Sea. The Project's environmental assessment indicates that recovery of the Beaufort Sea marine ecosystem from even a single major spill could take as long as a decade.

Given the scale of hydrocarbon development that is envisaged for the Delta–Beaufort region, a major spill is not only likely, it is inevitable over time. That must be our assumption, and it is based on the experience of spills elsewhere during exploration, and during production, transportation, handling and storage. We have not yet developed clean-up techniques adequate for major spills in temperate or tropical waters. We simply are not prepared for a major spill in the Beaufort–Delta region. The equipment we do have will not be effective; our present knowledge of the marine ecosystem, of ice conditions and of the behaviour of oil in arctic waters is quite insufficient to provide the information that is needed. What we do know simply reinforces this conclusion: we could not clean up a major oil spill in the Beaufort Sea.

ALBEDO, CLIMATE AND RESEARCH

On April 15, 1970, Parliament passed the Arctic Waters Pollution Prevention Act, a landmark in the development of legislation to protect the ecology of arctic waters. On that occasion, Prime Minister Trudeau used these words:

> The Arctic ice pack has been described as the most significant surface area of the globe, for it controls the temperature of much of the Northern Hemisphere. Its continued existence in unspoiled form is vital to all mankind. The single most imminent threat to the Arctic at this time is the threat of a large oil spill . . . [which] . . . would destroy effectively the primary source of food for Eskimos and carnivorous wildlife throughout an area of thousands of square miles. . . . Because of the minute rate of hydrocarbon decomposition in frigid areas, the presence of any such oil must be regarded as permanent. The disastrous consequences which its presence would have on marine plankton, upon the process of oxygenation in Arctic North America, and upon other natural and vital processes of the biosphere, are incalculable in their extent. [p. 5ff.]

What did the Prime Minister mean when he said that the arctic ice pack controls the temperature of much of the northern hemisphere?

What did he mean when he said its continued existence in unspoiled form is vital to all mankind?

He was referring to albedo, that is, to the reflective capacity of ice. The presence of oil would darken the ice, and lower its capacity to reflect light. More solar energy would be absorbed, which could lead to the ice melting earlier than usual. This change would enlarge the area of open water in the Arctic Ocean and lengthen the open water season to some degree, which in turn could bring about changes in climate. Whether a reduction of the ice pack by this means would ultimately have an effect on the climate that would exceed the effect from natural fluctuations in ice cover is something we do not know.

The Beaufort Sea Project considered this very question when it examined the risks of the Dome drilling program. E. R. Walker wrote:

> The effects of oil on the large-scale heat budget of the Beaufort Sea and Arctic Ocean are dependent on the scale of oil release. For the scenario for exploratory drilling, of one blowout, or even for a much larger release of oil, the area covered by oil would be too small to affect the large-scale heat budget of the Beaufort Sea, let alone of the Arctic Ocean as a whole. [*Oil, Ice and Climate in the Beaufort Sea,* p. 35]

However, the Beaufort Sea Project's terms of reference were limited to only the exploratory phase of Dome's drilling program. Walker was not prepared to say that he was certain there would be no impact on climate in the production phase. He put it this way:

> . . . it is certain that during the exploration phase of Beaufort Sea operations not enough oil is likely to be released to affect even local climate.
>
> The effect of oil release upon climate during a possible production phase is less certain. The writer's opinion is that while sizeable volumes of oil may be released, this oil will probably not spread over a sufficient area to affect anything but local climate. However as noted above several uncertainties remain. [p. 34]

These uncertainties relate to behaviour of oil in the ice, the migration of oil to the surface of the ice, the rate at which it evaporates, the rate at which it degrades, the circulation of the ice, the impact of open water on the weather and so on.

Milne felt that one major spill would not have any effect on the climate:

> . . . it is unlikely that oil discharged into the Beaufort Sea from a single oil well blowout running for several years would have any effect whatever on global or even local climate. [F18988]

But he entered a caveat:

> This is not to discount the possible climatic effects which might occur
> from a continuation of oil spills which might result from more wells being
> drilled and offshore production, and production spills and pipeline
> breaks. Now we're getting into a different order of magnitude there.
> [F19011]

Arctic oil and gas exploration and production would not be limited to
the Beaufort Sea. Drilling is also going on in the high Arctic, and there
are plans for offshore drilling in the Eastern Arctic. The Americans are
planning to drill offshore from Alaska's north slope. The Soviet Union
may soon be drilling off its immensely long arctic coastline. Drilling may
also take place off the Arctic coast of Norway and off the coast of Greenland. Do we have any idea of the impact of several major spills in arctic
waters around the globe? These events may be only five, 10 or 15 years
away.

Through the Beaufort Sea Project we now have assessed the risks
faced by an initial exploration of Canadian waters in the Beaufort Sea.
We are uncertain about the extent of the risks that production would
cause in those waters, and we have not yet attempted to appraise the
risks of simultaneous oil and gas exploration and development in arctic
waters by all the circumpolar countries.

To what extent might the climate be affected by a series of major spills
in arctic waters? No one can say. And no one is investigating the matter.
The Beaufort Sea Project has been terminated. There is no international
program underway to investigate this phenomenon. Canada, as the pioneer of arctic offshore drilling, ought to take the initiative.

A study must be made of the interaction of ice and oil, of the biological degradation of oil in icy waters, and of the possible influence of the
loss of the polar pack on climate. Who should carry out this research? I
say it should be fully funded by government, and carried out under government auspices. The Beaufort Sea Project will not do as a model. That
project was jointly sponsored by government and industry. That kind of
arrangement mixes up the functions of government and the goals of
industry.

The Prime Minister referred in 1970 to the critical role of the polar ice
pack in the world's weather system. Canada, having been the first to
warn of the risks involved in spilling oil in arctic waters, and having been
the first to drill in these ice-infested waters, should lead the way in call-
ing for an international program of research. Canada should propose
that research should be undertaken jointly by the circumpolar nations
into the risks and the consequences of oil and gas exploration, development and transportation activities around and under the Arctic Ocean.

The question of what effect oil spills in arctic waters will have on albedo and climate is one that is surrounded by controversy. I have cited the views of two Canadian scientists who take a conservative approach in the matter. It illustrates once again my general concern over the adequacy of scientific knowledge relating to oil and gas development in the North. It demonstrates the need for fundamental and applied research.

The albedo question is only one of a number of gaps in our knowledge that have hampered this Inquiry in conducting its assessment and in making the judgment that it has been called upon to make. Undoubtedly similar gaps in our knowledge will hamper the government's assessment of future petroleum development in Northern Canada for years to come.

I take as a basic principle that government ought to be in a position to make independent and enlightened judgments about engineering and environmental aspects of proposals advanced by industry for northern development. To be able to make such judgments, government must be capable of assessing the scientific and engineering research that industry has carried out. When fundamental questions of environmental impact are involved, government cannot leave it to industry to judge that impact. That is government's job and, to do this job, it must have advice of its own and competence of its own in the field concerned. Government must undertake whatever research is required to attain this competence.

It is my opinion, therefore, that government should initiate, plan and finance a continuing program of research to provide the knowledge that it requires and will require about northern development. Instant or crash programs will not adequately serve this need. Rather, such a program will require a continuity of support adequate to yield answers when they are needed. Although this research will necessarily deal with questions raised by individual projects, it should have the breadth and depth to deal also with the cumulative effects of successive developments and with questions of national or international importance.

VI

THE MACKENZIE VALLEY

THE PIPELINE GUIDELINES ENVISAGE TWO ENERGY CORRIDORS IN Canada's Northwest: one would cross the Northern Yukon, and the other would run the length of the Mackenzie Valley. I have recommended that no pipeline be built and no corridor be established across the Northern Yukon. In this chapter, I will address the Mackenzie Valley corridor.

The Mackenzie Valley is a transportation route that has seen several decades of industrial development. No major wildlife population is threatened by a pipeline along the Mackenzie Valley, and no major wilderness area would be violated by it—but that is not to say that a pipeline would have no impact. Clearly there will be impacts, but they will be superimposed on those that have already occurred in the region, and in many respects they can be ameliorated. So, setting aside the very important social and economic issues and the overarching question of native claims, all of which I shall treat in subsequent chapters, there is no compelling environmental reason why a corridor to bring oil and gas from the Mackenzie Delta and Beaufort Sea could not be established along the Valley. However, to keep the environmental impact of a pipeline to an acceptable level, its construction and operation should proceed only under careful planning and strict regulation. The corridor should be developed only on the basis of a sensible and comprehensive plan that accounts for and resolves the many land use conflicts that are apparent in the region even today.

THE REGION

The Mackenzie River not only defines the Mackenzie Valley, it dominates the entire Canadian Northwest. The Dene called the river *Deh-cho*, the Big River, Alexander Mackenzie called it the Great River, by which name it was known until John Franklin descended this river during his first overland expedition, 1819–1822. Since then, we have known it as the Mackenzie River. It is the longest river system in Canada, one of the ten longest rivers in the world, and one of the last great rivers that is not polluted. The Mackenzie drainage basin encompasses nearly one-fifth of our country, taking in northwest Saskatchewan, the northern half of Alberta, most of northern British Columbia, the eastern Yukon and, of course, all of the western part of the Northwest Territories. Included within this great drainage system are the Peace, Athabasca and Liard Rivers, as well as the Finlay, Parsnip, Nahanni, Great Bear, Arctic Red and Peel Rivers. It drains the great lakes of the North: Great Slave Lake and Great Bear Lake, both of which are bigger than Lake Ontario. Within the Northwest Territories alone, the Mackenzie River and its tributaries drain an area of some one-half million square miles—an area larger than the Province of Ontario.

Historically, the Valley has provided a home and subsistence for the native people. It provided the main transportation route and resources upon which the northern fur trade was built, and today it is a vital link between the people and the communities of the region. The river is also the route over which machinery and equipment are sent to the base camps and the drilling rigs of the oil companies active in the Mackenzie Delta and Beaufort Sea. Along this river Arctic Gas proposes to move pipe, material, equipment and supplies to its stockpile and construction sites. And along this Valley it is proposed to establish an energy corridor.

The Mackenzie Valley region that would be affected by the pipeline and oil and gas activities includes not only the Valley itself but also the basins of Great Slave Lake and Great Bear Lake. Despite the diversity of this large region, the continuity and definition given the region by the river make it a logical entity to deal with as a whole. Because it is a natural travel corridor, it now sees many competing uses by wildlife, traditional activities of native peoples, and the advance of industrial development.

When you fly along the Mackenzie Valley, you have the impression of immense distances and great isolation, but in some senses this impression is misleading. It leads to the assumption that the land is virtually empty and that its capacity to absorb impact is limitless. As each activity advances—seismic exploration, drilling, roads, highways, mines and pipelines—we tend to overlook their cumulative effects on the land, the wildlife and the native people.

THE PEOPLE AND THE LAND

Native land use within the Mackenzie Valley focuses on its renewable resources: moose, caribou, furbearers, fish and birds. Environmental impacts will, therefore, bear especially on them. It is only within comparatively recent years that the incremental changes to the environment caused by successive stages of industrial development have built up to a level that is obvious to the people who live in the Mackenzie Valley. The land has changed. A cut-line here and there, a drilling site, a road or highway where none existed before, airstrips, and more and more aircraft flying overhead. These things together are effecting a cumulative environmental transformation.

The initial incursions of white people into the Mackenzie Valley were limited both in number and extent. Engaged in the fur trade, they lived close to the major river routes and were dependent for their living on the native people's annual harvest of furs. The pattern of that relationship has survived for more than a century. But it began to change in the early 1900s when geological parties began to explore the Valley and surrounding area. Oil was found at Norman Wells in 1920; uranium and gold deposits were discovered in the region in the 1930s. Slowly the activities of industrial man moved farther from the main river transportation routes, away from the trading posts, into lands that had been the exclusive domain of the native people.

In recent years, many hitherto remote areas have come under intensive use. Consider what is happening in an area that is still regarded as relatively untouched, the Fort Norman–Fort Franklin region. The native people have always used the lands and waters of this area to hunt, trap and fish. The main area of long-term use by the people of Fort Norman extends inland past Brackett (Willow) Lake at least 250 miles from Fort Norman, and occasionally travel takes the people another 150 miles. The people of Fort Franklin still use all of the lands around Great Bear Lake.

There has been a fur trading post at or near Fort Norman for more than 150 years. Half a century ago, industrial development began in a limited way with the discovery of oil at Norman Wells, and a refinery has been there since the 1920s. But, more recently, there has been extensive industrial activity: now all of the lands around the communities at Fort Norman and Brackett Lake are held under petroleum exploration permit. The major permit holders include Aquitaine, Texaco, Decalta Group, Shell and Imperial Oil; some 25 wildcat wells have been drilled within 60 miles of Fort Norman, the nearest one only eight miles east of the settlement.

The oil companies have carried out widespread seismic exploration in the area for many years, and there are seismic trails everywhere. For example, Aquitaine has carried out 350 miles of seismic exploration on a block of land covering about 1,000 square miles.

There has been exploration for other minerals, too. Manalta Coal Limited of Calgary have exploration licenses on land covering some 240 square miles east and southeast of Fort Norman. They have put down about 30 shallow drill holes and found coal seams 20 feet thick at shallow depths. The same block of land is also held under a petroleum exploration permit.

There is barge traffic on the river in summer. The Mackenzie Highway alignment will pass along the north side of the village of Fort Norman, and its right-of-way is already partly cleared. The CN telephone land-line and a winter road run the length of the Valley. The feasibility of a hydro-electric development on the Great Bear River has been studied. There is extensive air traffic in the area, which rises and falls with exploration and development. A rash of activity by government and industry has anticipated construction of the pipeline.

The government regards the proposed pipeline as the key element of a transportation and energy corridor along the Mackenzie Valley. The pipeline issue has focused attention on the cumulative effects of other forms of development on the environment and peoples of the region. The consequences of these varied developments and changes on the way of life of the native people in the region was described by Chief Daniel Sonfrere of Hay River:

> ... after the white man came, well things look different, everything's changing now. I'm going to tell you a few things about that. . . .
>
> Look at it today. If we try to go in the bush and kill something, it's pretty hard for us to find [anything] because there are too many roads going different directions. There's too many people around. It's pretty hard for us to kill anything. We have to go quite a ways to get what we want off our land. Yes, even some people [are] complaining about the fish they're catching in this river because everytime they go and pull their net, when they want to have a feed of fish it always taste of fuel. . . . [We] have to go in the bush and do the hunting, [we] got to go quite a ways and got to get out quite a distance before [we] can get anything [we] want. [C588ff.]

ENVIRONMENTAL CONCERNS

Many parts of the Mackenzie Valley terrain are sensitive to disturbances. The region is distinguished by its silty, clayey permafrost soils that are vulnerable to dramatic thermal degradation, particularly along the many river valleys and slopes of the region. These concerns are of major importance because the north-south direction of the corridor cuts across the many east-west valleys and slopes that converge on the Mackenzie River.

Although the valleys crossed by the corridor may constitute only a small proportion of the total landscape, they are the locations of disproportionately high land use and are of particular environmental, aesthetic and recreational values. They define essential fish and mammal habitat and the vegetation along them is more varied and abundant than elsewhere. Valleys have always been and still are the preferred areas for many native people.

These factors give the location of pipeline compressor stations unusual importance, because many of the compressor station complexes would be located adjacent to the valleys that are the foci of the regional ecosystem. A gas pipeline would be a dynamic linear element across the northern landscape, with nodes of great activity at compressor stations at 50-mile intervals. These nodes would extend to include wharf sites, helipads, airfields and borrow pits. They generally lie at right angles to the pipeline right-of-way and corridor.

The immediate impact of industrial development would not necessarily be dramatic in a region like the Mackenzie Valley, where the influence of the white man has been evident for many decades. Wildlife populations are affected by the cumulative influence of such factors as weather, disease, predators and habitat conditions. But wildlife populations inevitably decrease as industrial activity takes over larger and larger portions of the landscape. This process is now well underway in the Mackenzie Valley, and it will accelerate as industrial development proceeds. Let me illustrate this point by referring briefly to some of the major wildlife species in the region.

BIRDS

Important areas for birds in the Mackenzie Valley are chiefly of two types: those that provide staging and nesting sites for waterfowl and those that are suitable sites for raptors, such as falcons, eagles and hawks.

The Mackenzie Valley is one of North America's great migratory bird flyways. Mills Lake near the head of the river, the islands and sandbars from Camsell Bend to Arctic Red River, and particularly the islands near Norman Wells and Little Chicago are heavily used by migrating waterfowl and shorebirds. These islands are an important link in waterfowl life cycles. River bars and flood plains, with their dynamic nature and early succession stage vegetation, are heavily used by migrating snow geese and swans in spring, because this is the first habitat available to them. The birds arrive immediately after break-up, landing on the exposed portions of the islands to feed and rest. Pair-bonding takes place during this part of their migration, and the pairs continue north to their nesting grounds in the Delta and beyond. With so short a season, they have no time to waste. Disturbance must be kept to a minimum.

Large numbers of ducks and some Canada geese, loons and shorebirds nest in the Mackenzie Valley. The most important nesting, moulting and staging areas for waterfowl along the Mackenzie Valley north of Great Slave Lake are the Ramparts River, Mackay Creek, Brackett Lake,

Mills Lake and Beaver Lake. As in the Delta and the Northern Yukon, the birds are susceptible to disturbance during these critical stages in their life, but the consequences probably would not be as great because the populations are not as concentrated.

The raptors that nest in the Mackenzie Valley, Mackenzie Delta and Northern Yukon are significant portions of the surviving North American populations of these birds, especially of the peregrine falcon and the gyrfalcon. There are nesting sites for the peregrine falcon, an endangered species, and other raptors all along the proposed corridor and, in particular, in the Campbell Hills and the Franklin Mountains. In recent decades, a number of factors, especially the widespread use of pesticides, have combined to reduce greatly the abundance of the peregrine falcon in most areas of North America. The plight of this bird is described by George Finney and Virginia Lang in the *Biological Field Program Report: 1975* prepared for Foothills Pipe Lines Limited:

> The population is at a dangerously low level and there is no indication that recovery is imminent. Due to the sensitivity of the peregrine population, developers have to face the fact that the destruction of a single nest site or interference with nesting in a single year is a serious and unacceptable impact. These constraints apply to no other birds species regularly nesting along the proposed pipeline corridor. [Vol. IV of IV, Section 4, p. 32]

MAMMALS

No populations of caribou in the Mackenzie Valley are directly threatened by a pipeline. The Bathurst herd, which ranges from the north and east shores of Great Slave Lake to the south shore of Great Bear Lake, is used by hunters from Yellowknife, Detah, Rae, Lac la Martre and Rae Lakes. The people of Fort Good Hope, Fort Franklin and Colville Lake rely mainly on the Bluenose herd, which ranges from Great Bear Lake north to the tree line. Some woodland caribou are taken throughout the Valley.

The calving grounds of the Bluenose and the Bathurst herds are far away from the impact area, and their main populations lie outside the corridor. Nevertheless, even though industrial activity in the Mackenzie Valley does not threaten the caribou populations, such activity will drive them farther from the Valley itself. Father Jean Amourous told us, when the Inquiry visited Rae Lakes, that this has already occurred to some extent:

> ... it's a fact that development means, in this country, the stop of development by traditional ways. For instance, when development took place with the mining, building of roads, cat roads, cat trains, on the lakes, at

about that time the caribou stopped migrating right through the Pre-Cambrian Shield and stopped going ... across to the sedimentary grounds, limestone country, like Lac la Martre, and all the way down to the other end of Lac la Martre, in 1956. No caribou there for the last 20 years. And that was about the time that the uranium mines grew up in the country, right on the caribou migrating roads.

... it was about that time that on an expedition to the barren land hunting caribou, we couldn't find any caribou that had fallen, but we found plenty of moose that had run away from this part of the country in between the Pre-Cambrian Shield and the limestone country, because of the industrial activity. And those moose have been pushed back by the noise to more isolated parts of the country.

And people here are witness to the fact that when the winter road is open, caribou don't come across it. And many times, certainly three or four times since the winter road is open to haul out to the South the minerals from around Great Bear Lake shores, it has spread the caribou pasturing in the country in between here and Great Bear Lake, and after the operation is going on of hauling that mineral ore outside, then you don't see the caribou alongside that road, or very few. [C8301ff.]

Moose, like caribou, are a heavily used resource in the Mackenzie Valley. They range widely over most types of habitat in summer and early spring. Hunting was the main cause for the decline in the moose populations. Such a decline occurred following World War I, when there was an influx of trappers, traders and prospectors into the Mackenzie Valley. While not immediately sensitive to encroachment on its habitat, successive disturbances will cause moose to move away. The effect is subtle and gradual.

The furbearers of the Mackenzie Valley region, like the other mammals, are threatened by successive developments that affect their habitat and tend to push them farther and farther away from the corridor. Localized depletions of beaver, lynx, marten and muskrat have been felt directly by many of the trappers who spoke to the Inquiry. Joe Martin told the Inquiry about conditions near Colville Lake:

There's parts around here, some areas where it used to be really good for trapping marten and stuff like that. Since explorations, all the seismic trails ... it's not so easy to go trapping and catch fur anymore. You have to really work for it, because it's really changed. Not so many furs like there used to be before.

[Horseshoe Lake] where [I] was trapping last winter, there's a lot of seismic cut lines around there. It used to be real good trapping area around there ... [but] just even cut lines like that can disturb the land, and the fur is not the same, and the wildlife is not the same. [C8338ff.]

FISH

The Mackenzie River is more productive and has more fish species than either the Porcupine River or the north slope drainage of the Yukon. Most fish in the Mackenzie Valley have specific migration routes and limited spawning, overwintering, nursery and feeding areas. Suitable water quality and food sources are obviously necessary. These habitats and conditions are particularly important because of the generally limited ability of northern fish populations to recover after a severe environmental disruption has reduced their numbers.

Of the many species of fish in the region, some are spring spawners, others are fall spawners and one species, the burbot, is a winter spawner. These species—grayling, yellow walleye, northern pike, longnose sucker, flathead chub, whitefish, cisco, inconnu, trout, goldeye, stickleback and others—have different sensitivities to disturbance depending on their life cycles and biological traits. The arctic grayling, for example, have a complex seasonal migration. Usually they spawn over gravel in small, relatively clear tributaries during spring break-up; then, it seems, the mature fish migrate to other feeding areas in the Mackenzie system, and they overwinter in lakes or in the mainstream channels. Nursery areas for fry and immature fish are generally in clear, swiftly flowing smaller tributaries. Changes in habitat, water quality (particularly by siltation of the clear streams), toxic spills and obstruction of channels could adversely affect species like the grayling.

We have limited knowledge of the population distribution and dynamics of fish in the Mackenzie drainage system. Jeff Stein of the Department of Fisheries told the Inquiry:

> Certainly we can identify the more significant populations and in some cases provide very specific measures for their protection. But for the vast majority of streams, especially small drainages, data are generally limited, thus requiring extrapolation from more intensively studied and hopefully similar watersheds. [F15723]

It is essential, therefore, that inventories and research on fisheries keep pace with industrial development in the Valley. Even so, we know that certain measures will have to be employed to protect fish habitat. These measures should include requirements for the design and construction of culverts, dykes, coffer dams, ice bridges, handling of toxic substances, siltation, water withdrawal and waste disposal.

Development of an energy corridor could interfere with the Mackenzie Valley fisheries by disturbance of the fishing sites or by direct disruption of fishing. The domestic fishery has traditionally been very important throughout the area as a source of protein. If the fisheries are to be retained, both the fish and the fishing sites must be protected.

CORRIDOR DEVELOPMENT

THE PIPELINE PROJECT

The route proposed by Arctic Gas along the Mackenzie Valley runs south from the Delta along the east side of the Mackenzie River. Starting from the Delta, it passes close to Inuvik, east of Travaillant Lake and then approaches the Mackenzie River near Thunder River. From here to Fort Simpson, the Mackenzie River and the route are generally parallel, except south of Fort Good Hope, where the pipeline route cuts through a gap in the Norman Range, and north of Fort Simpson, where the route crosses the Ebbutt Hills. The route crosses the Mackenzie east of its confluence with the Liard (east of Fort Simpson), and then continues southeast overland, to the Northwest Territories–Alberta border, just east of the Alberta–British Columbia boundary.

The pipeline will stretch 800 miles from the Delta to the Alberta border. But the project will not be just a line of pipe buried in a clearing through the bush; its effects will be felt in distance well beyond the right-of-way and in time far longer than the two winter seasons of pipelaying. All the material, supplies and equipment will have to be shipped down the river to the construction sites during the summer. The capacity of the fleet of tugs and barges on the Mackenzie River will have to be doubled. The Great Slave Lake railway and the Mackenzie Highway will be heavily used. Hay River, as a railhead, a road terminus, and with extensive trans-shipment facilities, and Fort Simpson, which is on the Mackenzie Highway, will both experience a boom.

There will be compressor stations at about 50-mile intervals along the pipeline. Arctic Gas proposes to have 18 in the Valley; with each station there will be a host of other developments. Let me described briefly what is planned for just one of the 18 compressor station sites that Arctic Gas proposes, the one at Thunder River.

The permanent facilities will comprise the compressor station itself, an airstrip (one of ten airstrips that Arctic Gas proposes to build in the Valley) seven miles of all-weather gravel road, and a wharf. Temporary facilities will include a construction camp to house an 800-man pipeline construction crew and, once the pipe is laid, the 200-man compressor station construction crew, a material stockpile site, two or three gravel pits and many miles of snow roads. The construction of this complex will require over two million cubic yards of gravel and other borrow material. The permanent compressor station will have between six and ten large steel buildings, which will house 30,000-horsepower turbine compressors, 17,000-horsepower refrigeration equipment, propane condensers to dispose of the waste heat from the refrigeration units, a workshop, garage, storage, control room, communications equipment, office area and living quarters for operation and maintenance staff. In addition, there will be outside storage areas for repair and maintenance material and vehicles, extra pipe, fuel and propane, a flare stack and an incinerator, a sewage lagoon and a communications dish to hook into the Anik Satellite. All this will require a fenced, gravelled pad about 1,000 feet square. According to Carl Koskimaki, an engineer who gave evidence for Arctic Gas, the operating noise of the station turbines and at the fence line of the station would be equivalent to the noise level within 100 feet of an urban freeway in mid-morning. The material stockpile site at Thunder River will be at the compressor station site and, together with the wharf, it will be able to handle tens of thousands of tons of supplies, including 88 miles of pipe, which alone will weigh about 85,000 tons. All this, including both the permanent and temporary facilities, will require the clearing of nearly 350 acres of land.

The pipeline companies told the Inquiry that the choice of the east side of the Mackenzie River for their pipeline and their selection of a route through this area were based on financial and engineering considerations. The shortest distance, with due regard to major terrain features, such as mountain passes, river crossing sites and soil properties, defined the route in the general sense. They took the proximity of transportation facilities into account and as site-specific engineering, environmental and, to some degree, socio-economic information became available, they progressively refined the routing and made some minor adjustments. Compressor stations were located at hydraulically optimum points that were chosen for pipe and station size and design gas volumes, then adjusted slightly as required by geotechnical considerations. For engineering reasons that involve the maintenance of hydraulic balance and throughput efficiency, the degree of flexibility in choosing compressor station sites was said to be limited.

People in all the communities along the proposed route expressed to the Inquiry concern over the location of the pipeline and its associated facilities. Their concerns were related to the location of the pipeline near the communities themselves and in or near traditional land use areas.

BALANCING DEVELOPMENT WITH THE ENVIRONMENT

The pipeline project has focused public attention on the need to resolve conflicts created by different demands on the environment. Dr. Ian McTaggart-Cowan of the Environment Protection Board summed this up:

> ... there is the oft experienced human tendency to argue that, now that some tolerable impact has been permitted, it becomes easier to argue for

each successive small increment—small change—each one on its own perhaps minor, but in the aggregate inducing serious impact. I have called this "destruction by insignificant increment." This process requires that proposals for initial incursions be viewed most thoroughly to determine particularly that the route designated for this project is the one least likely to be subjected to these incremental phenomena resulting from looping, from roads, from railways, from oil pipelines, etc.

[The Environment Protection Board] urges very strongly the preparation of a comprehensive land use plan for the Yukon Territory and the Mackenzie Valley area, taking into account the environmental and social components. The corridor concept makes this particularly important. [F6267]

Comprehensive land use planning can emerge only from a settlement of native claims. However, on purely environmental grounds, there are several areas of land that warrant immediate protection. I recommend that sanctuaries be designated to protect migratory waterfowl and falcons, and the sites that I recommend have already been identified under the International Biological Programme. They are the Campbell Hills–Dolomite Lake site, which is important to falcons, and the Willow Lake (Brackett Lake) and Mills Lake sites, which are of great importance to migratory waterfowl. Many islands in the Mackenzie River are also important to migratory waterfowl, and, in time, some of them should be designated as bird sanctuaries.

Many tributaries that feed into the Mackenzie River also warrant some degree of special protection from industrial impacts. These valleys, where the permafrost terrain and slopes are most sensitive, are the focal points for terrestrial and aquatic ecosystems that are important for traditional pursuits of the native people. These areas should be avoided by industrial development wherever possible, and any incursions that are permitted should be subjected to stringent assessments of impact and to special ameliorative measures.

We must recognize that land will become a scarce resource in the Mackenzie Valley. It will not be long before competition for land (and competition for access to the resources that land contains) will become much more intense than it is now. The wildlife species of the region have definite requirements, and the native people will continue to need extensive lands for their purposes. Industrial developers will need land for their purposes, and yet other areas may be designated in time for such purposes as conservation and recreation. All of these uses will increasingly press against each other, and there will be conflict.

In the Mackenzie Valley, a large number of events that affect the pattern and character of land use have already occurred, and more such events may occur before a comprehensive plan of land use has been formulated and implemented. Some things are now fixed. For example, many of the communities and most industrial developments are located on the east side of the river. But we are still at a relatively early stage of development. There is still time to consider a variety of options. It is not good enough simply to promise ourselves that we can serve a variety of divergent uses equally and simultaneously.

Measures must be instituted to limit the impact of industrial development on the land and wildlife resources of the Mackenzie Valley. This step is, after all, only good housekeeping, as the urgency of large-scale frontier development threatens to overwhelm the sustaining natural values of one of Canada's greatest river valleys.

This step cannot be taken unilaterally: there are too many interests involved—all of them legitimate. Industry, government and the local people all acknowledge the need for a comprehensive plan. As a start, the location of the proposed pipeline route and the ancillary facilities must be refined to avoid destruction of areas important to the native people and wildlife and areas important for conservation and recreation.

A settlement of native claims is the point of departure from which all other land uses, including major industrial uses, must be determined. A just settlement with the native people will not only give them the kind of protection they need to plan their own future, it will also involve them fully in planning the future of the Mackenzie Valley. If the valley environment is injured, they will be most affected.

If we take a long view of corridor development in the Mackenzie Valley and plan accordingly, the various demands on land use in the region can be successfully reconciled. There will have to be some environmental impact and some environmental change—it is unavoidable. But the existence of major wildlife populations would not be threatened, and no unique wilderness areas would be violated. The challenge we all face in the Mackenzie Valley is to maintain its environmental values with the same resolve that we plan the development of energy and transportation systems. I think, so far as environmental considerations are concerned, this challenge can be met.

CULTURAL IMPACT

CULTURAL IMPACT: A RETROSPECT

EARLY VIEWS OF THE NORTH

BEFORE CONSIDERING THE ECONOMIC AND SOCIAL IMPACT THAT the pipeline and the energy corridor will have, we should examine the history of the cultural impact of white civilization upon the native people of the North. The relations between the dominant society and the native society, and the history of that relationship from the earliest times to the present, should be borne in mind: they condition our attitudes to native people, and theirs towards us.

When the first Europeans came to North America, they brought with them a set of attitudes and values that were quite different from those of the original peoples of the continent. At the heart of the difference was land. To white Europeans, the land was a resource waiting to be settled and cultivated. They believed that it was a form of private property, and that private property was linked to political responsibility. This political theory about land was coupled with religious and economic assumptions. Europeans believed that the conditions for civilized existence could be satisfied only through the practice of the Christian religion and cultivation of the land. As an early missionary phrased it, "Those who come to Christ turn to agriculture."

To the Europeans, the native people's use of the land, based upon hunting and gathering, was extravagant in extent and irreligious in nature. But to the native people, the land was sacred, the source of life and sustenance, not a commodity to be bought and sold.

Chief Justice John Marshall of the Supreme Court of the United

States, writing in 1823, described the attitudes of the Europeans in this way:

> On the discovery of this immense continent, the great nations of Europe were eager to appropriate to themselves so much of it as they could respectively acquire. Its vast extent offered an ample field to the ambition and enterprise of all; and the character and religion of its inhabitants afforded an apology for considering them as a people over whom the superior genius of Europe might claim an ascendency. The potentates of the old world found no difficulty in convincing themselves that they made ample compensation to the inhabitants of the new, by bestowing on them civilization and Christianity, in exchange for unlimited independence. [*Johnson v. McIntosh* (1823) 21 U.S.543, 572]

It was to be the white man's mission not only to tame the land and bring it under cultivation, but also to tame the native people and bring them within the pale of civilization. This sense of mission has remained the dominant theme in the history of white-native relations.

In Northern Canada, even though the possibilities for agriculture were virtually non-existent in comparison with the prairie lands, the white man's purpose was the same: to subdue the North and its people. In the old days that meant bringing furs to market; nowadays it means bringing minerals, oil and gas to market. At all times it has meant bringing the northern native people within white religious, educational and economic institutions. We sought to detach the native population from cultural habits and beliefs that were thought to be inimical to the priorities of white civilization. This process of cultural transformation has proceeded so far that in the North today many white people—and some native people, too—believe that native culture is dying. Yet the preponderance of evidence presented to this Inquiry indicates beyond any doubt that the culture of the native people is still a vital force in their lives. It informs their view of themselves, of the world about them and of the dominant white society.

Euro-Canadian society has refused to take native culture seriously. European institutions, values and use of land were seen as the basis of culture. Native institutions, values and language were rejected, ignored or misunderstood and—given the native people's use of the land—the Europeans had no difficulty in supposing that native people possessed no real culture at all. Education was perceived as the most effective instrument of cultural change; so, educational systems were introduced that were intended to provide the native people with a useful and meaningful cultural inheritance, since their own ancestors had left them none.

The assumptions implicit in all of this are several. Native religion had to be replaced; native customs had to be rejected; native uses of the land could not, once the fur trade had been superseded by the search for minerals, oil and gas, be regarded as socially important or economically significant.

The moral onslaught has had profound consequences throughout Canada. Yet, since the coming of the white man, the native people of the North have clung to their own beliefs, their own ideas of themselves, of who they are and where they came from, and have revealed a self-consciousness that is much more than retrospective. They have shown a determination to have something to say about their lives and their future. This determination has been repeatedly expressed to the Inquiry.

THE FUR AND MISSION ERA

The penetration of European values in the North has been felt for nearly two centuries. In the early days of the fur and mission era, the native people were able to participate in the fur trade with comparatively little disruption to many of their patterns of social and economic organization, and with little change to their basic cultural values. For most of the year they still lived off the land, travelling in small groups of families in the semi-nomadic tradition of hunting and gathering peoples. Their aboriginal cycle of seasonal activity was modified to include visits to the trading post and mission to sell their furs, to buy tea, sugar, flour and guns, and to go to church.

Father Felicien Labat, the priest at Fort Good Hope, tracing a century of history through the diary of the mission, told the Inquiry about life during the fur and mission era:

> [The trading post] of Good Hope was deserted during the winter months. Christmas and Easter would see a good many of [the Dene] back in the Fort for a few days, but soon after New Year they would again go back to their winter camps. Then it would be the spring hunt, when beavers would start to come out of their houses and travel down the many rivers. Summer would bring nearly everyone back into Fort Good Hope. . . . The people lived close to nature, and their life pattern followed the pattern of nature. Winter and spring were times for working, when transportation into the heart of the land was easier. Summer, on the other hand, was a bit of a holiday, with drums echoing for days and days. That life pattern remained unchallenged until recently, when white people started to come down this way in greater numbers. [C1873ff.]

Even though contact with white civilization, the Hudson's Bay Company, the Church and, in later years, the RCMP was intermittent, its impact was pervasive. White society dictated the places and terms of exchange, took care to ensure that its rituals (social as well as religious and political) took precedence in any contact between native and white, and provided a system of incentives that was irresistible. Political, religious and commercial power over the lives of the native people came to reside in the triumvirate of policeman, priest and Hudson's Bay store manager.

Behind these agents at the frontier lay the power of the metropolis as a whole, a power that was glimpsed occasionally when a ship arrived, a plane flew overhead, or a law court with judge and jury came to hold court. White people in the North were powerful because of what they did, the goods they dispensed, and all that they represented. Their power became entrenched during the fur and mission era in the Macken-zie Valley and the Western Arctic.

Although the fur and mission era ended 20 years ago, the RCMP, Church and Hudson's Bay Company still possess considerable authority in the North, but their authority is no longer exclusive. Government has proliferated. The mining industry and the oil and gas industry have ar-rived. And these new authorities—governmental and industrial—possess a power that transcends the old order: a power to alter the northern landscape and to extinguish the culture of its people.

But make no mistake: the process of transformation has in a sense been continuous. With the fur trade, many native northerners became dependent on the technology and on some of the staples of the South, and this dependence gave outsiders a power quite out of proportion to their number. Although at that time many white people in the North needed the help of native people and had to learn local skills, they none-theless controlled northern society—or were seen to do so. The authority of traditional leadership was greatly weakened. The power and influence of traders, missionaries and policemen were noticed by many early ob-servers of the northern scene. No less an authority than Diamond Jen-ness believed that, "The new barter economy—furs in exchange for the goods of civilization" had caused great harm to the Inuit, and indeed had made them "economically its slaves."

But the native people did not always see it that way. They felt—and still feel—that they gained materially from the fur trade, even if at the same time they became dependent upon and subordinate to outsiders. The material culture of the fur trade did, in fact, become the basis of what is now regarded as the traditional life of the native people—and this is so throughout the Canadian North. It is not surprising that the fur trade era, dependent as it was on traditional skills and a blending of tech-nology with aboriginal ways, often seems to have been a better time, for it was a time when life still had a coherence and purpose consistent with native values and life on the land. Today, when Indian and Eskimo people speak of the traditional way of life, they are not referring to an unremembered aboriginal past, but to the fur and mission era. Most of today's adults in the Mackenzie Valley and the Western Arctic were raised in it and remember it vividly.

THE GOVERNMENT PRESENCE

The traditional way of life, based on the fur trade, lasted until about 20 years ago. As native people became increasingly dependent on trade goods and staples, so their economic well-being became increasingly tied to the fortunes of the fur market. It was the long depression in the price of fur in the years after the Second World War that led to the collapse of the northern fur economy in the 1950s. When the fur market failed, the federal government had to come to the aid of the native people.

It was at this time that the welfare state made its appearance in the North. Family allowances and old age pensions were paid to native northerners. Nursing stations and schools were built; then housing was supplied. All these things were provided by the federal government, which soon had a pervasive influence on the life of every native person. It offered what few parents anywhere would ever refuse—food, medicine and education for their children. Northern natives entered a system whose object—wholly benign in intent—was to reorder their daily lives.

In 1953 there were between 250 and 300 federal employees in the Northwest Territories. Today the Government of Canada (including its crown corporations) and the Government of the Northwest Territories have almost 5,000 employees there. What we are now observing in the North is a determination by native people to wrest from the government control of their daily lives.

THE GROWTH OF SETTLEMENTS

Federal policy in the North since the late 1950s has proceeded on the assumption that the traditional way of life was dying, and that native people had no alternative but the adoption of the white man's way. The short-run solution to the northern crisis was the provision of health and welfare measures. The long-run solution was the education of native people to enable them to enter the wage economy.

The native people who were still living in the bush and on the barrens had to live in the settlements if they were to receive the benefits of the new dispensation, and if their children were to attend school. Doubtless, the promise of greater comfort and ease made the move to settlements seem more attractive; but evidence given at the Inquiry reveals that many people do not remember the move as entirely voluntary. Many were given to understand that they would not receive family allowances if their children were not attending school. At the same time, the children in school were being taught a curriculum that bore no relation to their parents' way of life or to the traditions of their people.

What occurred on the Nahanni River exemplifies much of what happened as settlements grew. In the past the Dene did not live at Nahanni Butte but in camps along the Nahanni River. The government brought them all into Nahanni Butte so that their children could be taught at the school the government had established there. Nahanni Butte, though a beautiful place with an awesome view, is not a particularly good location for hunting, fishing or trapping. Neither the establishment of the school nor the arrangement of the school year and the curriculum—much less the location of the settlement itself—was planned in consultation with the native people.

The establishment of new government facilities in the settlements made available a few permanent and some casual jobs, especially in summer. Typically, these jobs were at the lowest level, such as janitor and labourer. Thus a hunter of repute, a man who might be highly esteemed in the traditional order, joined the new order on the lowest rung. Yet so depressed was the traditional economy that even the lowest paid native wage-earner lived with more security and comfort than most hunters and trappers. For those who wanted to continue living off the land, welfare was sometimes the only means of financing the purchase of ammunition and equipment. Whereas traders had previously extended credit to make sure families stayed on the land, now some administrators preferred the hunters to stay around the settlement to look for casual work rather than to give them welfare so they could go out hunting. Hence wage labour often came to be seen as antithetical to traditional life.

The building of the DEW Line accelerated this process in the Western Arctic. The DEW Line offered stores and medical facilities where there had been none. Many Inuit, such as those from Paulatuk, came to live in the shadow of the DEW Line stations. These sites had been chosen for strategic and military purposes, but they were often in areas without sufficient fish and game to sustain the native people.

When the people first moved into the settlements, they lived in tents or log cabins. The government, at the urging of those in the South who were disturbed by the plight of native northerners, decided that settlements should be modernized and new housing provided. These new communities were laid out to be convenient for services, such as sewage disposal systems, that were often never installed.

Along with the introduction of health, welfare, education and housing programs came new political models. Municipal government, derived from Southern Canada, was chosen as the institution for local government in the native communities. We ignored the traditional decision-making process of the native people, whereby community consensus is the index of approved action. Today in the Northwest Territories many native people sit on municipal councils, but the councils deal with matters such as water supply and garbage disposal, which the native people do not consider as vital to their future as the management of game, fish and fur, the education of their children, and their land claims. This is not to gainsay the usefulness of local government in the Northwest Territories. It is merely to remark that native people regard these local institutions as secondary to the achievement of their main goals. Their existence has not diminished in any way the growing native desire for self-determination.

Northern needs were defined by the government, or by Canadians concerned about northern natives. Programs were conceived and implemented in response to the sensibilities of southern public servants. And because few were able to find out how native people really lived or what they wanted, much less to heed what they said, many government programs were conceived and implemented in error.

This is not to depreciate the benefits that government has brought to the native people in the North. It is easy to discount these benefits now, but the attraction they held for the native people, and the need the people quickly felt for them, soon became apparent. Today housing, health services, schools and welfare are all made available by the government, and the native people have been continually and forcefully reminded of the advantages to themselves and their children of accepting these things.

As northern settlements have grown, white compounds have become established within them. In many places it is no exaggeration to speak of southern enclaves, occupied by whites who have no links with the native population, but are there to administer the programs of the Government of Canada and the Government of the Northwest Territories. Many native witnesses expressed the resentment they feel toward the white people within their communities who have large houses, clean running water and flush toilets, while they have none of these amenities.

It is important to recognize the speed with which these changes have come about: some of the children who were born in tents or log cabins and were raised in the bush or on the barrens, have gone to school; they now live in settlements and have entered the wage economy—all in just a few years.

THE WAGE ECONOMY

Wage employment and the greater availability of cash have had an impact on native culture. Much of the income earned by native people is, of course, used to buy provisions and equipment, such as snowmobiles, guns and traps. In this way, wage employment serves to reinforce the native economy and the native culture. But much of the cash that is earned is not so used, and this has had consequences that have been destructive and divisive.

Wage employment has, within the past decade or so, been important chiefly in the larger centres—Inuvik, Hay River, Fort Simpson, Yellowknife. Even in these places wage employment has created possibilities for men who wish to improve their hunting gear, and has encouraged the flow of consumer durables and processed foods into many families. But this has also meant that many native people have taken—at least temporarily—a place on the lowest rungs of the pay and status ladder. Because the number of such participants has grown considerably in recent years, and because there are persistent and increasing pressures on virtually everyone to participate in the wage economy, the cultural and social ramifications have been very wide.

THE IMPORTANCE OF THE LAND

There have always been indigenous peoples on the frontier of western civilization. The process of encroachment upon their lands and their way of life is inseparable from the process of pushing back the frontier. In the North, the process of detaching the native people from their traditional lands and their traditional ways has been abetted by the fact that fur trappers are at the mercy of the marketplace. There is no organized marketing system for their furs, no minimum price, no guaranteed return. Thus the fur economy is denied the support we accord to primary producers in the South. Nor is it comparable in any way to the network of capital subsidies, tax incentives and depreciation allowances that we offer to the non-renewable resource extraction industry in the North.

To most white Canadians, hunting and trapping are not regarded as either economically viable or desirable. The image that these activities bring to mind includes the attributes of ruggedness, skill and endurance; but they are essentially regarded as irrelevant to the important pursuits that distinguish the industrial way of life. This is an attitude that many white northerners hold in common with southerners. But the relationship of the northern native to the land is still the foundation of his own sense of identity. It is on the land that he recovers a sense of who he is. Again and again I have been told of the sense of achievement that comes with hunting, trapping and fishing—with making a living from the land.

Much has been written about the capacity of the native people to wrest a living from the country in which they live. Only to the southerner does their land seem inhospitable; to the native people it offers a living. In every village of the Mackenzie Valley and the Western Arctic there are people who use, and feel they depend on, the land.

The North is vast, and life in Sachs Harbour is altogether different from life in Yellowknife. In Sachs Harbour and in the villages that lie beyond the advance of industry—in Old Crow, Paulatuk, Holman, Colville Lake, Lac la Martre, Rae Lakes, Trout Lake and Kakisa Lake—the people still live off the land and take pride in their way of life. In these places, industrial development and the lure of the wage economy do not each day offer an immediate and continuing challenge to the legitimacy of native culture and native identity.

The Inuit of Paulatuk still live off the land. They store their caribou and fish on the roofs of their houses, away from the dogs. These people had earlier left Paulatuk to live near the DEW Line station at Cape Parry, where they eventually found themselves in decline. Now they have returned to the land they used to occupy, where caribou and arctic char are plentiful.

At Sachs Harbour the Inuit live off the land, and they live well. Some 23 trappers there cover a total hunting range as large as Nova Scotia to harvest white fox. They also live off caribou, seals, polar bear, muskoxen and geese.

At Kakisa Lake the Dene still make their living from the land. The people there have consistently resisted the idea that they should move from their tiny village to the larger Dene community of Fort Providence. They have built their own log cabins and have insisted on the establishment of their own school.

At Colville Lake, too, the Dene have maintained their annual cycle of activity, which sees them out in the bush for much of the year, supporting themselves and their families in the manner of their ancestors. They, too, have built their own log cabins and still burn wood in their stoves. They resist incorporation into the metropolis by continuing their traditional way of life.

Other people in Canada who live in rural and isolated settlements are having their lives changed by the impact of industrial development. White people who lived to some extent off the land by hunting, fishing and trapping, and whose wants were few, have been drawn into the path of industrial development. Their own rural way of life has been discarded under pressure from the metropolis. But we should remember that white people in rural Canada have generally shared the economic and political traditions that have led to the growth of the metropolis. The challenge the metropolis represents to their self-esteem is not as great as it is for the native peoples. Although the impact of rapid change on their communities and on family ties is often quite severe, there are possibilities for translating some of these traditions and values into an urban and metropolitan context. Few such possibilities exist for the native people of the North.

SOME IMPLICATIONS OF THE PIPELINE

In the days of the fur trade, the native people were essential. In the North today, the native people are not essential to the oil and gas industry, and they know it. The outside world may need the North's oil and gas resources, but it does not need the native people to obtain those resources. Outsiders know exactly what they want and exactly how to get it, and they need no local help. Now they can travel anywhere with tractors, trucks, airplanes and helicopters. They can keep themselves warm, sheltered, clothed and fed by bringing in everything they need from outside. They have, or claim to have, all the knowledge, techniques and equipment necessary to explore and drill for gas and oil, and to take them out of the country. They can bring all the labour they need from outside. The native people are not necessary to any of this work.

The attitude of many white people toward the North and native northerners is a thinly veiled evolutionary determinism: there will be greater industrial development in which the fittest will survive; the native people should not protest, but should rather prepare themselves for the challenge that this development will present. It is inevitable that their villages should cease to be native villages, for in this scheme, native villages are synonymous with regressive holdouts. "Progress" will create white towns, and the native people will have to become like whites if they are to survive. But this kind of determinism is a continuation of the worst features of northern history: southerners are once again insisting that a particular mode of life is the one and only way to social, economic and even moral well-being.

We must put ourselves in the shoes of a native person to understand the frustration and fury that such an attitude engenders in him. If the history of the native people of the North teaches us anything, it is that these people, who have been subjected to a massive assault on their culture and identity, are still determined to be themselves.

THE PERSISTENCE
OF NATIVE VALUES

The native peoples of the North have values that are in many respects quite different from our own. These values are related to the struggle for survival waged by their ancestors, and they persist in their struggle today to survive as distinct peoples.

There is a tendency for us to depreciate native culture. Many white northerners have argued that the native way of life is dying, that what we observe today is a pathetic and diminishing remnant of what existed in the past. The argument arises as much from our attitudes toward native people as from any process of reasoning. We find it hard to believe that anyone would wish to live as native people do in their homes and villages. We show indifference, even contempt, for the native people's defence of their way of life. We tend to idealize those aspects of native culture that we can most easily understand, or that we can appropriate to wear or to place on a shelf in our own homes. We simply do not see native culture as defensible. Many of us do not even see it as a culture at all, but only as a problem to be solved. But we must learn what values the native people still regard as vital today. Only then can we understand how they see their society developing in the future, and what they fear the impact of a pipeline and an energy corridor on that future will be.

THE NATIVE CONCEPT OF LAND

The native people of Canada, and indeed indigenous people throughout the world, have what they regard as a special relationship with their environment. Native people of the North have told the Inquiry that they regard themselves as inseparable from the land, the waters and the animals with which they share the world. They regard themselves as custodians of the land, which is for their use during their lifetime, and which they must pass on to their children and their children's children after them. In their languages, there are no words for wilderness.

The native people's relationship to the land is so different from that of the dominant culture that only through their own words can we comprehend it. The native people, whose testimony appears throughout this chapter—and indeed throughout this report—are people of all ages, from teenagers to the very old.

Richard Nerysoo of Fort McPherson:

It is very clear to me that it is an important and special thing to be an Indian. Being an Indian means being able to understand and live with this world in a very special way. It means living with the land, with the animals, with the birds and fish, as though they were your sisters and brothers. It means saying the land is an old friend and an old friend your father knew, your grandfather knew, indeed your people always have known . . . we see our land as much, much more than the white man sees it. To the Indian people our land really is our life. Without our land we cannot—we could no longer exist as people. If our land is destroyed, we too are destroyed. If your people ever take our land you will be taking our life. [C1183ff.]

Louis Caesar of Fort Good Hope:

This land it is just like our blood because we live off the animals that feed off the land. That's why we are brown. We are not like the white people. We worry about our land because we make our living off our land. The white people they live on money. That's why they worry about money. [C1790]

Georgina Tobac of Fort Good Hope:

Every time the white people come to the North or come to our land and start tearing up the land, I feel as if they are cutting our own flesh because that is the way we feel about our land. It is our flesh. [C1952]

Susie Tutcho of Fort Franklin:

My father really loved this land, and we love our land. The grass and the trees are our flesh, the animals are our flesh. [C684]

The native people in every village made it quite clear to me that the land is the source of their well-being today and for generations to come. This is how Bertram Pokiak of Tuktoyaktuk talked about the land in the best years of the fur trade, 40 years ago:

In Aklavik a lot of fur them days, just like you white people working for wages and you have money in the bank, well my bank was here, all around with the fur. Whatever kind of food I wanted, if I wanted caribou I'd go up in the mountains; if I wanted coloured fox, I went up in the mountain; in the Delta I get mink, muskrat; but I never make a big trapper. I just get enough for my own use the coming year. Next year the animals are going to be there anyway, that's my bank. The same way all over where I travelled. Some people said to me, "Why you don't put the money in the bank and save it for future?" I should have told him that time, "The North is my bank." But I never did. I just thought of it lately. [C4234]

Traditionally there was no private or individual ownership of land among the Dene and the Inuit. They have always believed that all the members of a community have the right to use it. That is why indigenous people do not believe they have the right to sell the land. It is not so much a limitation upon their rights over the land; it is rather something to which the land is not susceptible. Gabe Bluecoat of Arctic Red River addressed the Inquiry on this subject:

The land, who made it? I really want to find out who made it. Me? You? The government? Who made it? I know [of] only one man made it— God. But on this land who besides Him made the land? What is given is not sold to anyone. We're that kind of people. What is given to us, we are not going to give away. [C4587]

Dene and Inuit societies have also developed important values that centre on the welfare of the group or community. They are values that have survived many changes and are still strong today.
George Barnaby of Fort Good Hope, explained:

No one can decide for another person. Everyone is involved in the discussion and ... the decision [is] made by everyone. Our way is to try and give freedom to a person as he knows what he wants. [F22003]

At the community hearings of the Inquiry. I discovered what Barnaby meant. In the native villages there was an implicit assumption that everyone shared in forming the community's judgment on the pipeline.

Those who wonder why the feelings of the native people have not previously appeared as strongly as they do now may find their answer in the fact that the native people themselves had substantial control over the timing, the setting, the procedure and the conduct of the Inquiry's community hearings. The Inquiry did not seek to impose any preconceived notion of how the hearings should be conducted. Its proceedings were not based upon a model or an agenda with which we, as white people, would feel comfortable. All members of each community were invited to speak. All were free to question the representatives of the pipeline companies. And the Inquiry stayed in a community until everyone there who wished to say something had been heard. The native people had an opportunity to express themselves in their own languages and in their own way.

The tradition of sharing is seen by native people as an essential part of their cultural inheritance. Joachim Bonnetrouge told the Inquiry at Fort Liard:

We do not conquer, we are not like that. We are sharers, we are welcomers. [C1718]

Louis Norwegian at Jean Marie River:

If a person kills one moose, he shares and shares alike, and everybody have some amount, no matter how big the people around here. This is still carried out. If they kill one moose, everybody get a share of it. . . . If they go to fish, a few of them go to the lake and get some fish, everybody gets the same amount of fish. That's just the way we live here, at Jean Marie. [C2855ff.]

It is not only among the Dene that sharing is highly valued. In the Inuit communities the people told me the same thing.
Alexandria Elias at Sachs Harbour:

Long ago people helped one another all the time. They used to go down to Kendall Island every summer, and they go there for whaling, and lots of people go there. Once they got a whale everybody got together and ate. Nobody ever looked down on one another, everybody helped one another, the poor, and who had some and who didn't have. They never try to beat one another or try to go against one another. They were all just like one big family. . . .

The Delta used to be as full of people then, and [I] never ever remember government ever helping them. They never ever asked for government help. Everything they got was what they got themselves and what they shared with one another ... [I] never ever remember being poor. [I] didn't know what poor meant. [C4066ff.]

The observations of anthropologists provide additional support for the persistence of the sharing ethic in present-day native society. Joel Savishinsky, in *Kinship and the Expression of Values in an Athabascan Bush Community,* a study of the people of Colville Lake, writes:

> In addition to generosity in terms of food, the people's concept of inter-dependence and reciprocity extends into matters of hospitality, coopera-tion, and mutual aid. People adopt and care for one another's children, help each other in moving to and from bush camps, get one another fire-wood in cases of immediate need, do sewing for each other, camp with one another for varying periods in the bush, and also offer each other as-sistance for mending and operating boats, motors, chain saws and other equipment. Generosity, therefore, covers both goods and services, and these two aspects often are interchangeable in terms of reciprocity in-volved in the people's behaviour. [p. 47]

Although the tradition of sharing is still regarded as vital, it has of course undergone some adaptation, particularly over the last 20 years with the movement of the native people into permanent settlements. Thus, in the larger communities, a single moose may not be distributed among every single household, but it will be shared within the extended family group. Even in the larger communities, however, wherever cir-cumstances and the magnitude of the kill allow, communal distribution is still practised.

The native people have described not only how sharing characterizes relations among themselves, but also how it has characterized their rela-tions with whites. They told the Inquiry how, during the days of the fur trade, they shared with the traders their knowledge and their food, both of which were indispensable to the traders' survival in the North.

Joe Naedzo at Fort Franklin:

> The native people don't only share among themselves. There was one white man who lived among us. His name was Jack Raymond. He went to Johnny Hoe River with us. He had no money. He had five pounds of flour and that is supposed to last him for the whole year that they spent at Johnny Hoe River.... Before the end of November there was no flour. ...
>
> At the time ... there was a lot of people living in Johnny Hoe. And Jack Raymond and his family had no more food. And they had only six dogs left. And for five months we shared our food with him. From January to

April we fed them, we fed their dogs. And then at the end of April, with their six dogs, they went to Port Radium to find a job.

They have a job and they make money. But we never asked them to pay us back for all the five months that we took care of them. This is what our ancestors taught us. You know the kind of sharing we had with Jack Raymond. . . . The white man and the native people, no difference, we share our food. [C814ff.]

There exists among the native people a special respect for the old. The elders are their historians, the keepers of their customs and traditions. They are respected for what they are, for the experience and the knowledge that their age has given them, and for all that they can in turn give to others. George Barnaby put it this way:

Respect for the old people is another law, since all the laws come from the teaching by our elders, from stories that give us pride in our culture, from training since we are young; we learn what is expected of us. Without this learning from the elders our culture will be destroyed. [F22003]

The role of the elders and the respect they receive are important in the native people's attempts to deal with the problems that face them today. René Lamothe told the Inquiry at Fort Simpson about the activities of the Koe Go Cho Society, a community resource centre that serves the educational, cultural and social needs of the native people of Simpson. He explained the central role of the elders in the society's activities:

We don't look at senior citizens' homes as they are looked at in the South or by the industrial economy. . . . The reason for having senior citizens here is a service to them of course. If they choose to come here there would be no charge to them. We would ask them to come as leaders of the people, as people who have the knowledge of the ways of life of the people to teach to the young here. They would come, not as people who have no further productive reality in the existence of the people, but as the crucial element, the age which passes on the life to the young. One of the perspectives of life that is lacking in the industrial economy, which is a very real thing . . . in the Indian world, is the fact that we are born every day, and that every little bit of information that we learn is a birth. As we learn the way of life from the old, as we get older, we understand different things, we hear a legend, we hear it again, we hear it again, we hear it again, and every time at a given age this legend takes on new meaning.

So the senior citizens by their presence, their knowledge of the past, of language, of songs and dances, of the legends, the material aspects of their culture, such as the building of canoes, snowshoes, this kind of thing, will be very instrumental in creating the spirit, the atmosphere in which the culture thrives. The senior citizens will be present to give moral support to the adults in alcohol rehabilitation. They will be present to assist the research and information crews to build a library of native folklore. Their presence in the education system as it is developing will make it possible for them to take up their rightful and ancestral role as teachers of their people. [C2698ff.]

Until the signing of the treaties and the establishment under the Indian Act of the chief and band council model of Indian government, the Dene had no institutionalized political system as we understand it. However, as they made clear to the Inquiry, they did have their own ways of governing themselves. Chief Jim Antoine of Fort Simpson told the Inquiry:

Before 1921 people used to live off the land along the rivers . . . my people at that time were a nation. They had their own leaders, they had elders who gave direction, they had learned men who knew how to cure people and give good directions to the people, so that they could continue living off the land. [C2619]

Joe Naedzo, of the Fort Franklin Band, told the Inquiry:

In those days, too, the government wasn't there to tell them how to do this and that, to survive. So the Indian people chose leaders and these leaders were the government for the people. They decided in what way the people should go this year, what to do before the winter comes. . . . These chosen leaders were the government. [C640]

When the Dene were still living in semi-nomadic extended-family groups, their leaders were the most respected hunters. The acceptance of their leadership rested on the deference of others to their wisdom and judgment and on their ability to provide for the group. Guidance was also provided by the shamans, men knowledgeable in spiritual and psychological matters. Leadership, however, was not usually autocratic; it respected the basic egalitarian structure of the group. Dr. June Helm, an anthropologist who has specialized for many years in Northern Athabascan society, described its nature in a paper written in 1976:

The traditional Dene leader . . . is, on the basis of his superior abilities, consensually recognized by the group to serve as organizer, pacesetter and spokesman for the group. He is not the "boss" or independent decision-maker in group matters, as the Euro-Canadian might surmise. [*Traditional Dene Community Structure and Socioterritorial Organization,* p. 20, unpub.]

The Dene told the Inquiry about some leaders of the past. The Dogrib people of Fort Rae spoke of their great Chiefs Edzo and Monfwi, and the Loucheux people of Fort McPherson talked of the guidance given by Chief Julius. Both Chief Monfwi and Chief Julius were respected leaders when Treaty 11 was signed in 1921, and they became the first chiefs of their respective peoples under the system of elected chiefs instituted by the Indian Act.

Because no treaties were ever made with the Inuit, and because they were not brought within the framework of the Indian Act, they have not developed an institutionalized system for electing leaders. However, Inuit witnesses told the Inquiry that they, too, had their traditional leaders. Frank Cockney at Tuktoyaktuk described through an interpreter how, as a young man, he came to be aware of these leaders:

> At one time Eskimos used to get together in Aklavik after ratting and just before it was whaling season time. . . . He said he was big enough to understand, and that was the first time he saw the Indians there. And the Indians and the Inuit used to mix together, and that was the first time he also found out that there were chiefs. And he said the Eskimo Chief was Mangilaluk and there was other people there that got together with the Indians, Muligak and Kaglik, that was the Eskimo leaders. He said the other Indian people he found out only later were Paul Koe and Jim Greenland and Chief Julius. He said he used to wonder how they always got together, but later he found out they were making plans about their land. . . . He found out only later, even though he didn't see them very often, that the older people always used to get together. They always planned how they would look after their land, so he said now, after he grew up, he knew it's nothing new that people plan about their land and how they look after it. It was done a long time ago also. [C42512ff.]

Charlie Gruben also told the Inquiry at Tuktoyaktuk about Inuit leadership:

> When we were young we had a Chief Mangilaluk. He tell us not to kill this and that. We don't do that because we want to listen to our chief, so good, we don't overkill. It was better than game wardens we got today, I think. That's the way the people used to handle their game that time. We don't kill game just for the sport, we just kill what we need and that's it. [C4254ff.]

In the last few years the structure of native leadership seems, at first glance, to have changed. In many villages the Dene have elected young men to be their chiefs, and young people now play an essential role in the development of native political organizations. On closer analysis, however, the structure of leadership today can be seen to be continuous with traditional ways. In the old days, native leaders were chosen for their ability as hunters and as spokesmen in dealings with the white man. Today, the young and educated Dene and Inuit, who have learned to speak English and to articulate their aspirations to the outside world, have been chosen as leaders in the contemporary struggle for survival.

As leaders, however, the young people look to the elders for guidance. They seek to blend the knowledge they have acquired through education with the knowledge of the elders. Isidore Zoe, Chairman of the Settlement Council of Lac la Martre, a man in his early twenties, explained to the Inquiry the role of the new leadership:

> My position is to go between the young and the old. It is the sort of thing like you compare from the old to the young generation to see what is suitable for both. . . .
>
> We young people are the ear of the old people, to listen to what has been said. We hear what the politicians say—to pass it on to old people, in order for them to support and to make decisions.
>
> We young people are the eyes of the old people, to see what is happening down South, what we read, and to compare what is the best for the Dene people.
>
> We young people are the tongue of the old people . . . to say what they have to say. [C8197ff.]

There have been great changes in the life of the native people, particularly in the last 20 years, but they have tried to hold fast to the values that lie at the core of their cultures. They are striving to maintain these values in the modern world. These values are ancient and enduring, although the expression of them may change—indeed has changed—from generation to generation. George Erasmus, President of the Indian Brotherhood of the Northwest Territories, told the Inquiry at Fort Rae:

> We want to be our own boss. We want to decide on our land what is going to happen. It's not as some people keep referring to as looking back. We are not looking back. We do not want to remain static. We do not want to stop the clock of time. Our old people, when they talk about how the Dene ways should be kept by young people, when they talk about stopping the pipeline until we settle our land claims, they are not looking back, they are looking forward. They are looking as far ahead into the future as they possibly can. So are we all. [C8068]

The native people of the North insist that they have the right to transmit to future generations a way of life and a set of values that give coherence and distinctiveness to their existence as Dene, Inuit and

Metis. Frank T'Seleie, then Chief of the Fort Good Hope Band, expressed his hope for the future of his people:

> Our Dene nation is like this great river. It has been flowing before any of us can remember. We take our strength, our wisdom and our ways from the flow and direction which has been established for us by ancestors we never knew, ancestors of a thousand years ago. Their wisdom flows through us to our children and our grandchildren, to generations we will never know. We will live out our lives as we must, and we will die in peace because we will know that our people and this river will flow on after us.
>
> We know that our grandchildren will speak a language that is their heritage, that has been passed on from before time. We know they will share their wealth and not hoard it, or keep it to themselves. We know they will look after their old people and respect them for their wisdom. We know they will look after this land and protect it, and that 500 years from now, someone with skin my colour and moccasins on his feet will climb up the Ramparts and rest, and look over the river, and feel that he, too, has a place in the universe, and he will thank the same spirits that I thank, that his ancestors have looked after his land well, and he will be proud to be a Dene. [C1778]

It may be asked why I have devoted so much space to these statements of native values. It may be said that the task that is at hand is the development of the North. But I have given this space to the native people's own words because they felt it was essential to say these things. By these statements the native people have affirmed their belief in themselves, their past and their future, and the ideals by which they seek to live. These are the values and the principles that must underlie the development of the North.

THE NATIVE ECONOMY

ASSESSING THE NATIVE ECONOMY

The native people of the North have lived for generations in a world of their own, a world that has been obscured from the eyes of the rest of the world by the many myths our society has woven around it. Now they are emerging from the shadows, and they appear as themselves, not as imitations of us. And we can see that their world and their economy have a reality as tangible as our own.

Charlie Chocolate of Rae Lakes made this point quite explicit:

> This land is our industry, providing us with shelter, food, income, similar to the industries down South supporting the white peoples. [C8289]

We have always undervalued northern native culture, and we have tended to underestimate the vitality of the native economy. We have, at times, even doubted its existence.

Yet the evidence of the native people was altogether to the contrary. The Land Use and Occupancy Study, carried out by the Indian Brotherhood of the Northwest Territories, sets forth conclusions that are quite different from those of Gemini North. The Brotherhood claims there are 1,075 persons actively engaged in trapping in the Mackenzie District. Although not all of them are totally or equally dependent on the land, the evidence given in the communities by hundreds of native witnesses and the Land Use and Occupancy Study maps, all indicate the extent to which the native people are still engaged in hunting, fishing and trapping. These maps were presented and discussed at each community; the composite map, prepared by the Brotherhood, was introduced at the Inquiry's formal hearings in Yellowknife. The evidence I heard in the Inuit villages was similar. Like the Brotherhood, the Committee for Original Peoples Entitlement introduced a series of land use and occupancy maps to substantiate their claim of continued intensive native use of and dependence on the land. In the Yukon, the people of Old Crow presented similar evidence.

At every community hearing, the native people told me about their dependence upon the land. Such dependence is not just a question of what people say; it is founded on realities that we often have not seen or have not recognized. You can walk through any native village in summer, and at every home see fish drying on racks or being smoke-cured in teepees. Anyone who, like myself, has been to the native villages of the Mackenzie Valley and the Western Arctic is struck by the extent to which people still rely on the bush and the barrens: the "reefer" chock full of game at Fort McPherson, thousands of muskrat pelts at Old Crow, caribou carcasses butchered at Holman, hunting and fishing camps of the native people throughout the Valley and the Delta. In every community you find people eating country food: caribou, moose, arctic char, whitefish, trout, muktuk and sometimes muskox.

The fact is, the native economy exists out of the sight of white people: out of sight, out of mind. Furthermore, the true extent of the native economy is difficult to measure; it cannot easily be reduced to statistical form.

EVIDENCE FROM THE COMMUNITY HEARINGS

What then is the actual extent of the use by native people of the game, fish and fur of the land for subsistence and for cash? The Inquiry visited 35 communities in the Mackenzie Valley and the Western Arctic. At each hearing, native people spoke of their reliance upon the land, and what they said has been strongly supported by the evidence of social scientists. I will review this evidence in some detail because, as I have said, for more than a generation we have undervalued the native economy.

FORT FRANKLIN   For three days in June 1975, the Inquiry held hearings at Fort Franklin, a Dene village of approximately 400 people on the shore of Great Bear Lake. The evidence of the Dene there, together with the evidence of Scott Rushforth, an anthropologist who lived in Fort Franklin in 1974 and 1975, provides a detailed insight into the nature and extent of the native economy and of the native reliance on the land. These people traditionally lived in small kinship and family groups in camps around Bear Lake wherever fish and meat were abundant. If a group of Bear Lake people living at a fish camp received word that a large herd of caribou had been seen on the north shore, they might immediately pack up their essential belongings and move there to hunt. Abundant fish and game, and a strategic knowledge of these resources, gave the Bear Lake people security in a land that can be harsh and inhospitable. Following the changes the fur trade brought, their seasonal activity came to focus on trips to the trading posts at Fort Franklin or Fort Norman, at the mouth of Great Bear River, to sell furs for essential supplies. This way of life continued until the 1950s, when the people moved into the settlement of Fort Franklin. Liza Blondin, who was born in 1911, speaking through an interpreter, told the Inquiry at Fort Franklin about the traditional life of the native people during the fur trade era:

> [She] and her husband used to travel by boat with paddles.... When they get to the area where they want to go trapping, her husband gets their fishing net in the lake ... and then he goes hunting. And after he gets some meat for his wife to live off, he is away. Then he finally goes trapping ... he sets his traps [and usually] they trap right up until Christmas.... When she is alone after her husband goes trapping, she has to go out and visit the nets, she has to go hunting to feed her children, and ... sometimes her husband also gives her a few traps so that she can trap around the area that they are living in. When they are out trapping, she makes all of the dried fish and dried meat. And she prepares it for the long journey back to [Fort] Franklin. They usually come back to Franklin around Christmas ... all this time she has been preparing the food to come back to Franklin. She also makes all of the clothing for the children because coming back across the lake it is really cold.
>
> After spending Christmas in Franklin they go back in January. It is a very cold month. Nearly 60 to 70 [Fahrenheit] below in Franklin but ... they still have to set the net. They set four nets at a time and they still have to fish and they still have to hunt.... When you set four nets like that ...

if the ice freezes over with that temperature, [it] freezes . . . to at least a
foot. And you have to dig a hole right [through it. And when her husband
comes back from trapping,] he takes the fish for his dogs so that he can
feed them while he is on the trap line. And then while he is gone she has to
go fishing . . . [and] hunting and she sets snares for rabbits. She has to go
hunting for ptarmigan. . . . And it includes maintaining the home too.
Like getting brushes [spruce boughs] and putting the brushes on the floor
[of the tent], getting wood and sewing.

When her husband brings back a moose, she has to cut off . . . the meat
from the inside, and then they have to scrape the skin while it is still damp.
And then they have to tan it. . . .

When they go spring hunting they usually leave about May 7 . . . to fish,
hunt and get some wood . . . feed the children, make dry fish, paint the
boat and get the boat all ready. . . . When [the men] come back they
bring back beaver and muskrats. So you have to clean the beaver [skins]
off and the muskrats . . . until it is all smooth on the inside and then [you
have to nail it to a stretching board]. . . . While you are doing that, you
teach your children all of these things, how it is done. [C625ff.]

In the early 1950s the Bear Lake people moved into Fort Franklin. As
a result, they have faced many changes in their way of life, but, despite
these changes, they have retained much of their traditional culture and
many of their traditional values. In organizing their way of living, they
rely, for the most part, upon their own cultural knowledge and their own
values—not on those of white society. Rushforth, in his study *Recent
Land-use by the Great Bear Lake Indians,* concluded that the number of
people engaged in traditional land use activities has remained constant in
recent years, and that the people have not abandoned their traditional
means of making a living, despite changes in their life. Although many
aspects of social organization have changed since the days described by
Liza Blondin, the economic life of Fort Franklin still centres on hunting,
fishing and trapping.

Rushforth described the seasonal cycle of land use in Fort Franklin.
Nowadays, men leave the community in mid-October to go trapping.
With a few exceptions, their families no longer accompany them; instead
a trapper travels with a male relative or friend. Trappers who still use
dogs leave somewhat earlier than those who use snowmobiles. They
pitch camp near a fish lake, then set the nets to take advantage of the
late-October run of whitefish. They keep their nets in the water until
they have enough fish for themselves and their dogs and perhaps some to
send back to Fort Franklin. For example, the men who trapped at
Johnny Hoe River in November and December 1974 fished long enough
to feed themselves and at least 12 dogs and to send back approximately
1,000 whitefish, that is, over 3,000 pounds of fish, to Fort Franklin.

In addition to fishing while on their trap lines, the men also spend some time hunting for moose and caribou. If the hunt is successful, the trappers keep some of the meat for themselves and send the rest back to Fort Franklin to feed their families. During the 1974–1975 trapping season, at least ten caribou and four moose were divided in this way. The men go back to Fort Franklin in mid-December to trade their furs and to spend Christmas with their families. After the New Year, some, although not all, of the men go back out to their trap lines and stay until February. In addition to full-time trappers at Fort Franklin there are a number of men who trap part-time. By trapping every weekend, these part-time trappers can supplement their wage income by selling some furs, catching a few rabbits, shooting a few ptarmigan or grouse, and bagging an occasional caribou or moose; and—what is most important to many of them—they can maintain contact with life in the bush.

In the last few years, hunters at Fort Franklin have organized community hunts in February and March for barren ground caribou. In 1975 they made two such trips to the east end of Great Bear Lake. On the first, five men spent ten days at Caribou Point; on the second, 27 men spent three weeks in the Port Radium region. Altogether, these hunters killed at least 165 barren ground caribou and three moose. Approximately 90 of the caribou were stored in the community freezer for distribution among all of the people of Fort Franklin; the others were distributed among the individual hunters' families.

In fall and winter the Fort Franklin people sometimes go out to hunt moose; during 1974–1975, they took 17 moose.

During May, the men of Fort Franklin hunt beaver and muskrat on the rivers and lakes around Great Bear Lake. From the spring hunt, they get both fur to sell and plenty of meat to eat. Meat that is not consumed in the bush is dried and brought back to Fort Franklin. Like trapping in winter, the spring beaver hunt is undertaken almost exclusively by men because school is still in session and the women normally stay in Fort Franklin with the children.

During August, there is usually another community caribou hunt from Fort Franklin and, because school is out, the men take their families with them into the bush. In August 1974, about 25 hunters, many of them with their wives and children, making in all a party of about 120, went on a summer hunt to McGill Bay on the north shore of Great Bear Lake. While the men went hunting each day, the women remained in camp to scrape and tan hides, dry the meat, and mind the children. I visited that camp at McGill Bay, arriving while the men were out hunting. Everywhere caribou and fish were drying on racks and in teepees. After a meal of dried meat and fish, I flew in a small plane along the north shore of the lake, landing near "Nanook," the big schooner the Franklin people use to travel around the lake. As the plane landed, the men sighted caribou, turned back to shore and made a kill.

Fish are a major source of food for the Bear Lake people. In the vicinity of Fort Franklin itself, people fish throughout the year except during the two or three months of freeze-up and break-up. From December to May, they set nets under the ice for trout and herring, and they set hooks for trout. The nets are removed before break-up, then reset after the ice is gone. From July to September, they net hundreds of large trout. In July, a fisherman can catch between 50 and 100 grayling during a canoe trip to Great Bear River. The people make fishing trips throughout the year to many places around Great Bear Lake, during which they may catch hundreds of fish in a short time. For example, in June 1974, some fishermen went by snowmobile to Russell Bay; they set three or four nets under the ice for three days, and returned to Fort Franklin with approximately one thousand trout and whitefish.

Although the Fort Franklin people do not rely upon birds as much as, for example, do the people in the Mackenzie Delta, they do take many ptarmigan, grouse and ducks, and when they are at their spring camps, they can hunt the ducks and geese flying north to their breeding grounds on the shores of Beaufort Sea.

It has been assumed that, with the change to permanent settlement living, native people no longer use much of their traditional land base. The evidence challenges this assumption. Rushforth stated that, although the Bear Lake people no longer live in small dispersed groups at places like Johnny Hoe River, Hottah Lake, Caribou Point, Dease Bay, Bydand Bay and Mackintosh Bay, they continue to use all of these places, as well as others, to hunt, trap and fish. For example, at Johnny Hoe River there are six cabins that are used every year during the winter trapping season, during the spring beaver hunt, and during the seasonal fish runs. The Bear Lake people continue to use the entire area that their ancestors used and that they themselves used as recently as 25 years ago. At the hearing in Fort Franklin, Chief George Kodakin's 15-year-old son Paul showed me on a land use map where he and his father had travelled on hunting trips—the places were the same as those the older people of the village had identified as important traditional territory. New technology, such as snowmobiles, larger boats and chartered aircraft, and differently organized work units, such as community hunting groups, permit the Bear Lake people to reach quickly areas far from Fort Franklin, and to spend a shorter time at areas in which, in the old days, they would have camped for a whole season.

Chief Kodakin told the Inquiry:

> The whole lake is like a deep freeze for Fort Franklin. Our ancestors have used it as a deep freeze and we will use it as a deep freeze for the future children. [C751]

**MACKENZIE DELTA AND BEAUFORT SEA COM-
MUNITIES** Dr. Peter Usher, a geographer who has had a long
association with the region, reviewed the season of 1973–1974 (the last
for which he had comprehensive data) in the Western Arctic communities of Aklavik, Inuvik, Tuktoyaktuk, Paulatuk and Sachs Harbour (but
excluding Holman). He estimated that the native people harvested over
$800,000 worth of fur and nearly $1.6 million worth of food in the
region. For a population of about 2,000 Eskimos, comprising some 300
families, these figures represent an average income of about $8,000 per
family from the land. Although Usher properly used replacement value
as the standard of measurement, the values he imputed were somewhat
high. At the same time it should be remembered that 1973–1974 was a
very good year for trapping. Notwithstanding these qualifications,
Usher's evidence established that the value to be imputed to the native
economy in the Western Arctic is greater than has generally been
thought. Continued and widespread use of country food is confirmed in
a general way by survey of the diets of northern households carried out
by the federal Department of National Health and Welfare.

In three of the Western Arctic communities, Sachs Harbour, Holman
and Paulatuk, virtually all families make their living from the land. Roy
Goose, who is an Eskimo and the local Wildlife Officer at Holman, described to the Inquiry the extent of the people's use of the land:

> There [have] been approximately 200 to 225 caribou killed in Holman Is-
> land since October of this year. That's an average of six per family. . . .
> Most of the people . . . are professional hunters and trappers. They are the
> people that know the land, that know the ocean, that know everything
> relating to the environment. And up to date, the white fox catch is ap-
> proximately 900 by approximately 25 serious trappers. . . . Their seal
> catch . . . would be approximately 1,700 ringed seals. . . . Their income
> from the seals would be approximately $60,000 and their income from the
> white foxes . . . $39,000. As you can see from these figures . . . they're
> very wealthy people, they're well off, they're happy. The full use from the
> land and from the ocean that these people have can be shown from their
> income and from the way they live.
>
> Now to go over to the fishing, the people do all of their fishing in the
> fall of the year, in October when the snow comes over and the ice freezes
> over on the lakes enough for them to travel to the Fish Lakes. . . . It's a
> three-chain lake and these chain lakes empty into the Minto Inlet. . . . The
> approximate pounds per hunter that are harvested from the Fish Lakes
> would be approximately 300 to 350 pounds of arctic char. . . . So that's
> 5,000 to 6,000 pounds harvested per year. . . .
>
> The settlement of Holman Island has a quota of 16 polar bear per year
> . . . and 99 percent of the polar bear taken this year was taken within a 25-

to 30-mile radius of Holman. . . . The income from these polar bear would be $700 to $800 per hide this year. . . . A few years ago [the Japanese] raised the price right up to $2,000 or $3,000 in some cases for a hide and that was only for one year. . . .

A long time ago the Eskimo utilized the muskox quite a bit for food and for clothing . . . the early explorers started killing muskox because of the similarity to beef in taste, and since then the numbers have gone down to very little, and this made the Canadian Wildlife [Service] and other government agencies involved close off the hunting of it as an endangered species. For the past few years there have been sightings of these animals. The sightings continue to be more frequent . . . and the people here have been continually asking for a quota.

Generalizing now, the total of all the income from the land and from the ocean would be in the near figure of $100,000 for the settlement of Holman Island, and that's the income only from fur-bearing animals. That's not counting the other monies that they make from handicrafts and/or carvings. [C3963ff.]

This figure relates only to cash receipts. It does not include the replacement value of all of the country food upon which the Holman people depend.

I have been to Holman in winter. I have seen the meat and furs that are everywhere in the village. I understand what Roy Goose means when he says the people of Holman are "well off."

At Sachs Harbour, in addition to the food obtained from the harvesting of caribou, muskox, fish, geese and polar bear, the income derived from the trading of white fox and polar bear skins is normally higher than that which the villagers could earn if they were employed as wage labourers.

Even in Tuktoyaktuk and Aklavik—communities where urban and industrial influences are considerable—people do some trapping as well as wage employment. But even those who work for wages full-time often spend weekends and holidays hunting. Moreover, this is not mere recreation, but an attempt to secure both the foodstuffs and the sense of identity that are so important to native people throughout the Western Arctic.

In Inuvik, virtually no one lives exclusively by hunting and trapping, partly because the native people who chose to move there did so in response to wage opportunities, and partly because Inuvik is essentially an urban community. Nonetheless, native men in Inuvik go out hunting and trapping. Many of them told the Inquiry of their continued commitment to the land.

Colin Allen said:

[We] are not like . . . the people that come from South and have government jobs; they go down South and have a rest on their holiday, whereas the Eskimos—they use a holiday to hunt as much food as they can so that they don't have to buy from the store, and that will help them to live through the winter. Even though they have a job, they need to get their food in order to keep up with themselves. [C3455]

Ishmael Alunik, President of the Inuvik Hunters and Trappers Association, added:

We do not think of our jobs as a substitute for living off the land. Jobs are another way to help us live. We still want to trap and eat the food from our land. [C3448]

Usher, on the basis of his work on the Inuit Land Use and Occupancy Project, concluded that, although there had been a reduction in trapping by the Inuit of Inuvik, Tuktoyaktuk and Aklavik, their dependence on fish and game for subsistence was still considerable. He pointed out that even the shift toward limited wage employment had not reduced the use of land. Key hunting areas still include the Richardson Mountains for caribou and sheep, the whaling areas in Shallow Bay and near Whitefish Station, the goose-hunting areas along the main channel of the Mackenzie River, and the Delta itself for trapping.

Colin Allen described for the Inquiry his land use patterns before moving to Inuvik, and he explained how, although he has taken up permanent residence in town, he still uses many of his old hunting and trapping areas on a part-time basis:

Today I work in Inuvik for about 15 years altogether, but still all these hunting grounds, goose-hunting area, caribou-hunting area, whale-hunting area, I still use them even though I worked that long. The hunting has never changed for me from the time I was driving dog team and paddling canoe. Now today I've got no dog team, [so I] use skidoo, and today I use the outboard motor . . . and still I go to them places today that I used to go to when I was walking and dog team. [C3768]

Usher also pointed out that, in the Tuktoyaktuk region, after construction of the DEW Line and the movement of the people into the village, there had been a contraction of the general hunting and trapping areas for a few years, but since the introduction of the snowmobile the people once again hunt and trap areas they had temporarily abandoned. The Tuktoyaktuk people now cover their traditional hunting areas as effectively from the one settlement as they did many years ago from the various camps along the Arctic coast between Kittigazuit and Cape Bathurst.

There was evidence of this increase in hunting effectiveness in the other villages on the Beaufort Sea, as we saw when the Inquiry visited Paulatuk. On the very day of the hearing there, two young trappers returned to the village, and pointed out to me on a map where they had been trapping. They included an area that was not marked on the maps that indicate the most recent areas of land use, but which did appear on the maps that indicate land use 20 years ago, when the people were still living in camps. These men, both in their twenties, are now using again, with the help of modern technology, trapping areas used by their fathers and grandfathers.

Usher's evaluation of the importance of the native economy is supported by the work of Dr. Derek Smith in his study, *Natives and Outsiders: Pluralism in the Mackenzie River Delta, Northwest Territories.* Smith states that, in the Delta:

> More people are engaged in casual labour and are living in the settlements in improved housing. But this does not mean that the land and its resources have become less significant for Native people. There is less fishing, since there are fewer dogs to feed, but there is more hunting (and more effective hunting) for meat for human consumption. [p. xiii]

The survival of the native economy has depended primarily on the native people's special relationship with the land. To native people, the land is more than just a source of food or cash: it is the permanent source not only of their physical, but also of their psychological well-being and of their identity as a people.

Rushforth, in his evidence on Fort Franklin, offered these observations:

> The Bear Lake people work in the bush not only because they derive income from their land, but also because that work represents a link in their cultural tradition to a way of life characterized by industrious activity and the acquisition of knowledge through bush experience, independence and self-reliance, and generosity and mutual support. These values help explain why Bear Lake people maintain strong ties to the bush in spite of increasing pressures from outside of their socio-cultural system which undermine their continued economic use of the land. [F22668]

The independence and self-reliance characteristic of life in the bush are highly prized by the native people. Dr. Peter Gardiner, an anthropologist who spent 15 months with the people of Fort Liard, told the Inquiry that the transformation in them as they left the settlement for the bush could be clearly observed:

> . . . going with them, I have seen them change as they leave town and the pressures of town life behind them. Faces are simply more relaxed . . . they're more open . . . when you get out of town, there's no boss. And this is a tremendous relief. In the world of towns, you have people asserting themselves in authoritarian ways constantly. That's just the white world. [C1705ff.]

Jim Pierrot of Fort Good Hope told the Inquiry:

> That is the way how we live our life on our land. We like to be free. [C1814]

Some white people are inclined to romanticize the bush and the barrens. But make no mistake, it is a hard life—the native people have no illusions about this. Abe Okpik told the Inquiry in Aklavik about hardships and bad times in the Mackenzie Delta:

> . . . when we have severe cold winters . . . and there is hardly any snow, the lakes freeze to the bottom, and all the muskrats . . . will disappear. . . . In the springtime, when we are out hunting muskrat with the canoe . . . and when the weather turns cold, especially around Shallow Bay, the ice gets about two inches thick and you can't walk out on it . . . you can't paddle on it, so sometimes we will be stuck for a whole week trying to live off what may be around. . . . [In the summer] we used to go down to Fish Station, and we hunted gulls . . . and you got nothing to eat for about three days. And maybe the dogs screaming for life [from the mosquitoes], and you tried to build smudges to keep them alive. . . . In the fall sometimes . . . when it is heavy rain . . . you go knee deep or lower in the mud . . . and we didn't have the rubber boots like we have now. . . .
>
> Some years, when there is a big west wind before freeze-up, the water flows back around Shallow Bay . . . and all the fish that are supposed to go up the creeks hardly come up, and you have a hard time getting any good load of fish, and you really have to work to get that. . . .
>
> Although all these things that we strive and struggle with, we like this land. [C140ff.]

Life in the bush and on the barrens is hard; it also demands industriousness. There is always something that must be done. Food must be obtained, fires must be kept, clothing and shelter must be looked after, dogs must be fed, and boats, snowmobiles and toboggans must be repaired. Trapping is not a mechanical activity in which a trapper simply sets his traps and hopes the animals will walk into them; the trapper must be able to predict where the animals are likely to go and to set his traps accordingly.

The native people told the Inquiry that life in the bush requires constant learning. Randy Pokiak, the young President of the Hunters and Trappers Association of Tuktoyaktuk, explained that point:

> One thing I learned about trapping, one thing I learned about hunting, is that we never know everything all at one time. No matter how old you get, I believe you keep learning—you find out something new, and this is what I like about it. Because sometimes you figure you know everything, and then again there's times you find out that it's not true, and you are sort of happy that there are other things to learn. [C4227]

Among the northern native people, there is a powerful commitment to the land that is their home. Native people of the Western Arctic and the Mackenzie Valley regard their environment as rich and productive.

THE PLACE OF WAGE EMPLOYMENT

The Dene, Inuit and Metis are proud of their history, traditions and identity. They are now trying to adapt to the modern world in ways that will not destroy their culture and that will not lead only to their assimilation into white society—or to relegation to the fringes of that society. They are seeking means of earning a living from the land and participating in the wage economy without becoming entirely dependent on wage income. They want to achieve a measure of control over their own lives and their land to ensure that their communities remain essentially native communities.

Dr. Charles Hobart, a sociologist who testified for Arctic Gas, feels that, if we build a pipeline, the native people's movement away from trapping to a wage economy will likely reach its ordained result. Hunting, fishing and trapping as a way of life will receive their quietus. If we do not build the pipeline, the Dene and the Inuit will be condemned to a life of idleness and dependence. Given the events of the last two decades, there is, according to this argument, no choice for us or for the native people; the die has already been cast.

The question comes down to this: are traditional customs and values essential to the native people's sense of identity and well-being today? Or have they fallen into desuetude?

Dr. Michael Asch and Scott Rushforth, anthropologists called as witnesses by the Indian Brotherhood of the Northwest Territories, criticized Hobart for relying too heavily on changes in technology as an indication of acculturation. They said that, merely because native people have adopted certain items of western technology, they do not necessarily adopt western values with them to replace their traditional values. Dr. Derek Smith, in *Natives and Outsiders: Pluralism in the Mackenzie River Delta, Northwest Territories,* has also cautioned against equating technological adaptations with a change in values:

> Technological change, which is very visible, should not be allowed to obscure the less visible, but very important, continuities in reliance upon traditional resources. [p. iii]

The fact is that, without modern equipment, including rifles and snowmobiles, the native people would find it virtually impossible to continue their traditional land-based subsistence activities in the contemporary situation because, in some cases, they live in villages far removed from traditional hunting grounds and, in others, the concentration of population has led to a depletion of game nearby.

The evidence heard at the Inquiry has led me to conclude that the selective adoption of items of western technology by the Dene and the Inuit is, in fact, one of the most important means by which they continue to maintain their traditional way of life. These items, like other modern or southern elements in the native society, have become part of the life that native people value.

THE NATIVE PEOPLE'S OWN VOICE

English has not been wholly an instrument of acculturation: rather, Dene groups have used it as a lingua franca to achieve a measure of unity among themselves that was never possible when they spoke only the five Athabascan languages. They have used English, not to become like us, but to tell us that they wish to be themselves. English has become one of their principal means of expressing their desire for self-determination. It is English that has, paradoxically, helped the Dene to insist upon their identity as a distinct people.

Some recent studies have thrown a good deal of light on native preferences. Between 1971 and 1973, for example, Hugh Brody carried out, under the auspices of the federal government's Northern Science Research Group, more than 150 interviews in communities of the Canadian Eastern Arctic to see how the white and native populations regarded each other. Having interviewed members of each generation, Brody found that Inuit of all ages identified themselves with their land, and they regarded continued use of the land as central to their identity. He found that most of the men wanted to spend an important part of their time hunting, fishing and trapping; and this included those who had only recently returned from training schools in Churchill and elsewhere and who, on the evidence of appearance and material culture, would be regarded as highly acculturated. Brody found, too, that all of them, old and young alike, regarded land use activities in quite modern terms: they consider that good hunters are men who can use snowmobiles, high-quality rifles and other recent technological developments that might be useful in hunting.

The Inquiry's hearings revealed the same attitudes among Dene and Inuit in the Mackenzie Valley and the Western Arctic. Expressions of native pride and identity returned many times to the importance, and therefore to the defence, of the land.

I do not want anyone to think that I regard the evidence of these social scientists as decisive by itself. They, like other white people in the North, have been willing to tell me what they think the native people want. But if we are truly to understand what the native people want and what kind of life they seek, we must let them speak for themselves. They must describe their own preferences. Their testimony, heard in community after community, is the best evidence of what really are the native goals, the native preferences and the native aspirations. In village after village, the witnesses made one point clear: they do not want to become white men with brown skins.

Here is how some of them expressed their deeply-felt conviction on this subject. Richard Nerysoo at Fort McPherson:

> We do not have to become brown white-men to survive. We are Indians and we are proud to be Indians. All the education, all the schooling that you have given us cannot destroy that in us.
>
> We are Indian people. We will survive as Indian people, and we will develop our own ways based on the strengths and traditions of the old ways. We will always see ourselves as part of nature. Whether we use outboard motors or plywood for our cabins does not make us any less Indian. . . . The young people from Fort McPherson hunt and fish and get out into the bush whenever they can. We are Indians just like our fathers and grandfathers, and just like our children and grandchildren will be. [C1187ff.]

Peter Green at Paulatuk:

> I have sat down many times and thought over the differences or the distinction between my people's way of life and your way of life. It's pretty hard for me to say that your way of life is superior. . . . I would prefer the Inuit way of life, our way of life. . . . Your way of life, down South as white people, is a way of life I myself would not want to live. We are people who are free to go hunting every day. [C4444ff.]

Paul Andrew, Chief of the Fort Norman Band:

We do not want any other way of life. We do not know enough of any other way of life. We cannot go into the white man's world and expect to live like him. . . . We wish for the upcoming generation . . . to carry on our identity, our language and our culture. [C878]

Alexis Arrowmaker, of the Dogrib people:

It seems that the government's intention is . . . to persuade native people to become like or act like white people. And there is no way that we native people want to lose our culture. . . . There is no way they are going to change native people or have them like white man. [C8081ff.]

George Erasmus, President of the Indian Brotherhood of the Northwest Territories:

The decision that is before the Dene people today, as it has been now since Confederation, since the beginning of Canada as a nation, for the original people, for the native people, is: do we assimilate? Do we remain distinct people?

For us in the valley here, it's a decision: do we want to continue on as Dene people? Or do we want to forget that and become like everybody else? The decision before us, I think, has been made already, and people are acting on it. Clearly we want to remain as Dene people. We do not want to assimilate. [C8067]

The programs of the Government of Canada and the Government of the Northwest Territories have conferred some real benefits on the native people. But the critical result of these programs has been to create a dependence on them. And this dependence, in turn, creates in the native people a frustration that is almost palpable.

Native people have expressed this frustration to the Inquiry. Mary Elias at Sach's Harbour:

Long ago [our] parents they didn't have nobody, [no] Government to tell them what to do or ask them anything. They used to have a real good life because they lived only the way they wanted to. Nobody told them how to live, and they knew how to make a good living, and they were good people then. But now [it is] just like they are having government substitute the way of life, everything is government. [C4063]

Robert Clement at Fort Norman:

I remember a few years ago, the people lived in their homes. They cut their own wood and hauled their own water. People were happier then, when they didn't have to depend on the government all of the time. We were happier then and we could do it again.

But look what has happened. Now the government gives the people everything, pays for the water and the fuel and the houses, the education. It gives the people everything, everything but one thing—the right to live their own lives. And that is the only thing that we really want, to control our lives, our own land. [C897]

This time native people say they want to decide their future for themselves. And they want to be allowed to choose a life that is still connected to the land and their own tradition. So many hundreds of people came forward at the hearings and said these things that I must regard them as an expression of the people's deepest convictions.

Many white people in the North ask how the native people, after all that has been done for them, can now be dissatisfied or ungrateful. The native people reply: "These are things you chose for us. We did not choose them for ourselves."

The old and the young alike are of one mind on this issue. Mary Kendi, an elderly woman from Fort McPherson, told the Inquiry:

We would like to see our children and theirs carry on the ways of our ancestors and ourselves. We don't want to be changed into something we don't understand. If we must make some changes, we don't want it through someone pushing us into it. We must be given time to think and do it our own way. [C1135]

These thoughts were echoed by Isaac Aleekuk, a young trapper at Holman:

I want you people to understand [that] the way of life I am leading is very important to me, and I would like to keep it and use it to the best of my knowledge. I don't want it to be taken away from me or from anyone else here living at Holman. I am 24 years old now. I got married at an early age, and I do feel strongly about this, my way of life, and the way I am living it. I want my children to live that way if they want to. I'll teach them what I know. I still want them to keep this land long after we have gone. [C3948ff.]

If the native people are given the right to make their own choices, the future will be hard and difficult—both for them and us. The question is, ought we to give them that right? And the next question must be, is it possible to give them that right? Here the moral, political and economic questions intersect. Here the industrial system impinges directly upon the native people, and the values of the two ways of life are in opposition. Here we are faced with the fundamental problem of the future of the North: whose preferences should determine the future of the North? Those who think of it as our last frontier? Or those who think of it as their homeland?

Harry Deneron, Chief of the Fort Liard Indian Band, told the Inquiry:

> This is not a virgin land, it is not a pioneer land, it is the Indian [and Inuit] land. [C1664]

TWO DIFFERENT VIEWS

The industrial system is now impinging on the northern native people. History and perceived economic necessity have brought the white and the native societies into contact on our northern frontier, a frontier occupied from time out of mind by the native people.

White people, in general, are driven by economic and social values that are very different from those that motivate native society. White people have always regarded the North as a land rich in desirable commodities: first furs, then gold and uranium, and now oil and gas. The white man, therefore, has progressively encroached upon the land and life of the Dene and the Inuit to secure for himself those commodities that he believes the native people leave unused or underused.

In all the years of contact between the two societies, the white man still sees the North from his own point of view, and he still wishes to conquer the frozen and waste spaces that he sees, with roads, mines, drilling rigs, gas wells and pipelines. He dreams of the technological conquest of the northern frontier.

The Dene and Inuit see their land as unbounded in its ability to fulfil their deepest needs. They see moose, herds of caribou and rivers and lakes teeming with fish. To them the frozen sea does not cover riches, nor is it an obstacle to shipping, but it is a storehouse from which they can take what they need: fish, seals, walrus and whales. The native's preferences and aspirations are formed by his way of looking at the North. Even though many Dene and Inuit have adopted southern dress and speak English, they retain their own ways of thinking about the land and the environment and their own idea of man's destiny in the North.

It has been difficult for the native people to convince us that their preferences and aspirations are real and worthy of our respect. Deeply rooted conceptions underlie the responses that have revealed themselves in the dealings of Europeans with aboriginal groups throughout the world. Hugh Brody, in his evidence, described this devaluation of native people in the European's terms of nature and culture:

[We regard] the native person [as] at the very edge of, or just beyond, the world of culture. Insofar as he is beyond the frontier and stays outside the economy and society that the frontier is seeking to advance, he remains a part of nature. . . . Peoples in that condition do not know what is best for them (they cannot understand progress) and can only learn by acquiring religion, schooling, housing, money, modern conveniences, jobs. This picture of the native beyond culture, beyond the frontier, suggests that he has no real religion, no effective schooling, no proper houses, still less conveniences, money or jobs. As these are supposed to be the very hallmarks of culture, of civilization, and as they are the indices by which we measure progress, then if people do not have them, and do not get them, they cannot progress. [F25873ff.]

Hence many southerners—including policy-makers and administrators—arrive at a moral imperative to bring industrial development to the frontier.

It is for reasons of this nature that the oil and gas companies and the pipeline companies are convinced that their activities will greatly benefit the people of the North. The representatives of the companies regard their presence in the North as benign. They are, therefore, shocked and disbelieving when native people suggest the contrary: they attribute any negative response to their proposals to ignorance or sometimes to the influence of white advisers on the native organizations.

Those who represent the industrial system have a complete and entire commitment to it, as a way of life and as a source of income. This is so whether we are public servants, representing a government whose goals are based on ideas of growth and expansion, or executives and workers in the oil and gas industry.

Seasonal employment that oil and gas exploration offers in the Mackenzie Delta has become an important source of income to many Inuit. Yet that does not mean that they—any more than the Dene—are prepared to give up their claim to the land. If our specialized vision of progress prevails, it is likely to prevail with indifference to—or even in defiance of—native aspirations as they have been expressed to this Inquiry.

ECONOMIC IMPACT

DISCUSSION OF THE NORTHERN ECONOMY IS ALWAYS BEDEVILLED by two related problems. In the first place, the relationships between social, cultural and economic problems of the native people are so intimate and intricate that it is not possible to separate the narrowly economic from the more broadly social. It is impossible, for example, to assess the problems of employment and unemployment in the North in isolation from the kinds of lives that the native people want to lead, or without regard to the present condition of their culture. The discussion in this chapter must, therefore, draw on that of the last and must anticipate some of the discussion in the next.

The second and more serious problem is the quality of the statistical information that is available. Louis St-Laurent once remarked that, for a long time, Canada had seemed to govern its North in a state of absence of mind. Although he was referring to the 1930s and 1940s, his judgment may cast some light on the situation today. Despite the expenditure of millions of dollars and the efforts of thousands of public servants, data on some crucial aspects of northern economic life are either simplistic or are not to be found at all. I shall in this chapter have occasion to use employment figures, but I am bound to conclude that those made available to the Inquiry by the Government of the Northwest Territories are so flawed by conceptual error that they are almost useless. I shall also, both here and in a later discussion of renewable resources, need precise information on the present and potential productivity of the land. But such information, despite the enduring importance of hunting, fishing and trapping, is inadequate.

The absence of data is, of course, an indirect consequence of policy. We have been committed to the view that the economic future of the North lay in large-scale industrial development. We have at times even persuaded the native people of this. We have generated, especially in northern business, an atmosphere of expectancy about industrial development. Although there has always been a native economy in the North, instead of trying to strengthen it, we have, for a decade or more, followed policies by which it could only be weakened or even destroyed. We have believed in industrial development and depreciated the indigenous economic base. Indeed, people who have tried to earn a living by depending on that base have often been regarded as unemployed.

The consequences of federal policy priorities in the past go beyond the problem of inadequate statistics. The development of the non-renewable resources of a region can bring serious pressures to bear on its population: people who try to continue to live on the renewable resources experience relative poverty, and may be faced with the loss of a productive way of life. Gradually more and more people give up one kind of work, and therefore relinquish the way of life associated with it, in favour of another kind of work and life. Where this has happened, they often feel they had very little choice in the matter. If the neglected sector of the economy represents a preferred or culturally important way of life, if it is a means of self-identification and a source of self-respect, then the devaluation of that way of life can have widespread and dismaying consequences. These consequences are exacerbated if the industrialized economy offers rewards that are only short-term.

Long ago, the native people of the North developed an economy based on the seasonal harvesting of renewable resources, which was for centuries the sole basis of their livelihood. That economy is still a vital part of their livelihood today, but the growth of industries based on non-renewable resources has created an imbalance in the northern economy as a whole. The traditional or native economy has come to be associated with relative poverty and deprivation. To the extent that a person tries to live off the land, he must often accept a low income and, in relation to the values of the white world, a lower social status than those who do not. Because success in hunting, fishing and trapping are the hallmarks of traditional native values, this imbalance may all too easily undermine the native people's whole way of life.

In this chapter, I shall refer to the total intrusive effect of the industrial economy on native society. By this process, the native people are pushed and pulled into the industrial system. The process, which is caused by several economic and social factors that will be spelled out, begins with the depreciation of a way of life and ends with the demoralization of a whole people. If a pipeline is built and an energy corridor established before the present severe imbalance in the northern economy is redressed, its intrusive effects will be total.

I do not mean to suggest that native people will not want to participate in the opportunities for employment that industrial development will create. Some native people already work alongside workers from the South. Many native people have taken advantage of opportunities for wage employment on a limited or seasonal basis to obtain the cash they need to equip or re-equip themselves for traditional pursuits. But when the native people are made to feel they have no choice other than the industrial system, when they have no control over entering it or leaving it, when wage labour becomes the strongest, the most compelling, and finally the only option, then the disruptive effects of large-scale, rapid development can only proliferate. Eventually the intrusion of the industrial system is complete, and the consequences for the native people disastrous.

Southern views of "development" and "progress" have resulted in distorted data on unemployment; consequently, many non-renewable resource projects have been at least partially justified on the grounds that they would create jobs for the native people. Government subsidies have been sought and obtained because it seemed appropriate for government to help solve the unemployment problem. But the fact is that large-scale projects based on non-renewable resources have rarely provided permanent employment for any significant number of native people. Even in its own terms, therefore, the policy of the past two decades has not been a success, and there is abundant reason to doubt that a pipeline would or could provide meaningful and on-going employment to many native people of the Mackenzie Valley and the Western Arctic.

It is important to understand the main point of this chapter. The failure so far of large-scale industrial projects to provide permanent wage employment for large numbers of native people had led to expressions of indignation by government spokesmen and by native people. But the real danger of such developments will not be their continued failure to provide employment to the native people, but the highly intrusive effects they may have on native society and the native economy. The real failure of the past lies in a persistent refusal to recognize, and therefore to strengthen, the native economy and native skills. This failure is evidenced by our tendency, perhaps our compulsion, to adopt solutions that are technologically complex. We, as members of an industrial society, find it difficult, perhaps impossible, to resist technological challenge. Technology and development have become virtually synonymous to us. In the North new technology or technology-for-its-own-sake may sometimes inhibit solutions. It seems easier to ship prefabricated housing units from the South than to build log cabins from local materials. When that kind of thing happens, local skills rust or remain undeveloped.

The real economic problems in the North will be solved only when we accept the view that the Dene, Inuit and Metis themselves expressed so often to the Inquiry. We must look at forms of economic development that really do accord with native values and preferences. If the kinds of things that native people now want are taken seriously, we shall cease to regard large-scale frontier industrial development as a panacea for the economic ills of the North.

This consideration of economic impact leads inexorably to the conclusion that the interests of native people are in conflict with those of large-scale industrial developers. In the short run, the strengthening of the native economy in the Mackenzie Valley and Western Arctic should take first priority; otherwise its very foundations will be undermined by the intrusive effects of pipeline construction. But, once the native economy has been strengthened, the Mackenzie Valley corridor could be developed as a pipeline right-of-way. Only by this means can we ensure that these interests will not be in conflict in the long run as well as in the short run.

In the end, it is the native people who will have to live with the economy that is developed in the North; their interests must, therefore, be kept very clearly in mind. I do not mean by this that the white business community, or any economic interest in the Mackenzie Valley or the Western Arctic, should simply be ignored. In this chapter, I shall try to assess the impact of a pipeline on these other interests; both in estimating the consequences of a decision to proceed with the pipeline now and in estimating the consequences of a decision to postpone its construction. But we must face the fact that where interests conflict, and only one choice can be made, priorities must be set.

If we build the pipeline now, the native people's own land-based economy will be further weakened or even destroyed, and many of them will be drawn into the industrial system against their will. They strongly oppose this prospect. We must recognize now that if we remain indifferent to their opposition, that indifference will bring yet more severe deformation of the native economy, serious social disarray, and a cluster of pathologies that will, taken together, constitute the final assault on the original peoples of the North.

THE DEVELOPMENT OF THE NORTHERN ECONOMY

By North American standards the regional economy of the North is not large, complex or mature. Both its demographic base and the number of industrial sites are small. Viewed from the perspective of the hydrocarbon potential upon which hopes for its growth and elaboration are so often pinned, it is not only an economy with a brief history, it is also an area of production remote from the main markets of Canada and from the homes of those who own and invest in its resources. In all these respects it is a frontier economy—but its frontier aspect is not quite as new as many in the South believe.

Much of Canada's history is related to the export of staples from successive geographic frontiers to serve the needs of advanced industrial centres. The great Canadian export commodities have been fish, fur, lumber, wheat, pulp and paper, minerals, and oil and gas. All of these staple industries have been created to serve the needs of the metropolis —once France, then Britain, and now the great industrial centres of Canada and the United States. H. A. Innis, in his work *Empire and Communications,* wrote:

> Concentration on the production of staples for export to more highly industrialized areas in Europe and later in the United States had broad implications for the Canadian economic, political, and social structure. Each staple in its turn left its stamp, and the shift to new staples invariably produced periods of crises in which adjustments in the old structure were painfully made and a new pattern created in relation to a new staple. [p. 5ff.]

The first great staple industries in the North were the fur trade and whaling; then followed mining; now there is oil and gas. But the impact of exploration for oil and gas has not been the same as the impact of the fur trade, which depended on the Indian, the Eskimo and the Metis. The fur trade did not sever the age-old relationship between man and the land, nor did it call into question the ownership of land.

Dr. Melville Watkins, a witness for the Indian Brotherhood of the Northwest Territories, described some aspects of the fur-trade economy:

> The prosecution of the fur trade depended, at least initially in each region into which the trade expanded, on the Indian as fur-gatherer. As such the Indian was a commodity producer, not a wage-earner, and the fur trade was literally a trade, or a commercial activity, not an industrial activity. The Indian became dependent to the extent that he became vulnerable to the exigencies of the trade, but he did not have to make two critical and traumatic adjustments.... Firstly, he did not have to become a wage-earner, and secondly, which is really the opposite side of the coin, he did not have to yield up his ownership of the land. To put the matter differently, neither his labour-time nor his land had to become themselves marketable commodities. [F23582ff.]

Dr. Peter Usher's evidence also dwelt on the characteristics of the early staple economies of the North. He pointed out that although whaling, which was extremely profitable in the Western Arctic between 1890 and 1906, brought disease to the Inuit of the area, from the strictly economic point of view,

> . . . had the whalers simply left the country and not been replaced by outsiders . . . the Eskimos could have reverted to their traditional means of livelihood and survival. [F25894]

The whalers were quickly followed into the Western Arctic by fur traders. Usher, like Watkins, emphasized that the fur trade brought relative economic stability, cultural continuity, and some real prosperity, at least to the Inuit of the Delta:

> At the best of times, good trappers had far higher incomes than the average southern Canadian. The fur trade economy permitted a significant increase in regional output and wealth, although the dramatic increase in both the production of surplus and the return on it, far higher than elsewhere in the Arctic, must be balanced against the shortage of some country foods, which was the legacy of over-hunting during the whaling era. [F25895]

The fur trade economy lasted, in effect, until the 1950s. It was the fur traders who explored and established the lines of communication and transportation in the North. And it was the fur trade that brought the northern peoples within the purview of the western world's economy and into the metropolitan sphere of influence.

Even during the fur trade, however, the non-renewable resource potential of the North was important. The Klondike gold rush led to an interest in the base metals of the region. When the first great flush of enthusiasm for gold had subsided, prospecting and mining became a recognized part of northern economic life in certain areas, although they employed comparatively few people.

In the Mackenzie Valley, however, oil has, for some time, seemed to offer the prospect of economic development. In 1912, oil was found near Fort Norman and, in 1914, the geologist T. O. Bosworth staked three claims to seepages that Alexander Mackenzie had seen in 1789. In 1920, Imperial Oil drilled a well there, a year after acquiring Bosworth's claims, but according to Imperial Oil, the well did not become economic until 1932.

In the 1930s, economic activity also centered on rich mineral deposits at Yellowknife and Port Radium, and mines in the Great Slave Lake and Great Bear Lake areas have had continuing importance. In the 1960s, base metals became the focus of renewed and, at times, fervent economic interest in the Northwest Territories. Before 1964, no more than 6,000 claims were staked North of 60 in any one year. Between 1964 and 1969, approximately 90,000 claims were staked in the Pine Point and Coppermine areas alone. In 1970, the value of mineral output for both the Yukon Territory and the Northwest Territories was in the region of $200 million.

Other activities that preceded the oil and gas industry in the North included the construction of highways, the Pine Point railway, and the DEW Line stations. Each of these projects required the transportation of large volumes of material and supplies and large numbers of men, and each of them, as we have already seen, had some influence on the native people's cultural and economic situation. Each of them represented an advance of metropolitan and industrial interests into the hinterland.

In their historical development, the fur trade, mining, and the oil and gas industry have overlapped one another. Some capital-intensive projects, based on the exploitation of non-renewable resources, were taking place while furs were still being harvested and exported from the Northwest Territories. From the native people's point of view, however, whenever an area or a community became involved in a new staple such as mining, that staple left its mark upon their economic and social lives. The mining and petroleum industries, in particular, have raised the issues of land ownership and of wage employment, and these questions obviously bear directly on the interests of the native people.

If we return to Innis' historical view of the Canadian economy, we can see the succession of economic ventures in the North in a clearer perspective. The impact of each of the staple industries is, of course, what Innis referred to as its "stamp." And, as Watkins said in applying Innis' theory to the economic development of the North:

> The impact of the proposed pipeline is simply the "stamp" of the oil and
> gas industry on Canada in general and the North in particular. The North
> is experiencing "the shift to a new staple," the result is a "period of crisis"
> and of "painful adjustments." [F23579]

In fact the real impact of the oil and gas industry on the North takes us back only to the late 1960s and early 1970s. Although an exploratory well was drilled on Melville Island in 1961, only after 1968 did attention focus on exploratory drilling wherever oil reserves might be found. This surge of interest has been reflected in increased expenditure on exploration—from $34 million in 1970 to $230 million in 1973—and by the fact that, by the beginning of 1973, petroleum leases covered almost 500 million acres of the Northwest Territories.

Oil exploration does not need local labour: it is the land, not the people who live on it, that has now become important. Of course this was also true of mining, but the difference between mining and the hydrocarbon industry is one of scale. The impact of mining is limited to a comparatively restricted area; the hydrocarbon industry, because of the nature of both exploration and its delivery systems, is likely to have a much greater impact.

The establishment of an economy based on mining or, more particularly, on the oil and gas industry could deprive the people who live on the frontier of their rights to their lands, and it could offer them employment for reasons that have nothing to do with their real needs. Because the oil and gas industry does not depend upon them, the native people cannot depend upon it. And if they can no longer rely upon the land for their living, they will cease to have any essential relation to any form of economic activity. The native people's assertion of their claims must, in this historical perspective, be seen as an attempt to negotiate an alternative course of economic development.

The history of the North illustrates the relation that often exists between the metropolis and the hinterland: large-scale frontier projects tend to enrich the metropolis, not the communities on the frontier.

The pipeline project is of a piece with this pattern, but we must remember that the pipeline project is of extraordinary proportions. For example, Stelco's plant at Hamilton is the only steel plant in Canada where the pipe itself can be manufactured. Northern businessmen cannot participate in manufacturing the pipe, nor can they supply any of the machinery or equipment essential to the project. The construction of the pipeline will demand the most advanced technology, machinery and transportation systems. The project will be so huge that only companies that function on a national or international scale will be able to participate in many aspects of the work.

The development of the northern economy is sometimes viewed as a model of the political and economic formation that has taken place in other parts of the country. In this view, frontier development leads to secondary economic growth. The theory that underpins this has to do with spin-offs and multipliers, which affirm the connections between investment, investment returns, and a spreading through reinvestment of these returns into other economic activities. In this way, an economy expands, diversifies, and eventually becomes the base for towns, cities and large political entities. It was in this way that the western provinces were carved out of the old Northwest.

The necessary condition for secondary economic growth, however, is the retention of earnings and of returns on capital within the frontier region. This condition has not been met in the Northwest Territories. The profits from the fur trade and from whaling were earned in the markets of Europe and America and they generated secondary activity only in France, England and Southern Canada. Only a fraction of the profits were returned to the Indians and Eskimos. The mining industry has also taken its profits out of the Northwest Territories, and the oil and gas industry will do the same.

The present state of the northern economy shows two continuities. On the one hand, the native people are being drawn into the dominant economic modes that originate in the metropolis, and they are now faced with the possibility of large-scale industrial development that will disturb the land on which the native economy is based. On the other hand, primary economic activity in the North has been and continues to be frontier in character. Local economic formation has persistently been isolated; the returns have been taken south. The local impact of frontier development has been great, but it has not resulted in a shift towards a broadly based, self-sufficient regional economy.

In the rest of this chapter, I shall consider whether or not a Mackenzie Valley pipeline would alter or consolidate these trends.

OBJECTIVES OF ECONOMIC DEVELOPMENT

When the Honourable Jean Chrétien addressed the House of Commons Standing Committee on Indian Affairs and Northern Development in March 1972 to introduce the *Statement of the Government of Canada on Northern Development in the 70s,* he said:

> Fundamental to the Government's statement is our belief that native northerners should derive early, visible, and lasting benefits from economic development. Our efforts must not only be turned to developing the natural resources of the North for the benefit of Canada as a whole. The development of northern resources must first improve the standard of living and the well-being of northern residents. All too often the economic activity of the past was at their expense. [*Introductory Remarks,* p. 8]

Like Mr. Chrétien, I have found that native northerners have not in the past realized "early, visible, and lasting benefits from economic development." Will the construction of a Mackenzie Valley pipeline provide such benefits?

I can recommend some terms and conditions that would provide early and visible benefits from the construction of a pipeline to native northerners, but I do not think any terms and conditions could be imposed on any pipeline built today to ensure that native northerners would derive *lasting* benefits from it. Indeed, it is my judgment that the social costs of the pipeline to native northerners would outweigh any economic benefits they may derive from it.

I am speaking, as the Minister was, of native northerners and of wage employment for native northerners. I can recommend terms and conditions that would enable northern business to achieve real and substantial growth during the construction of a pipeline. But these benefits would not accrue to native northerners, except to those few—and they are very few—who possess the capital, the knowledge and the inclination to take advantage of the business opportunities that pipeline construction would offer.

We have always assumed that large-scale industrial projects, in the North as elsewhere, are good in and of themselves. Our whole economic history, which is one of earning and spending, saving and investing, encourages this belief. If a project achieves a measurable surplus or gain, such as increased profits, additional tax revenues or higher employment, that is thought to be sufficient justification for it; no other test need be met.

This assumption should be looked at more closely. Can the pipeline project and its aftermath be subjected to any realistic cost-benefit analysis? What is the purpose of the project? In whose interest is it being undertaken? What economic gains will be made? How should the gains be shared? Is anyone likely to be hurt by it? Can the negative impacts be ameliorated?

We have already begun to ask these questions. Sometimes we asked them in the past, but we did so diffidently because of the complexity and imprecision of the concerns we were addressing. Moreover, merely by raising such questions, we implicitly suggested that curbs or limitations might have to be placed on large-scale industrial development, a suggestion that is regarded as inimical wherever the industrial system is seen as the great engine of progress.

We must take a hard look at what our objectives in the North really are. For example, it may be important to build the pipeline as quickly and as cheaply as possible. Certainly the pipeline companies would regard this as vital: rapid construction and an early flow of gas would generate income sooner. Once the capital has been borrowed, every month and year that passes before the gas begins to flow will increase the interest to be paid.

But suppose we consider the project from the point of view of its external economics—from the point of view of society's profits and losses. We might then urge that the project be delayed, that its construction phase be spread over a longer period to maximize employment and income for northerners. We might urge the building of a smaller diameter pipeline in order to conserve gas and extend the operating phase. These measures might well reduce social costs and result in a net saving to the Government of Canada. Federal welfare and other programs for northerners and northern business could be curtailed if they did not have to respond to the boom-and-bust cycle that the market, unaided or undeterred, would set in motion.

But if one of our objectives is to provide gainful employment for native northerners, is a pipeline the best way to do it? Native people have insisted that, because the resources of the land and sea have always provided a living—and still do for many of them—ways should be sought to make that living more productive. These ways can be tried only if construction of the pipeline is postponed.

ECONOMIC DEVELOPMENT AND SELF-SUFFICIENCY

Many white northerners have asserted that the northern economy could become self-sufficient if the pipeline were built. But the northern economy is the product of its history. It is paradoxical to suggest that a large-scale frontier project designed to supply energy, the modern staple, to the metropolis will result in regional self-sufficiency. The pipeline will not serve regional objectives; it will serve national and international demands for energy.

Federal policies and programs have not resulted in a regional economy in the North that will capture and regionally contain a significant proportion of the income that is generated by major private and public investment there. Most capital and consumer goods are still imported into the region, and most of the industrial labour needed is also brought in from the South. By and large, the persons making up this imported labour force have little or no commitment to the North. They do not, generally, bank their money there or invest surplus earnings in any way that would expand employment within the region; nor do royalties, profits, or taxes stay in the North.

But federal policies have brought industrial development to the North. Mining and the oil and gas industry have responded to government initiatives by undertaking some large investment programs. Some of them, such as Pine Point, have been highly profitable. With others, investment still awaits a major return, but a large part of the cost of these ventures has been publicly absorbed. Mining companies and the oil and gas industry have found the North an attractive place in which to invest. But such federally supported investment, which has no long-term multiplier effects, will not secure the economic self-sufficiency of the Northwest Territories.

The northern economy is not going to become self-sufficient, no matter what support systems are devised for it. Indeed, there is no reason why the Northwest Territories, any more than any other region, should have a self-sufficient economy. Regional interdependence is part and parcel of Canadian economic life. Mr. Chrétien's goal, of encouraging economic development that would provide real and lasting benefits to the people of the North is one that can be rationally pursued. It is a goal that we can reach if we are prepared to diversify the northern economy by strengthening the renewable resource sector.

THE   MIXED   ECONOMY

The development of the northern economy has successively given rise to
mixtures of economic activity, to overlapping modes of production, consumption and exchange. The fur trade added a new layer of activity to
the original subsistence economy. The governmental presence provided
some opportunities for wage employment and transfer payments. Mining
and the oil and gas industry have added industrial wage employment to
the mixture of economic elements in the North.

The northern economy is often thought of as dual, consisting of a native sector and a white sector. This duality emphasizes the differences
between the native way of life, with its long roots in the region's
aboriginal past, and the white way of life, which represents the extension
of the southern metropolis into the northern hinterland. The first is the
traditional economy, based on renewable resources; the second is the industrial economy, based on the exploitation of the non-renewable resources of the frontier.

The differences between the two sectors today are accentuated by the
scale and technological complexity of the industrial sector of the economy. Extractive industries located in a harsh environment and far from
their markets can be economic only if they are large. This has given rise
to the sharp contrast that is now coming to exist between the ways of the
life preferred by most native people and the scale of industrial development. In his evidence, Hugh Brody referred to the striking contrast:

> . . . when industry does come to the North, we find the smallest, most iso-
> lated societies alongside some of the most costly and technically complex
> development projects in the world. Hence the paradox: the smallest
> alongside the largest, the most traditional alongside the most modern, and
> the most remote becoming involved with national or even international
> economic interests. [F25780]

This concept of a dual economy in the North may, however, be misleading. Dr. Charles Hobart and Dr. Peter Usher both pointed to
changes and adaptations in traditional life; it has absorbed and now even
depends upon some elements of the economy of the newcomers. Usher
pointed out that this dependence upon outsiders, especially when it is reinforced by great (if at times unseen) political authority, has inevitably
given rise to some flexibility in the native society. This does not mean, of
course, that there are no limits to this flexibility, but this ability to accommodate to change reveals the danger in oversimplification: looked at
in one way the northern economy is a dual economy, yet looked at in another way, it is rather more complicated.

In fact, the native people's own idea of traditional economic activity does not correspond to the idea of an economy that is dual in nature. Neither Dene nor Inuit regard the aboriginal past, when they were isolated from and independent of southerners, as their traditional life. Ever since the first days of the fur trade, they have willingly adopted new techniques and equipment, and some of the social practices that the white man brought to the North. These elements were amalgamated into the native economy, and have to some extent become integral to the way of life that the native people are now trying to maintain and defend. At every stage there have been the dual aspects to the northern economy: the native society, with its emphasis on hunting, fishing and trapping, has stood apart from the white society that has gradually established itself in the North. This duality has never become fixed, and it continues to evolve.

At the present time, the clash between the interests of the oil and gas industry on the one hand, and the native (though not the aboriginal) economy on the other, does invite us to see two distinct economic modes. But Dr. Melville Watkins argued that the whole idea of a dual economy erroneously emphasized a separation between the "traditional" and the "modern":

> According to this view, the North is a two-sector economy, consisting of a "modern" sector and a "traditional" sector, and these two sectors are substantially separate. The "modern" sector is seen as essentially an "enclave," where "development" takes place, while the "traditional" sector is stagnant and full of problems, and is not experiencing the benefits of "development." The logic of this position is that the solution lies in moving people out of the "traditional" sector and into the "modern" sector. The transition, though painful, is necessary. At the end of the road— or in this case, at the end of the pipeline—what will be created is a one-sector "modern" economy with everybody experiencing the benefits of "development." [F23604]

There are, in reality, four sectors in the northern economy: subsistence, trading of renewable resource produce, local wage employment, and industrial wage employment. We can trace the history of the native economy along a spectrum that has subsistence activities at one end and industrial wage labour at the other. But we must bear in mind that overlapping or mixed economic forms are now integral to the native economy.

The question with which we are faced here can then be stated as, how will the mix look as a result of the pipeline?

The native economy includes a large subsistence-harvesting component. In general, the native people harvest the renewable resources without fundamentally affecting their populations or the land that produces them. How much a man can produce and consume (and, in the case of furs and other trade items, exchange) depends upon the productivity of the land, local knowledge of the land gained through long experience of it, and the technology used. The bush and the barrens do not at present produce surpluses, but they still provide a living—or the greatest part of a living—for many families.

The native economy today also includes the production of fur for the market. The Dene, Inuit and Metis view of traditional life includes all of the economic activities upon which the fur trade is based.

In some ways, wage employment has been useful to the native economy. The jobs made available by settlement growth and the government presence, along with some transfer payments, have substantially increased the flow of cash into native hands, and hunters and trappers have used this cash to improve their equipment. But in other ways wage labour has had adverse effects on the traditional life: a regular schedule of work conflicts with a hunter's need to respond quickly to weather and to animal movements; cash tends to flow to the men who are least committed to a life of hunting, fishing and trapping; and employment in a settlement may put a man at a great distance from his hunting and trapping areas. But it seems fair to say that local and limited wage labour was included in an economic mix that was compatible with the realization of many native values and aspirations.

In the native economy, the individual or the family combines production, exchange and consumption activities, at least during certain parts of the year. But in the cash economy, which is based on production for the market, these activities tend to be divided. An individual does not consume what he produces, nor does he sell his product directly to the ultimate consumer. Specialization of activity has enabled the industrial economy to become extremely productive; surpluses are produced that, when re-invested, promote the growth of further productive and consumptive capacity. An ever higher degree of specialization is one of the basic principles on which the industrial economy operates.

In the North today, the lives of many native families are based on an intricate economic mix. At certain times of the year they hunt and fish; at other times they work for wages, sometimes for the government, sometimes on highway construction, sometimes for the oil and gas industry. But if opportunities for wage employment expand and the pressures to take such work increase, the native economy may be completely transformed. Men will then leave the small communities to work at locations from which they cannot possibly maintain a mixed economic life. Many people have expressed the fear that, if the industrial economy comes to every settlement, if wage employment becomes the only way to make a living, then the native economy will be debased and overwhelmed.

The native economy should not be preserved merely as a curiosity.

The northern peoples have demonstrated before this Inquiry that their economy is not only a link with their past, but it is also the basis of their plans for the future. The continued viability of the native economy should be an objective of northern development, not its price.

IMPACT ON THE NATIVE ECONOMY

What is the place of the native people in the northern economy today? Many of them receive welfare, old-age pensions and family allowances, but most of them are at the edge of the capital and income flows that dominate the northern economy. Native people earning wages are engaged mainly in low paid, unskilled, casual or seasonal employment.

In 1972, Dr. Chun-Yan Kuo prepared *A Study of Income Distribution in the Mackenzie District of Northern Canada,* which revealed that in 1969–1970, the mean annual per capita cash income of whites living in the Mackenzie District was $3,545, of Metis $1,147, of Inuit $840, and of Indians $667. The study also indicated that 22 percent of the native people of the Mackenzie District received a cash income of less than $4,000; only one percent of the native population had an income in excess of $10,000. In contrast, 22 percent of the white families had an income above $10,000. Mean income for white families was $9,748; for Indian families $2,568. There is no reason to believe there has been any significant change in the proportional distribution of income in the Northwest Territories since Kuo's study was made.

These differences in income show the extent to which the developed money economy of the North is confined to urbanized enclaves. Kuo's figures did not, of course, take into account the extent to which the native people still live off the land: income in kind is still vital to native people. If they were to be totally absorbed into the industrial system, whether employed or unemployed, they would lose their income in kind.

Such wage employment as the native people have had has not suddenly put an end to their reliance upon country food, nor to their earnings from trapping and the sale of furs. Indeed, because wage-earners can afford to improve their equipment, a wage income can actually be beneficial to the traditional economy. But, in the longer run, the trend toward an industrial economy leads to a decline in the use of land and in the harvesting of country food.

This trend has its influence on income distribution within small communities. The native people have always shared the food they obtain from the land. Such produce is shared more readily than money, and the land is generally regarded as communal. The shift towards a money economy has created new possibilities for poverty: those in want are more likely to stay in want, and inequalities in native communities can become more marked. If income in whatever form it may take is not shared, it is possible for the average per capita income to rise at the same time the number of households experiencing poverty is also increasing. The number of poor people and a community's total cash income may rise concurrently. No assessment of the economic gains and losses of oil and gas development in the North can overlook a predictable decline in the native economy and the losses that decline will entail for virtually every native family in the North. Economic development will make native communities poorer in some ways as they become richer in others.

The impact of large-scale labour recruitment on the small communities will be felt by everyone in them: its intrusion into village social life will not be selective but total. With small-scale economic developments, persons who are particularly qualified for, or inclined towards, wage labour are selected or select themselves; with large-scale developments, all available manpower is recruited and moved to the place of work. Because the hunters and trappers who work only occasionally are usually regarded as partially or wholly unemployed, there will be pressures exerted on them to take wage employment, with results that will be felt throughout the traditional sector of the northern economy. These pressures are intensified by the fact that the men whose lives are most firmly committed to the harvesting of renewable resources also suffer from recurrent cash problems. So it is that the persons—or even whole communities—that have the strongest cultural and personal links with the land and its resources are the ones that are most firmly pushed towards participation in industrial activities. Hence the effect of total intrusion into community life.

Of course, if the pipeline is built, it will tend to justify itself in the statistical tables. The gross domestic product of the region will increase substantially. Per capita income will rise. Consultants who now recommend the construction of the pipeline on the grounds that it will benefit the native people of the North, will be succeeded by consultants willing to support whatever conclusions government and industry are then anxious to justify.

Statistics enable you to keep the problem at one remove. When using figures, you do not have to consider the reality of what is happening on the ground; with pages of text, flow charts and graphs, you can express ideas about cash income and gross domestic product and avoid all consideration of what is really occurring among the families of the native communities.

Any community, in the North or in the South, would bear certain social costs if it were associated in any way with a project of the magnitude of the proposed pipeline. These costs, which include urban congestion, shortage of housing, separation of families, alcoholism, violence and crime, and problems of mental health, are magnified in the North. The social and health services that are provided to deal with these ills are a spin-off from the project, and they, too, are sometimes categorized as a form of economic growth. The federal and territorial governments will provide these services, but their cost should be regarded as a debit, not a credit, in any cost-benefit analysis.

You may question why I am pessimistic about the prospect of the pipeline as a means of bringing the native people more fully into the industrial system. Can they not participate in some way or other in such a project and reap the benefits that so many people firmly believe can be realized? If the native people cannot be painlessly transformed into industrial workers, is it not, nevertheless, inevitable that they must become industrial workers, albeit painfully?

The fact of the matter is, however, that if the North continues to be regarded solely as a frontier for industrial development, there will not be an assimilation that is either more or less painful. On the contrary, the North will become the home of a demoralized, confused and increasingly angry people who believe that they have been oppressed and weakened ever since white men came to their land.

The impact on the native economy of pipeline construction in the near future would be serious, perhaps irreparable. Pipeline construction now, and all that it would bring, would impel the northern economy during the next generation or more toward further industrial development. If that shift occurs now, before the native economy has been strengthened, the very possibility of strengthening it will have been undermined. All northerners seek a diversified economy, but the possibility of diversification, which depends upon strengthening the renewable resource sector, will be lost if we build the pipeline now.

EMPLOYMENT AND THE PIPELINE

THE QUESTION OF UNEMPLOYMENT

Jack Witty, Chief of the Employment Division, Department of Economic Development, Government of the Northwest Territories, told the Inquiry that there is a labour force of 17,000 in the Northwest Territories. This figure represents all persons, male and female, between the ages of 14 and 65, in the Northwest Territories. According to Witty, there are between 10,000 and 12,000 jobs, and he concluded, therefore, that 5,000 or more people have no jobs. Most of those employed work for the Government of Canada, the Government of the Northwest Territories, local municipal bodies, the mining industry, and the oil and gas industry, a largely white work force. When, therefore, we talk about unemployed northerners, we are talking about 5,000 or more native people in the Northwest Territories whom the government regards as unemployed.

But these calculations have an unreal flavour. The labour force figure of 17,000 comprises all persons, male and female, between the ages of 14 and 65—including housewives, many children in school, the disabled and ill, and even able-bodied adults engaged in hunting, fishing and trapping. It can be seen at once that such a figure is an unsound basis for determining what the potential labour force really is. Calculations derived from it obscure, rather than reveal, how many able-bodied persons are working or might actively be seeking work.

The concept of endemic unemployment among the native people of the Northwest Territories has been one of the primary justifications for the pipeline project. Official willingness to justify construction of a pipeline on the basis of an inflated figure for unemployment complements the official tendency to discount the importance of the native economy. Witty's testimony is an example of this tendency:

> ... there is no equality of opportunity for employment—because the employment simply does not exist. Of 67 communities in the Northwest Territories, only 9 [Yellowknife, Hay River, Pine Point, Tungsten, Inuvik, Arctic Bay, Resolute Bay, Echo Bay and Norman Wells] ... could be considered to have a substantial economic base outside government support. . . .
>
> The population of the 67 communities ... is estimated at 45,488 [May 1976]. The population of the 9 communities that I consider to have a reasonable degree of employment stability is 20,251 or slightly less than 50 percent of the total. [F31223ff.]

This analysis does not take into account the continuing strength of the native economy that sustains communities like Sachs Harbour, Holman, Paulatuk, Colville Lake and Trout Lake. Hunting, trapping and fishing for subsistence are simply ignored.

Of course, many native people do seek wage employment, and many of them find it. But what they seek is employment on a seasonal basis, as part of a wage-and-subsistence economic mix. Very few are seeking permanent employment in the industrial system.

Public servants who have perceived an overriding necessity to provide industrial wage employment for the unemployed native people have also tended to regard the native economy as moribund. This perception became fixed in the 1960s, when the native economy was at its nadir because of more than a decade of low fur prices, administrative neglect, and rapid social change.

Although it is a mistake to talk about a pool of 5,000 or more unemployed persons in the Northwest Territories today, it is nevertheless true that a significant number of native persons may properly be classified as unemployed or underemployed. I do not pretend to know how many such persons there are, and I venture to say that no one knows for sure.

Even were we to assume that the number of unemployed is large, and that it will be increased by the entry into the labour market of a large school-age population, certain questions would still remain. Without increased wage employment, will the native people have to choose between a life in the North on welfare or relocation to Southern Canada? Can pipeline construction offer them opportunities for meaningful and productive employment? Or, as the native people themselves have argued in the testimony quoted in these pages, does that opportunity lie in the strengthening of the native economy?

Only now is it becoming apparent that no skilled jobs will be open to the native people. Skilled jobs on the pipeline will not be available to them because they have no training for these types of jobs and, even were they to qualify for these jobs, once the pipeline was finished, they would have to travel to other parts of the world to pursue their specialized trade. In fact, very few native northerners have ever left the North to pursue successfully a career in the South.

There will be severe limitations on the type of work native northerners can do. During clearing and grading, some native people would operate heavy equipment and drive trucks, but most of them would be employed in cutting brush. During pipelaying, some native workers would be employed in semi-skilled jobs, but most of them would be employed in various unskilled capacities.

EMPLOYMENT AND UNEMPLOYMENT

Except during the construction phase of a project, the petroleum industry is capital- rather than labour-intensive. Those who argue that the employment of native people on a project like the pipeline will equip them with skills that will be of lasting use to them and to the North have not made their case. What is more, that case is based on an idea of native aspirations and needs that is at odds with what so many of the native people themselves have expressed to this Inquiry. The pipeline, even if it were to provide many long-term jobs, would not solve the problems of the northern economy.

It is, perhaps, worth considering at this point the employment of native people in the government sector. At present the Government of Canada, including crown corporations, employs about 1,900 in the Northwest Territories: only about 250 of these jobs are held by natives, and their work is mainly clerical or unskilled labour. It is now 10 years since the Government of the Northwest Territories transferred its headquarters from Fort Smith to Yellowknife. Yet, in 1976, out of 3,069 people on the payroll of the Government of the Northwest Territories, only 603, or 20 percent, were native and of these 603, most worked at clerical or unskilled labour.

Both government and business have insisted on the importance of introducing the native people into wage employment. This has been one of the reasons for the subsidies provided to industrial development in the North. Quotas requiring a certain number of native employees have been imposed but have not, however, been met, and all concerned have expressed dismay. No one yet has been ready to examine the false assumption that lay behind the quotas. If the creation of jobs for native northerners is really a primary objective, there must be better ways of achieving it, from the point of view of northern development, than the past and present emphasis on the extraction of non-renewable resources.

In the past few years, Imperial, Gulf and Shell together have been employing about 250 native people at any one time in the Mackenzie Delta at the peak of their winter drilling season. Although the average length of employment is only nine weeks per worker, these jobs have assumed a real importance for Delta people, especially for the Inuit. It should not be forgotten, however, that there are grave social problems in Inuvik and Tuktoyaktuk, and that many of these problems are closely associated with the intrusion of the oil and gas industry into them. The most serious problem of all may, in the end, turn out to be the dependence that the native people are coming to have on industrial employment. In the absence of an alternative source of income, people may become locked into a dependence on the oil and gas industry—whatever its relation to their environment or to their culture and aspirations. They may, therefore, quickly come to the point where they feel unable to oppose further industrial development. People who are locked into an economic condition because of their dependence on it can only acquiesce in the perpetuation of that condition.

When we consider the creation of employment for northern native people, we must be quite clear, however, about the unemployment that may also be created. Policy-makers in Ottawa and Yellowknife have tended to underestimate the extent to which native northerners are gainfully employed. Men who support their families—and even have surplus to share among other families—can hardly be said to be idle. Yet, there has been a tendency—and it seems to be one that persists—to classify such persons as unemployed, the result, obviously, of equating the category "employed" with that of "wage-earner." But, in native economic life, there are persons who, at any given time, may not be wage-earners, but who are nonetheless productively employed. I suggest that such persons should be regarded as "self-employed."

If, however, communities in the Mackenzie Valley and Western Arctic are made to depend exclusively on industrial wage employment—if the production of country food for local consumption ceases to be an important component in the economy, then the self-employed will certainly become the unemployed. The point is simple enough: the extension of the industrial system creates unemployment as well as employment. In an industrial economy there is virtually no alternative to a livelihood based on wage employment. Those who are unable or unprepared to work for wages become unemployed and then dependent on welfare. To the extent that the development of the northern frontier undermines the possibilities of self-employment provided by hunting, fishing and trapping, employment and unemployment will go hand-in-hand.

So, employment on the pipeline for native people will be seasonal. Seasonal employment, offering native people an opportunity to acquire cash to supplement their income from hunting, fishing and trapping, can, of course, be extremely useful. In some respects the seasonal wage employment available in the Delta has been just that. The danger lies, however, in the way that the intrusion of the industrial system leads to undermining and abandonment of the native renewable resource economy. This process has already been observed in the Delta, despite the fact that the seasonal wage employment available there (with the exception of Inuvik and Tuktoyaktuk) has, even over the past six years, been comparatively limited. The pipeline would offer seasonal employment for only two or three years. But it would intrude throughout the Mackenzie Valley and the Western Arctic in a way that would threaten the native economy to an unprecedented extent. Seasonal employment will be of little use to those who wish to maintain their own economic life: the very possibility for that economic life will have been removed.

IF THE PIPELINE IS NOT BUILT NOW

I have indicated that the economic impact of the pipeline will not bring lasting benefits to native northerners. In the next chapter, I shall outline the social costs of the project. They will be very high. And I shall have to say that construction of the pipeline now would irremediably compromise the goals embodied in native claims. All of these considerations lead inexorably to the conclusion that the pipeline should not be built now.

I speak of a postponement of the pipeline, not of its cancellation. Although the oil and gas reserves discovered so far in the Mackenzie Delta have been disappointing, the Government of Canada is committed to an exploration program of the oil and gas potential of the Beaufort Sea. The drilling program undertaken there by Dome Petroleum will continue and, if sufficient reserves of gas are discovered, in due course a pipeline may be built along the Mackenzie Valley to deliver this resource to market.

In their final submission, Arctic Gas urged the Inquiry to address this question: What will be the impact of a decision not to build a Mackenzie Valley pipeline now? They offered their own answer: they said that without a pipeline there would be no development of business opportunities, of employment, of economic growth in the Mackenzie Valley and the Western Arctic. They were supported in this answer by the Northwest Territories Chamber of Commerce and the Northwest Territories Association of Municipalities.

Jim Robertson, the Mayor of Inuvik, on behalf of the latter Association said that at least 50 percent of the present labour force in the Mackenzie Delta is employed directly or indirectly in oil and gas exploration and development. He insisted that, rightly or wrongly, education over the past 15 years has prepared the native people to take their place in the wage economy, and that there would be no alternative to out-migration from the Mackenzie Delta, if the pipeline did not proceed.

Robertson maintained that the pipeline would provide an urgently needed tax base for the larger centres in the North. He argued that there would necessarily be a reduction in the level of local services if the pipeline were not built, because there are not sufficient funds to pay for them. He pointed out that Northern Canada Power Commission, Northern Transportation Company Limited and other crown corporations have invested money in preparation for anticipated growth. If such growth does not occur, these companies will have to recover their capital and their operating and maintenance costs from a much smaller market than they had anticipated. Robertson said that this situation would lead to economic hardship in communities like Inuvik. He also argued that the erosion of the local tax base could have as great, if not greater, adverse impact than that predicted as a result of pipeline construction:

> Without prospects of growth, capable persons in all areas of expertise together with many dedicated civil servants would again invariably have no option but to pursue their careers in geographic areas where personal fulfilment and family advancement could be obtained.
>
> While many families, especially in the smaller communities, could continue to provide for themselves with an existence from the land, it is doubtful that many would freely elect to live off the land on a full-time basis for an indefinite period of time.

Robertson concluded:

> Mr. Commissioner, the foregoing ideas are placed before you not to assume a disaster if resource development is discontinued, but to illustrate what the Association perceives could be some serious problem areas arising as a result of an indefinite moratorium on resource development. [F29713]

However the case is put, it reflects the concept that, without a pipeline, there will be no economic development in the Northwest Territories. I find this point of view an oversimplification of what might happen. It reflects a decade of insistence by political figures and spokesmen for the oil and gas industry that there can be no form of northern development except a pipeline; *ergo,* without a pipeline there will be no development in the North.

If the pipeline is not built, the northern economy will not come to a sudden halt. To begin with, the native economy will not be seriously affected. The program of modernizing and expanding the native economy, which the native people have called for, can be undertaken. The mining industry will not be affected. The oil refinery at Norman Wells will not shut down. The Mackenzie River transportation system will continue to supply and resupply the communities of the Mackenzie Valley and the Western Arctic. The government bureaucracy, which is the largest employer and main source of income for both white and native northerners in the Northwest Territories, is not likely to diminish significantly in size simply because a pipeline is not built now.

Finally, a decision to postpone pipeline construction would not necessarily mean that oil and gas exploration in the North would be ended. As I said earlier, Dome's exploration program in the Beaufort Sea will continue, and exploration by independents is not likely to stop. I do not think the majors will necessarily cease drilling altogether: they would run the risk of losing their leases. In any event, if the federal government were to decide that, in the national interest, exploration should continue, Petro Canada is the instrument by which such a policy could be carried out.

Nevertheless, there would be a serious setback to Inuvik and perhaps (although this is less certain) to other Delta communities. Many northern businessmen, encouraged by spokesmen for the Government of Canada, have proceeded with their investment programs on the assumption that the Minister of Indian Affairs and Northern Development would grant a right-of-way, and the National Energy Board would grant a Certificate of Public Convenience and Necessity, to enable the pipeline project to proceed. Both government and the oil and gas industry have encouraged businessmen in this belief. If the pipeline is postponed, the losses that northern businessmen would suffer would be as attributable to the raising of these expectations as to the postponement itself.

I am proceeding on the assumption that the oil and gas in the Mackenzie Delta and the Beaufort Sea will, in due course, be delivered to the South by a pipeline. Given this assumption, the setback ought not to be as severe as many northern businessmen have predicted. Although a number of businesses may suffer from a postponement, the fact is, the decline in oil and gas activity in the Delta over the past two years has already resulted in a significant reduction in business activity.

According to John MacLeod, an economist from Inuvik, most of the businesses in Inuvik were established between 1970 and 1973. They have operated at a very high level of activity because of the high level of exploration work that went on in the early 1970s. It is not necessary to start construction on a pipeline tomorrow to keep these businesses alive. What is necessary, according to MacLeod, is to keep the prospects for pipeline construction positive enough to maintain drilling activity. He said that these businesses would be healthy if drilling activity were maintained at its 1974 level.

Nevertheless, if expectations of ever building a pipeline are dampened, there will be a decline in business activity in the Mackenzie Delta, and some businesses may be forced to liquidate. But I do not think the decline would be as severe as Arctic Gas predicts, because the drilling program in the Beaufort Sea will continue. This program has already created an unprecedented level of economic activity in Tuktoyaktuk, a level well above that reached during the peak years of oil and gas exploration in the Mackenzie Delta in the early 1970s. We are not contemplating the end of oil and gas activity in the Western Arctic. Exploration and related activities may be more strictly controlled, and development may be spread over longer periods of time than some have recently anticipated, but investment in the North will undoubtedly continue at moderate levels. This investment will continue to generate a range of economic opportunities that may fall short of a boom, but will certainly not be anything like the recession that many white businessmen seem to fear. The business community's disappointment would be real, but many of its gloomy economic forecasts would not.

SOCIAL IMPACT

THERE IS A TENDENCY, IN EXAMINING THE IMPACT OF A LARGE-scale industrial project, to accept the prospect of negative social impacts and to make recommendations for remedial measures that could or should be taken. There is also a tendency to minimize the importance of conclusions that are unsupported by "hard data." Usually those in favour of the project are able to say approximately how much it will cost, although experience with some other large-scale frontier projects, such as the James Bay hydro-electric project and the trans-Alaska pipeline, has indicated that the early estimates of costs have been completely unreliable. But at least there is a set of figures to work with, and they offer the comforting illusion that you are dealing with hard data.

In considering the social impact of large-scale developments, very few figures are available. All that can safely be said is that the social costs will be borne by the local population and that the financial costs will be borne by industry and the government. There is a strong tendency to underestimate and to understate social impact and social costs, and there is a tendency to believe that, whatever the problems may be, they can be overcome. The approach here is curative rather than preventive. No one asks for proof that the problems anticipated really can be ameliorated in a significant way—the assumption is that they can be. This assumption has been made with respect to problems of the proposed pipeline, and I think this assumption is demonstrably false.

Let me emphasize one thing at the outset: changes occur in the lives of everyone, changes that we have come to look upon as either necessary or inevitable. Everyone agrees that life is not static: each individual and every society has to accept change. A home owner may find that he has to give up six feet of land because a street is being widened, or his home may even be expropriated to make way for a new road. The location of a new airport near an urban centre may mean that hundreds of people must give up their homes. A farmer may have to agree to an easement across his land for hydro-electric transmission lines—or for a pipeline.

But the proposal to build a pipeline and to establish an energy corridor from the Arctic to the mid-continent will bring changes to the native people far greater in magnitude than the examples just mentioned. The pipeline and the energy corridor would change the North, alter a way of life and inhibit—perhaps extinguish—the native people's choices for the future.

The social impact that I foresee in the Mackenzie Valley and the Western Arctic, if we build the pipeline now, will be devastating—I use the word advisedly—and quite beyond our capacity to ameliorate in any significant way.

THE NORTHERN POPULATION

There are two populations in the North, a native population and a white population. Although the latter has increased dramatically since the early days of the fur trade, the native people are still in the majority in the Northwest Territories. Native people fear that the pipeline and the energy corridor will bring with them an influx of white people into their homeland, with consequences that will be irreversible. Richard Nerysoo made that point in Fort McPherson:

> The pipeline means more [white people] who will be followed by even more white people. White people bring their language, their political system, their economy, their schools, their culture. They push the Indian aside and take over everything. [C1190]

It is important to understand the composition of the northern population and how it has changed under the impact of industrial development and the proliferation of government. Only on the basis of such an understanding can we predict the social impact of the pipeline on the people of the North.

A Hudson's Bay Company trading post was established at Fort Resolution in 1786, three years before Mackenzie's journey to the Arctic Ocean. Other posts along the Mackenzie River followed in the early years of the 19th century. James Anderson, in his 1858 census of the Dene trading at Forts Liard, Rae, Simpson, Wrigley, Norman, Good Hope and McPherson, estimated their total number at 3,000.

In the Delta, in 1840, the Hudson's Bay Company erected a trading post on the fringes of Inuit territory at Fort McPherson. At that time, according to Diamond Jenness, there were 2,000 Inuit inhabiting the

Arctic coast between Demarcation Point (at what is now the international boundary between Alaska and the Yukon) and Cape Bathurst.

During the 19th century, the Metis became established in the North. They trace their ancestry through two sources: as descendants of the Metis who moved into the Mackenzie Valley from Manitoba and Saskatchewan after the Northwest Rebellion; and as descendants of unions between the early fur traders and Dene women.

Until the middle of the 19th century, except for a few European explorers, the only whites in the Mackenzie Valley were Hudson's Bay Company traders and their clerks. In the 1860s the missionaries came. The native people adapted their traditional life of subsistence hunting and fishing to a trapping and hunting economy, which included seasonal visits to a trading post and, later, to a mission near it. Although the fur trade introduced many technological innovations to native life and some dependence on manufactured goods, the people still lived on and from the land.

THE GOLD RUSH

Toward the end of the 19th century, large numbers of whites poured into the North in search of gold: in 1898 alone, some 30,000 prospectors and others joined the Klondike gold rush and headed for Dawson City. Two anthropologists, Dr. Catherine McClellan and Julie Cruikshank, described to the Inquiry the effect of this influx on the Indians of the Southern Yukon:

> Indians along the route to the gold fields became temporarily involved in packing, guiding and providing food for the white prospectors. Some became deck hands on the river boats. A few Indian women married white prospectors and left the country. The Tagish, who were themselves involved in the discovery of gold, and the Han, who lived at the mouth of the Klondike River, were the natives most affected. The latter were virtually destroyed. [F23094]

When the excitement died away, at the turn of the century, most whites left the area. In 1900 the population of the Yukon had climbed to 27,000 (of whom about 3,000 were Indians), but by 1912 it had shrunk to 6,000, and by 1921 to 4,000.

The gold rush of 1898 also affected the native people of the Northwest Territories. One of the routes to the Klondike was down the Athabasca and Mackenzie Rivers to the Mackenzie Delta and then overland via the Rat River to the Porcupine River, or via the Peel River to the Wind River and thence across to the Yukon. By the end of 1898, some 860 prospectors had reached Fort Smith, and an estimated 600 of them camped that winter in or near Fort McPherson. Some turned aside from their rush to the Klondike when news spread of rich gold deposits at the eastern end of Great Slave Lake. The influx of prospectors into the Mackenzie Valley played a significant part in the government's decision to make a treaty with the Indians in 1899. Charles Mair, a member of the Halfbreed Commission, which was established to deal with those Metis who chose not to sign the treaty, described what happened:

> The gold-seekers plunged into the wilderness of Athabasca without hesitation and without as much as "by your leave" to the native. Some of these marauders, as was to be expected, exhibited on the way a congenital contempt for the Indian's rights. At various places his horses were killed, his dogs shot, his bear-traps broken. An outcry arose in consequence, which inevitably would have led to reprisals and bloodshed had not the Government stepped in and forestalled further trouble by a prompt recognition of the native's title. . . . The gold seeker was viewed with great distrust by the Indians, the outrages referred to showing, like straws in the wind, the inevitable drift of things had the treaties been delayed. For, as a matter of fact, those now peaceable tribes, soured by lawless aggression, and sheltered by their vast forests, might easily have taken an Indian revenge, and hampered, if not hindered, the safe settlement of the country for years to come. [cited in R. Fumoleau, *As Long As This Land Shall Last,* p. 48ff.]

Anglican missionaries were appalled by the corruption that accompanied the invasion of prospectors. One wrote:

> The influence of the class of people now rushing into the country in search of gold is worse than I can describe.

And another added:

> I have always dreaded the incoming of the mining population, on account of the effect it would have upon the morals of our people, but did not think it would touch us so closely. [cited in Fumoleau, op. cit., p. 49]

The prospectors who reached the Klondike by the Rat River left their imprint on the minds of the native people of Fort McPherson. They still remember the location of Destruction City, the miners' winter camp on the Rat. Some of the native people from Fort McPherson, who guided miners over the mountains to the Klondike, stayed there for a few years, earning their living by supplying Dawson City with meat.

WHALERS, TRADERS AND TRAPPERS
In the 1890s, the American whaling fleet from San Francisco entered the Beaufort Sea, and Herschel Island and Baillie Islands, off Cape Bathurst,

became the focal points for the whaling industry in the Western Arctic. Native people were attracted to these harbours where the whaling ships wintered, and they were hired to gather driftwood to conserve the ships' stocks of coal, and to hunt caribou and muskox to supply the whalers with fresh meat. Some winters there were as many as 600 white people at Herschel Island. Whaling took a heavy toll not only of the bowhead whales but also of muskoxen and caribou. But it was not just the animals that were affected. Diamond Jenness, in *Eskimo Administration: Canada,* provides us with a graphic description of the effect of the whalers on the Inuit of the Delta:

Whaling ships churned the waters of the Beaufort Sea until about 1906. . . . By that date not only had the number of whales and caribou gravely diminished, but the number of Eskimos also. A little earlier influenza and other diseases introduced by the whalers had produced a similar diminution in the population of the Eastern Arctic; but there, for some reason which is not yet clear, the whaling captains had carried only limited stocks of intoxicating liquor, and had restricted its consumption very largely to their own crews. In the Western Arctic, on the other hand, they not only distributed liquor to the Eskimos with full hands, but taught them how to make it by distilling molasses or potatoes from one five gallon coal-oil can to another. . . . Syphilis took root among them, increasing the death-rate, especially of infants, and causing apparently widespread sterility. Then in 1902 some Indians who had contracted measles in Dawson City conveyed it to Fort McPherson, whence it reached the Eskimos of the Delta, carrying off nearly 100 persons, about one-fifth, Stefansson estimated, of the surviving population. This population continued to decline after the whalers departed, though the decline was masked by a stream of immigration from Arctic Alaska, set in motion by the depletion of the caribou in that region. [p. 14]

Dr. John Stager of the University of British Columbia told the Inquiry that, when the whaling industry collapsed in 1908, out of an original population of 2,500, there were only about 250 Mackenzie Eskimos left in the region between Barter Island and Bathurst Peninsula.

Yet in 1901 the resident white population of what is now the Northwest Territories was still only 137. It included Hudson's Bay Company factors, free traders, white trappers, missionaries and some church and residential school personnel. The first Northwest Mounted Police detachment was established in 1903; then came Indian Agents, nursing sisters and game officers.

By 1919–1920, fur prices had achieved a very high level, and white trappers and traders entered the Mackenzie Valley and Western Arctic in large numbers. There were 110 trading stores in 1920 in the Northwest Territories; the number doubled by 1927. In Fort Rae alone, 41 trading licences were issued in 1926. Statistics compiled by the RCMP in 1923 show that there were 118 white trappers in the area around Fort Smith and Fort Resolution.

During this period of intense competition, the Hudson's Bay Company's trade monopoly was broken, and the nature of the fur trade was altered. In particular, the old practice of outfitting the native hunters on credit was replaced by the cash system.

THE RISE OF INDUSTRY

The discovery of oil at Norman Wells in 1920 brought another surge of white people into the Mackenzie Valley. In the winter of 1921, some 24 parties travelled by dog team from Edmonton to Fort Norman to stake claims, and other parties came overland from Dawson City and Whitehorse. Before the first steamer reached Fort Providence that summer, boats of every description had passed the village on their way north. Most of these white people left as quickly as they had come. In 1921, after the signing of Treaty 11, the census for the Northwest Territories indicated there were nearly 4,000 Indians living in the Northwest Territories, but only 853 "others"—a category including Metis, non-status Indians and whites.

In the years after the signing of Treaty 11, the native population was increasingly ravaged by the diseases the white people had brought. Father René Fumoleau told the Inquiry:

A discouraged Doctor Bourget, Indian Agent at Fort Resolution, wrote in 1927, "We seem to be in a period of readjustment which will show seriously on the Indians." Deaths from tuberculosis alone outnumbered births in most places. Many infants died a few months after birth. Most families lost parents and children alike. Periodic outbursts of smallpox, measles and flu took a heavy toll over the years. In 1928, the influenza epidemic struck the Mackenzie District. While all the whites recovered, the sickness killed 600 Indians, one-sixth of the Indian population. At Goulet's camp near Yellowknife, 26 Indians died and the seven survivors fled in panic. [F21835]

Prospecting and mining brought a significant increase in the white population. The richest uranium mine in the world opened at Port Radium in 1932. When gold was discovered at Yellowknife in 1933, prospectors and miners rushed to stake claims there. In 1937, there were 400 prospectors searching for minerals in the Mackenzie District. Census figures for the Northwest Territories have always been unreliable, but we know that during the 1930s the number of people classified as "other" stood at 1,007 in 1931, and swelled to 4,000 by 1941. In the same decade, the population classified as Indian and Eskimo rose by only 700.

Since the Second World War, the white population in the Northwest Territories has increased rapidly. Hay River, for example, which is now an important transportation centre, has changed from a small Indian community into a predominantly white town of 3,500, with the Indian village on its periphery. The Mayor of Hay River, Don Stewart, described the changes since the Second World War:

> I came to the Territories in 1946, as a young married man and have remained, with the exception of two years since that date, in Hay River. Through this period of time we have noted many changes. . . . When I first came to Hay River there was only the Indian village on the east bank of the river, one small Imperial Oil tank, a dirt runway with an American Quonset hut, a leftover of the Northwest Staging Route, an emergency landing field for aircraft going to Alaska during the last war. . . . The Americans had come and gone. . . . There were five white people in Hay River. We found a village that was self-sufficient, we found people with pride . . . we found people living in the same type of housing . . . everything was similar. . . . Everybody had the 45-gallon barrel in the corner that sufficed for [a] water supply, and this was, for the most part, ice that was cut during the winter time and used in the summer time. There were no vehicles to speak of. I think we had one truck in Hay River at that time. [C409ff.]

Mining, development of transportation facilities and oil and gas exploration have all contributed to the growth of the white population in the Mackenzie Valley and the Western Arctic.

THE GOVERNMENT ERA

The proliferation of government in the North has been the chief cause of the growth of the white population since the Second World War. An increasing number of white people administer the health, education and welfare services now provided to the native people in various regional centres. In 1953, there were between 250 and 300 federal employees in the Northwest Territories. In 1966, there were about 2,600. With the establishment of the territorial government in Yellowknife in 1967 came a further increase. By 1976, there were something like 3,000 employees on the payroll of the Government of the Northwest Territories alone, and in addition there were approximately 2,000 employees of the Government of Canada and of federal crown corporations in the Northwest Territories. Of these 5,000 government employees, 80 percent or more are white; they and their families account for the majority of the white population of the Mackenzie Valley and the Western Arctic, if not the Northwest Territories as a whole. And, unlike earlier waves of white immigration into the North, this one has not receded.

Although the white population in the North has increased dramatically in the last 20 years, the majority of whites who go North still think of home as somewhere in the South. They soon leave, to be replaced by others. This is characteristic of the employees of the Government of Canada, the Government of the Northwest Territories, and of the mining and the oil and gas industries. Indeed, in the three years since the Inquiry was appointed, the Department of Indian Affairs and Northern Development has had three Regional Directors of Northern Operations and three Regional Representatives, Indian Affairs Program, in the Northwest Territories. Members of the RCMP and the Canadian Forces perform a tour of duty, then they too return south. At Fort Resolution, in a graveyard 85 years old, only two white adults and two white children are buried.

A large percentage of the white population in the North is on rotation: the numbers increase, but the faces constantly change. Some individuals do remain who have decided to make the North their permanent home. Their numbers are increasing slowly, but not in the dramatic way that the white population as a whole has increased.

NORTHERN POPULATION TODAY

What is the composition of the population of the Northwest Territories today? In 1974, the latest year for which figures from the Government of the Northwest Territories are available, there were 7,533 people classified as Indian, almost all of whom lived in the Mackenzie Valley and the Mackenzie Delta; 13,932 classified as Inuit, of whom some 2,300 resided in the Mackenzie Delta and Beaufort Sea communities; and 16,384 "others."

This ethnic breakdown into Indian, Inuit and "others" is not, however, as helpful as it may appear. The people classified as Indian are only those whose names are on the band lists. The number of Indians does not, therefore, include non-status Indians—persons of Indian ancestry who have become enfranchised under the Indian Act. An Indian might, in the past, have sought enfranchisement for a number of reasons: to vote, to buy liquor—things that treaty Indians then had no legal right to do. The most common example of enfranchisement has been by the operation of law when a treaty Indian woman married a non-status Indian, a Metis or a white man. Such marriages are not uncommon, and when they occur, the woman ceases to be an Indian under the law; she and her children are henceforth enumerated as "others." Virtually all of non-status Indians still regard themselves as Dene, just like their treaty relatives, and at the community hearings their views were indistinguishable from those of Dene who are still treaty Indians. The distinction, therefore, between treaty and non-status Indians, for my purposes, is not significant. Virtually all of these people regard themselves as Dene. Nor does the category described as Indian in the census include people of combined white-and-Indian ancestry who regard themselves as Metis and distinct in their heritage from the Dene and the white populations. These people, too, are included in the census as "others."

Because the Indian Act was never applied to the Eskimos, the distinction between status and non-status categories has never been legally relevant to them. The children of non-Eskimo fathers married to Eskimo women acquired "disc numbers"—the method of identifying the Eskimos until the 1960s—and they were counted as Eskimos.

To arrive at an accurate count of the native peoples, we must add to the figures for Indian and Inuit a portion of the number designated "others," because these "others" include non-status Indians and Metis. The number of non-status Indians and Metis is a matter of dispute. In attempting to determine actual figures I have considered the evidence of the Government of the Northwest Territories, the Indian Brotherhood, the Metis Association, and Dr. Charles Hobart. I have also examined the 1976 Preliminary Counts of the Census Divisions of the Government of Canada. I do not think there are more than 4,500 non-status Indians and Metis altogether.

The number of Metis is a matter of some confusion. Following the signing of Treaty 11 in 1921, 172 Metis took scrip. This would suggest that the number of native people who saw themselves as distinctively Metis was comparatively small at that time. That this is still the case is indicated by the federal government's study entitled *Regional Impact of a Northern Gas Pipeline,* published in 1973, which says, "The Metis formed only an estimated 10.5 percent of the total native population of 17 [Mackenzie] Valley communities in 1970." [Vol. 1, p. 35] This statement is based on the number of persons who said that they were Metis when questioned about their ethnic affiliation for the purposes of a manpower survey. Applying it to the present native population of the Mackenzie Valley and Western Arctic suggests that the population that regards itself as distinctly Metis would lie currently somewhere between 1,000 and 1,500 people. This analysis of the figures would correspond with the evidence at the community hearings, where the vast majority of people of Indian ancestry who spoke identified themselves as Dene.

Taking natural increase since 1974 into account, there must be about 12,500 people of Indian ancestry in the Northwest Territories today, virtually all of whom live in the Mackenzie Valley and Mackenzie Delta. Again taking natural increase since 1974 into account, there must be about 2,500 people of Inuit ancestry living in the Mackenzie Delta and Beaufort Sea communities.

I estimate the number of white people living in the Mackenzie Valley

and the Western Arctic today to be about 15,000. Thus the native population and the white population are more or less equal. But the figure for
the white population is in a sense misleading because it includes so many
people—undoubtedly the majority—who do not regard the North as
their home and who have every intention of returning to the South.
These are heavily concentrated in Yellowknife and the larger centres.

The native population in the Northwest Territories is a young one.
Statistics show that live births per 1,000 population rose from a low of
about 20 in 1931, to about 40 in 1947, and peaked at almost 50 between
1960 and 1964. This figure may have been among the highest in the
world at that time. The birthrate has declined since then to 40 in 1970
and to 27.8 in 1974. This figure can be compared to a rate of about 10
per 1,000 for Canada as a whole. It seems safe to say that 50 percent of
the native population of the Northwest Territories is under 15 years of
age today.

SOCIAL IMPACT AND INDUSTRIAL DEVELOPMENT

The pipeline companies and the oil and gas industry maintain that a
pipeline will have a beneficial social impact on the people and the communities of the North. In particular, they say a pipeline will reduce the
unemployment, welfare dependence, crime, violence and alcoholism that
are at present characteristic of many northern settlements.

Dr. Charles Hobart, analyzing social malaise in the North, attributed
it to two main factors. First, massive government intervention in the
people's lives over the past two decades has undermined their traditional
independence and self-esteem, creating social and psychological dependence. Second is the frustration and anger that many young people, who
have been brought up in the white man's educational system, experience
on leaving school. They find that the promise of useful and dignified employment is an empty one. Hobart suggested that new employment opportunities associated with the pipeline and the oil and gas industry will
offer a positive response to both causes of social malaise. He argued that
stable employment will "facilitate native identification with new
identities, which are prideful and relevant to the world in which native
people must live today." Here is how he put it:

> The lack of opportunities to experience employment demanding responsi-
> bility and commitment, to obtain the training that would lead directly to
> such employment, and to aspire towards such employment, tends to per-
> petuate anti-social patterns. Without more stable employment becoming
> available, there are no opportunities for the structural and motivational

reasons for such anti-social behaviours to change, nor are there generally effective mechanisms for reinforcing more socially constructive behaviour. However, increased stable employment opportunities, with opportunities for training, upgrading and advancement, would provide alternative motivations and reward alternative constructive behaviour. [F25109ff.]

I disagree with Hobart on this point. I have come to the conclusion that in this instance his analysis will not hold up. Our experience so far with industrial development in the North has been recited. That experience has revealed two things: first, that native people have not participated in the industrial economy on a permanent basis; and secondly, that the native people have paid a high price in terms of social impact wherever the industrial economy has penetrated into the North.

Stable employment and an ever-increasing disposable income are part and parcel of what we regard as progress and prosperity. We see wage employment as the answer to the problems of our urban poor. Why, then, do so many native people in the North view the pipeline in such negative terms, as something that will undermine their communities and destroy them as a people? For, as the following statements show, many native people do see the pipeline in this way.

Fred Rabiska at Fort Good Hope:

If the pipeline is built we will be very unhappy people. We will drift farther from each other as well as [from] our land. [C1787]

Mary Rose Drybones, a Dene social worker, at Fort Good Hope:

It will destroy their way of life, their soul and identity. We have enough to cope with without another big issue [such] as the pipeline. It will touch everybody at all levels. It will not leave [any] one alone. [C1947]

Edward Jumbo at Trout Lake:

Talking about the pipeline . . . that is just like somebody telling us they're going to destroy us. [C2398]

Bruno Apple at Rae Lakes:

If this pipeline should get through, there's going to be a lot of people here. When this pipeline gets through, it's going to be like the end of the world here. [C8255]

I think the basic reason for this gulf between our belief in the benefits of industrial employment and the native people's fear of it is that the native people of the North are not simply poor people who happen to be of

Indian, Inuit or Metis descent. They are people whose values and patterns of social organization are in many ways quite different from those that underlie the modern industrial world. Solutions based on the industrial system may easily become problems when they are applied to native people.

THE FORT SIMPSON EXPERIENCE

We can get some idea of the impact of industrial development in the Northwest Territories by examining the experience of the native people at Fort Simpson. The Mackenzie Highway was completed to Fort Simpson in 1970, and the Inquiry was told of the social consequences it has had in that community. People in Fort Good Hope, Fort Norman and Wrigley told me that their deepest fear was that, if the pipeline went through, their communities would become like Fort Simpson. Native witnesses at Fort Simpson told me that their people's involvement in the construction of the Mackenzie Highway, through the Hire North project, has resulted in major social problems such as high rates of alcohol abuse, crime and violence, and family breakdown.

Betty Menicoche gave the Inquiry her own family's history as an example of what the native people mean when they say, "We don't want to become another Fort Simpson." She explained how her parents, after leading a traditional life in the bush, had moved into Fort Simpson to earn wages to supplement the living they earned by hunting and fishing. She told of the hardships her parents endured while trying to cope with the two ways of life, and she described the social pressures brought about by the construction of the highway:

> By 1970, things in Simpson had reached a point of social disorder and ultimately of breakdown in [the] cultural value system. The scene in Simpson for natives was one of excitement, and one way they began enjoying this fun was through alcohol, [thus] beginning misuse through misunderstanding . . . it was since 1970 that I found the breakdown of our family as a result of alcohol, stress and strain, created by this need to achieve an economic base, a wage economy. At this time my family experienced the biggest social disaster . . . that was the ultimate breakdown of my mother. She had kept our family going despite the thin threads of the family. The strain of trying to tie two ways of life into one another was too much to bear. . . . All the frustrations and the difficulty of coping with this transition are easily remedied by the bottle. That was the final breakdown of a once solid family. . . .
>
> We have been accused of being young radical Indians, only repeating ideas of left-wing people. These are just a few examples of what has occurred in Simpson. Further social and economic injustices will be experienced if the pipeline goes through. Tell me, is it wrong to begin standing

on two feet, [telling] what you yourself and your people have truly experienced? [C2667ff.]

Theresa Villeneuve was born in Nahanni Butte and spent her early years living with her parents in the bush. In those days her father came to Fort Simpson only to sell his furs and buy supplies. She has lived most of her married life in Fort Simpson and has seen the changes that have occurred:

Since 1968, things have been happening too fast, and people cannot put up with them. The Dene people are not involved in what things are happening. They have never helped in planning for future development . . . because Dene don't think like the white man. [C2656]

Seen through the eyes of the native people of Fort Simpson, their experience with wage employment during the construction of the Mackenzie Highway was debilitating. Jim Antoine, the young Chief of the Fort Simpson Indian Band, summed up the views of the Dene on the impact of the pipeline:

I'm not worried about the money or jobs that this pipeline is going to give because, as Indian people, we don't think about the money. We think about the lives of the people here because, the way I see it, if this pipeline goes ahead, it's just going to destroy a lot of people. It's going to kill a lot of people indirectly. . . . I don't want the pipeline to come in here because, with the highway coming in in the last five to six years, it has changed Simpson altogether. A lot of problems arose out of this highway. If this pipeline comes through, it's going to cause problems to be a hundredfold more. We're the people that live here, and we're the people who are going to suffer. [C2624]

NATIVE VALUES AND THE FRONTIER

René Lamothe, a Metis, described to the Inquiry some of the deep-seated reasons for the confusion and frustration that have beset the native people of Fort Simpson. In his view, the assumption that native people will adapt to and benefit from industrial development is too easily made. He argued that, in the Northwest Territories, the philosophy of life, the values, and the social organization that have been developed by a hunting-and-gathering society, together with the modifications introduced by a trapping economy during the last century, go very deep.

As we have seen, the native values and the native economy persist. But the values and expectations of the industrial system push in a different direction. Hugh Brody described the process in his evidence:

Inuit and Dene peoples are proud of the ways in which they share the produce of the land. The activity of hunting may be comparatively individu-
alistic, but its produce tends to be communal—at least insofar as those in
want are able to approach successful hunters and ask for food. Also, the
basic means of production—land—is regarded as communal. Requests for
food were never refused; the right to use land was rarely disputed. Money,
however, is not so readily shared. It tends to be regarded as the earner's
own private property, and spent on his or her immediate family's personal
needs. Moreover, it tends to be spent on consumer durable goods, which
cannot be divided among neighbours. [F25787ff.]

The result of this difference is not only that the sharing ethic is undermined, but the cohesion and homogeneity of the community are
threatened when new inequalities begin to develop.

When those who live by hunting and trapping are seen to experience
poverty, they tend to lose their status within the society. Once again, the
native community's sense of cultural distinctiveness is eroded, and the
traditional ways of according respect are undermined. Wage labour is
not necessarily an adequate substitute for the traditional social system,
once the values of the traditional system have been eroded by the industrial world. René Lamothe explained this danger to the Inquiry:

. . . the hunting economy permitted a man to support an extended family;
whereas the wage economy does not adequately support an immediate
family within the expectations that the industrial economy raises. . . . We
have elders alive now who in their youth supported up to 40 people. Etoli,
an old man living in the hospital right now, in his youth supported up to
40 people by hunting. Who of us with our salaries today can support 10?
Etoli is living in the hospital here primarily because the expectations of
ourselves, his relatives, have been changed by education, the churches, the
industrial economy; and secondly because the wage economy . . . does not
generate enough cash to support more than one nuclear family . . . young
women are raised among the Dene people to expect specific benefits from
a husband. However, these benefits are found in a hunting economy, not
in a wage-earning economy. Young men are raised to believe that to be a
man one must provide these benefits, and again these benefits are not
found in a wage-earning economy. . . .

We are a people caught in an industrial economy with a mind prepared
for a hunting economy. The expectations women have of their men [and]
the men of the women [are] not being realized in everyday life [which] results in frustrations, confusions, misunderstandings and anger that net
broken homes. [C2687ff.]

Lamothe's views may seem, at first glance, out of keeping with modern notions of industrial motivation, but there is a hard practicality to what he said. His views are especially relevant in the North, because there the disruptive effects of the industrial system on native values are intensified by the particular kind of industrial development that the pipeline represents—large-scale industrial development on the frontier. The values of white people working on the frontier are opposed to and inconsistent with the values that are embedded in native tradition in the villages and settlements of the North. The community life of native people emphasizes sharing and cooperation between generations and among the member households of an extended family. The native community has a profound sense of its own permanence. The place is more important than economic incentive.

The frontier encourages, indeed depends upon, a footloose work force, mobile capital and all their ideological concomitants. It is not any particular location that matters but the profitability of an area; attachments are to reward, not to place, people or community. Individualism, uncertainty and instability are part and parcel of the frontier.

The native people are well aware of the difference between their own attitudes and values and those of a frontier work force. Agnes Edgi at Fort Good Hope told the Inquiry:

> We, the Dene people, were born on this land of ours. We are not like the white people who go wandering around looking for work. They are not like us . . . who have a home in one place. They, the white people, move from one town to another, from one country to another, searching for jobs to make money. [C2003]

The frontier mentality exacerbates the processes whereby traditional social controls are broken down and pathological behaviour becomes a feature of everyday life.

Ethel Townsend, a native teacher from Fort Norman, told the Inquiry that construction of a pipeline will impose a great strain on the people of the Northwest Territories:

> The adaptability of our people will be stretched to its limits, and there is a breaking point. [C4388]

I have been describing here a complex process, one that may be difficult for people who have grown up within the industrial system to comprehend. Let us turn now to some of the easily understood and highly visible effects of industrial development on the northern people to date, and let me suggest what the social impact of the pipeline would be.

SPECIFIC IMPACTS

THE COSTS OF WELFARE

Transfer payments in the North are made for a variety of purposes, which include payments to people who are in ill health, to single parents with dependent children, to persons caring for dependent relatives, to wives of men in prison, to the blind and to the aged. These payments also include "economic assistance" for people who would normally support themselves, but who cannot do so for lack of employment.

It is commonly believed that welfare payments are inversely related to the size of the employment base: the larger the employment base, the lower the welfare payments. This idea is widely accepted among northern policy-makers; it is one of the foundations of policies designed to expand northern industrial wage employment and, more generally, to industrialize the North. The reasoning is simple: people in the North require economic assistance because they lack employment. They believe that the traditional life based on the land has collapsed and that nothing has taken its place. The native people therefore require welfare—but only as a "transitional measure." When opportunities for wage employment have been sufficiently enlarged, they will no longer need economic assistance. Quite predictably, white northerners complain that native people are receiving too much welfare, and that industrial development is not proceeding fast enough to relieve the public of the substantial burden that native welfare represents.

What is the real relationship between welfare payments and the economic base of the North? Have welfare payments declined as industrial activity has expanded? The evidence strongly suggests that the conventional wisdom is wrong. So far, the expansion of industrial activity in the North has been accompanied by a marked increase in economic assistance and in other types of welfare payments.

The recent increase in welfare payments and in related social problems that we have observed in the North has one basic cause: the force and suddenness with which industrial development has intruded into the region. During the past two centuries, the native people of the North have had to change a great deal and, by and large, they have shown a remarkable ability to adapt. But never before has there been such a sustained assault on their social institutions and relationships, on their language and culture, and on their attitudes and values. Never before have there been greater strains on the families. Should a husband and father stay in his community or work far away? Should the young people choose one way of life or another? Under the accumulated force of these pulls and pressures, communities are bound to disintegrate, families are bound to come apart, and individuals are bound to fail. The rising figures for welfare payments reflect to a considerable degree the impact of the industrial system on the native people of the North today.

CRIME AND VIOLENCE

Welfare and economic assistance payments may be regarded as the economic aspect of a much larger problem. We must also consider a range of social disorders, each of which, like dependence on welfare, can be seen in economic or in broader human terms. Crime and violence are already problems in northern native society; will the advent of large-scale industrial development ameliorate or compound these problems?

Native witnesses maintained that there is a correlation between social disorders and industrial development. Crime in the Northwest Territories increased between 1969 and 1975, a period of industrial expansion. The native people assert that the communities least involved in wage labour and least dominated by the frontier mentality are the communities with least crime and violence. Indeed, many native witnesses emphasized to me their fear that their particular settlements might become more like the "developed" communities.

All of the evidence indicates that an increase in industrial wage employment and disposable income among the native people in the North brings with it a dramatic increase in violent death and injuries.

I am persuaded that the incidence of these disorders is closely bound up with the rapid expansion of the industrial system and with its persistent intrusion into every part of the native people's lives. The process affects the complex links between native people and their past, their culturally preferred economic life, and their individual, familial and political self-respect. We should not be surprised to learn that the economic forces that have broken these vital links, and that are unresponsive to the distress of those who have been hurt, should lead to serious disorders. Crimes of violence can, to some extent, be seen as expressions of frustration, confusion and indignation, but we can go beyond that interpretation to the obvious connection between crimes of violence and the change the South has, in recent years, brought to the native people of the North. With the obvious connection, we can affirm one simple proposition: the more the industrial frontier displaces the homeland in the North, the worse the incidence of crime and violence will be.

HEALTH AND HEALTH SERVICES

During the 1940s and 1950s, the health of the native people was one of the major problems confronting government in the North. By that time, the spread of infectious diseases, especially tuberculosis, had assumed appalling dimensions, and it was evident that medical services would have to be extended to even the remotest camps and villages. The extension of these services was one of the reasons for the rapid growth of settlements in the 1950s and 1960s. However, improved medical services did not solve the native people's health problems. Certainly the devastation of pulmonary disease was eventually brought under control, and epidemics of influenza, measles and whooping-cough no longer caused so many deaths. But the former causes of sickness have, to some extent, been replaced by new ones—less deadly, but nonetheless debilitating.

The Inquiry heard evidence from doctors and dentists with wide experience of the health situation in northern communities. They told us that during the past decade venereal disease rates have risen rapidly in the Northwest Territories and are now many times higher than those for Canada as a whole. Dr. Herbert Schwarz, a physician from Tuktoyaktuk, told the Inquiry:

> Mr. Commissioner, if we apply these 1975 Inuvik percentages and figures for the seven-month period only [the first seven months of 1975], showing that one person in every six was infected with gonorrhea, and transpose these figures on a per capita basis to a city like Ottawa, then [it] would have from 80,000 to 100,000 people suffering with venereal disease. [The] city would be a disaster area and a state of medical emergency proclaimed.
>
> The incidence of venereal disease for the whole of the Northwest Territories was up 27 percent for the first seven months of 1975 over a similar period of a year ago. The Inuvik region contributed much more than its share to the territorial average. Cases reported and treated in the Inuvik zone were up 58 percent over a similar seven-month period last year, with 537 cases confirmed and treated to 339 confirmed cases treated last year. [C7532ff.]

In testimony, the medical authorities gave particular attention to changes in diet: native people are eating less meat, more sugar, and mothers have been encouraged to bottle-feed rather than breast-feed their babies. Dr. Elizabeth Cass said the shift from country food to southern food has resulted in widespread myopia; Dr. Schaefer associated the change in diet with extremely high rates of child sickness in general and with middle-ear disease in particular. Dr. Mayhall described an epidemic of dental disease and the very high rates of tooth decay and gum disease in the North. We understand that a change in diet may cause such problems when we realize that local meat has a higher food value than meats imported to the North. Some changes in diet are plain to see, such as the consumption of great quantities of pop. (It has been estimated that in Barrow, Alaska, the average consumption of pop is seven cans a day for each man, woman and child.)

Change will come to the North, as it does everywhere. There will be problems related to the delivery of health services in the North, pipeline or no pipeline. What we must understand is that the impact of a pipeline, with increased wage employment, rapid social change, and new ways and diet, will produce among the native people of the North particular and unfortunate effects that cannot be mitigated by any conventional means. There are real limitations to any preventive and curative measures that can be recommended.

I do not wish to leave the impression that I believe wage employment and an increased availability of cash to be the proximate cause of health problems. They are perhaps more generally attributable to rapid social change. But the situation is all of a piece: when the native people's own culture is overwhelmed by another culture, the loss of tradition, pride and self-confidence is evident in every aspect of personal, family and social life. The advance of industrial development has affected every part of native life, and there is every reason to believe that the construction of a pipeline and its aftermath would lead to further deterioration in the health of the native people.

ALCOHOL

The subjects of heavy drinking and drunkenness recur in every discussion of social pathology in the North. Both native and white people regard the abuse of alcohol as the most disruptive force, the most alarming symptom, and the most serious danger to the future of northern society. François Paulette of Fort Smith expressed the feelings of many native people in saying:

> Today I feel sad when I see my people, the people who were so close together in the past . . . fragmented with booze. [C4747]

Alcohol was introduced to northern natives by the fur traders in the Mackenzie Valley and by the whalers on the Arctic coast. Alcohol and other drugs were used in the Americas before the advent of Europeans, but only among agricultural peoples, not among hunters and gatherers. There is no evidence of the use of alcohol in any form by northern Indians and Eskimos before the coming of the white man.

The fact is, drinking has become an enormous problem throughout the Northwest Territories. When a traditional community becomes a drinking community, the whole atmosphere can change. Drunks can be seen staggering around the village, and people begin to lock their doors. People are apprehensive every time a plane lands: is it carrying liquor?

ALCOHOL AND THE PIPELINE

If we build the pipeline now, what will be its impact on native drinking?

What might happen in Northern Canada? Dr. Ross Wheeler, a Yellowknife physician, outlined the problems he saw in the North. He mentioned suicide, mental illness, crimes of violence, and the exploitation of native women, and he concluded:

> The common theme running through all these social problems is alcohol. This single drug, more than any other factor, has been, is, and will be at the root of most of the social problems in the Territories. Facilities for dealing with alcoholism are in their infancy. More time and money are needed if the programs are to be built up. This need can only increase in the future.
>
> While treatment programs are necessary, they do not affect the basic problem causing alcoholism. Only the restoration of self-respect and a meaningful place in a society to which a person can relate, only basic dignity as a human being will reduce the problem of alcoholism. [C3401ff.]

Wheeler, like so many other witnesses, insisted upon the connection between the abuse of alcohol and industrial development. How, therefore, can we suppose that the construction of the pipeline will do anything but make the present situation worse?

The mindless violence and the social disarray that accompany drinking in the native communities are matters of grave concern to the native people themselves. They have spoken frankly to the Inquiry about the use of alcohol in the villages and of the measures they have taken to curb the problem.

Historically, measures to limit or prevent the misuse of alcohol have taken two forms: legislative sanction and remedial and educational activities. These efforts have not succeeded generally in North American society and they have largely failed in the North. But recently the native people have had some success with both methods: at Fort Rae and at Lac la Martre the people have adopted local prohibition, and in many native villages programs of self-help are underway. In my view, these programs will succeed only to the extent that the increasing self-awareness, self-confidence and self-respect among the native people provide a foundation upon which these programs can be built. I believe that the native organizations have created positive role models—exemplars, even heroes —for native people. These models may now be replacing the southern stereotype of the drunken Indian.

At the moment, it is impossible to say whether or not the native people's attempts to control the use of alcohol will succeed. But the construction of the Mackenzie Valley pipeline will certainly make the struggle more difficult, not easier.

The alcohol problem is bad now, but it could become far worse. There are communities in the Mackenzie Valley where alcohol-associated problems are severe, but there are other communities where these problems are relatively minor, still kept at bay by the enduring vigour of native society and its values. In the language of sociology, there continue to be well-integrated native families and communities. Rapid and massive change poses two threats: to communities of well-integrated families, whose satisfying lives may suddenly be disrupted, and to communities whose families have already been broken, and who will find attempts to improve their situation made more difficult or impossible.

The alcohol problem is secondary to other and more basic issues. Why should people not drink heavily when they have been separated from all the things they value? To the extent that the native people are obliged to participate in the type of frontier development that separates them from their traditional life, their chances of containing, and finally of ameliorating, the problems of alcohol grow worse and worse.

SOCIAL INEQUALITIES

During the early 1950s, the swift growth of a strong governmental presence in the North was intended to bring to the native people the benefits of the modern liberal state and to give them equal opportunity with other Canadians. Paradoxically, it had the effect of producing yet deeper inequalities in the social structure of the North. The establishment and growth of Inuvik illustrate this point vividly.

Inuvik was intended to replace Aklavik as a centre for federal administration. All major commercial and government services were transferred to Inuvik, and new research and defence establishments were built there. Dr. Hobart described what the move from Aklavik to Inuvik entailed in terms of social impact:

When whites first came to the Arctic, if they were to survive, much less live in comfort, they had in many ways to adopt the life-style of the native people. Thus, there was a basic similarity in the everyday living and survival patterns of everyone in the same community. As I heard people in this area say ten and more years ago, in Aklavik, the honey bucket was the great equalizer. At the risk of over-simplification, we could characterize the shift from Aklavik to Inuvik as the shift from egalitarianism to discrimination, from attitudes of acceptance to attitudes of prejudice against native people. . . . If in Aklavik the honey bucket was the great equalizer, in Inuvik, particularly during the early years, the utilidor was the great discriminator. The planning of Inuvik provided that some would have to continue to carry the honey bucket and [others] would no longer have to. Thus, discrimination was built into the piling foundations of this community. You could see it from the air, before ever setting foot in town, in terms of where the utilidor did run, the white serviced end of town—and where it did not—the native unserviced part of town. [F17160ff.]

Such inequalities have not gone unobserved by the native people, for they are to be seen in almost every community. Philip Blake, a Dene from Fort McPherson and a social worker there for five years, talked about the changes in that community:

I am not an old man, and I have seen many changes in my life. Fifteen years ago, most of what you see as Fort McPherson did not exist. Take a look around the community now and you will start to get an idea of what has happened to the Indian people here over the past few years.

Look at the housing where transient government staff live. And look at the housing where the Indian people live. Look at what houses are connected to the utilidor. Look at how the school and hostel, the RCMP and government staff houses are right in the centre of town, dividing the Indian people into two sides. Look at where the Bay store is, right on the top of the highest point of land. Do you think that this is the way that the Indian people chose to have this community? Do you think the people here had any voice in planning this community? Do you think they would have planned it so that it divided them and gave them a poorer standard than the transient whites who came in, supposedly to help them? [C1078]

We must ask ourselves, how will these inequalities be affected by the construction of the Mackenzie Valley pipeline? The likelihood is that the native people will be employed as unskilled workers on jobs that will not last beyond the period of construction. The social implications of this likelihood can be stated baldly: industrial expansion into the Western Arctic means the extension northward of southern wage-and-status differentials. The native people will find themselves on the bottom rungs of the ladder, and most of them are likely to remain there.

Any claim that equality of opportunity at the work place will prevent the coincidence of low pay and low status with brown skin is, to say the least, naive. Inequalities of income and of occupational level are intrinsic to the industrial system, and they will no doubt be features of its extension to any frontier. Nevertheless, it is not easy to accept the racial inequalities at the work place. Still less easy is it to accept the social tensions and disorders that such inequalities bequeath.

Only time and the establishment of options available to the native people will go any distance toward preventing such inequalities. Once again we must remember that industrial development of the frontier, without a parallel development of native self-determination and the native economy, will bring to bear on the native people immense pressure to give way to a style of life that they regard as alien and destructive. If we create a society in which the native people of the North are deprived of social and economic dignity by a process of development that they regard as an assault on their homeland and themselves, they will see this assault in racial terms and will protest and oppose it in the years to come.

IDENTITY AND SELF-RESPECT

By cataloguing the pathologies of society in the North today, I have tried to show the North as I see it. I have tried to predict what will happen in terms of social impact, if a pipeline is built now.

It should be plain enough that one of the most pervasive social problems in the North today is the loss of self-esteem that many native people have experienced. It may be no exaggeration to speak at times of a despair that has overwhelmed whole families, even whole villages. I want this point to be well understood because it is integral to many of the social pathologies of northern people, and the problem must be faced if we are to develop a rational social policy for the future of the North.

Many of us cannot easily imagine what it is like to be a member of a subject race. When you see your race, or a member of it, denigrated or insulted, then you too are diminished as an individual. The expression can be subtle and insidious, or it can be overt; it can be part of deliberate behaviour, or it can be unintentional. The disorders that such discrimination involves cannot be eliminated by psychiatric, health and counselling services. Although such services may palliate the disease, they will never cure it.

Dr. Pat Abbott, a psychiatrist with the Division of Northern Medicine, Department of Health and Welfare, made a point that is vital to understanding these problems. The establishment of new programs, the recruitment of personnel, the delivery of improved health services and social services by themselves are and will be an exercise in futility; it is the condition of the people that we must address. And here we have come full circle to return again to the question of cultural impact. Abbott elaborated upon the difference between disorders that are individual, and therefore amenable to treatment at the individual level, and those that are social, and therefore unamenable to individual treatment:

In the same way that psychiatry throughout the world differs in its approach [in] different cultures, psychiatry in the North must also take into account the cultural and social conditions of the people. The vast majority of the problems that I have seen as a clinical psychiatrist cannot, in all honesty, be classified as psychiatric problems. Some problems such as the major psychoses occur in all people, and the treatment is largely medical in the sense of medication. So at least in its initial stages, southern psychiatry is appropriate. However, many of the problems seen are so closely interwoven with the life-style of the native people in the North, which in turn is closely bound to such problems as economics, housing,

self-esteem and cultural identity, that to label them as psychiatric disorders is frankly fraudulent and of no value whatsoever, as the treatment
must eventually be the treatment of the whole community rather than [of]
the individual. [F28437]

SOCIAL IMPACT AND THE PIPELINE

The process of rebuilding a strong, self-confident society in the Mackenzie Valley has begun. Major industrial development now may well have a
disastrous effect on that process. With the pipeline, I should expect the
high rate of alcohol consumption to persist and worsen. I should expect
further erosion of native culture, further demoralization of the native
people, and degradation and violence beyond anything previously seen
in the Mackenzie Valley and the Western Arctic.

The presence of a huge migrant labour force and the impact of construction over the years will mean that alcohol and drugs will become
more serious problems. It is fanciful to think that greater opportunities
for wage employment on a pipeline will stop or reverse the effects of past
economic development.

Let me cite what Dr. Wheeler said of the Dene, because this statement
applies to all the native peoples of the Mackenzie Valley and the Western
Arctic. His views exemplify those of every doctor and nurse who spoke
to the Inquiry.

> The Dene have great strength as a people. Part of this strength lies in their
> extended family ties which they have been able to maintain in close-knit
> communities. We white people know the value of these kinds of ties, as we
> are now feeling the loss of them in terms of the depersonalization and
> dehumanization of southern urban living. How long will the Dene family
> survive the loss of its young men and the degradation of its women?
>
> We want to hear what plans the territorial and federal governments
> have or are developing for these kinds of social problems. But perhaps the
> answer lies not with increasing government bureaucracy, with all its con-
> trols. The solution to these problems, and with it the survival of the Dene,
> lies within the Dene. They must be allowed to develop these solutions
> within a time frame of their own choosing before we get stampeded into a
> social disaster from which the North may never recover. The people need
> time and freedom in order to survive. [C3402]

THE LIMITS TO PLANNING

I have been asked to predict the impact of the pipeline and energy corridor and to recommend terms and conditions that might mitigate their

impact. Some impacts are easier to predict than others: there is a vast difference between the effects that are likely to occur in the first year and those that will be important in ten years. And there are difficulties in prediction that involve more than time or scale, for even short-term causal chains can be intricately connected. Moreover, some consequences of the pipeline will be controllable, but others will not. Just as there are limits to predicting, so also are there limits to planning.

I can recommend terms and conditions that will to some extent mitigate the social impact of the pipeline and energy corridor, but some of the consequences I have predicted will occur no matter what controls we impose. Other consequences can be predicted only in a vague and general way: we can anticipate their scale, but cannot adequately plan for them. There is a gulf, therefore, between the nature of the predictions and the nature of the terms and conditions I am asked to propose. The one is imprecise and often speculative; the other, if the terms and conditions are to be effective, must be very precise. We must never forget their limitations; it is all too easy to be overconfident of our ability to act as social engineers and to suppose—quite wrongly—that all problems can be foreseen and resolved. The nature of human affairs often defies the planners. In the case of a vast undertaking like the Mackenzie Valley pipeline, overconfidence in our ability to anticipate and to manage social problems would be foolish and dangerous.

I am prepared to accept that the oil and gas industry, the pipeline company, and the contractors will be able to exercise a measure of control over the movement and behaviour of their personnel. I am prepared to accept that government will expand its services and infrastructure in major communities to serve the requirements of pipeline construction in the Mackenzie Valley and of gas plant development in the Delta. Where actual numbers of people can be predicted, planning is possible and orderly procedures and cost-sharing arrangements can be worked out. However, there are obvious limitations to planning of this sort. The cost of the project or the number of workers required may be so far in excess of the figures we have now that it will seem as though we had planned one project but had built another. There is the question of how many people will be involved in secondary employment: their number will be large, no matter what measures are taken to discourage them, and the costs associated with their presence in the North will be very high.

There are also political limits to planning. The impacts that lead to social costs vary in the degree to which they can be treated. There are matters over which government and industry can exercise some control; there are other matters over which control would not be in keeping with the principles of a democratic society. And there are social impacts over which no control could be exercised even under the most authoritarian regime.

211

Finally, I am not prepared to accept that, in the case of an enormous project like the pipeline, there can be any real control over how much people will drink and over what the abuse of alcohol will do to their lives. There can be no control over how many families will break up, how many children will become delinquent and have criminal records, how many communities will see their young people drifting towards the larger urban centres, and how many people may be driven from a way of life they know to one they do not understand and in which they have no real place. Such problems are beyond anyone's power to control, but they will generate enormous social costs. Because these costs are, by and large, neither measurable nor assignable, we tend to forget them or to pretend they do not exist. But with construction of a pipeline, they would occur, and the native people of the North would then have to pay the price.

X

NATIVE CLAIMS

THE PARAMOUNT CRY OF THE NATIVE PEOPLE OF THE NORTH IS that their claims must be settled before a pipeline is built across their land. In this chapter, I shall outline the history of native claims in Canada. This history is important because the concept of native claims has evolved greatly in recent years: they have their origin in native use and occupancy of the land, but today they involve much more than land.

When treaties were signed during the 19th century, the settlement of the native people's claims was regarded primarily as surrender of their land so that settlement could proceed. The payment of money, the provision of goods and services, and the establishment of reserves—all of which accompanied such a surrender—were conceived in part as compensation and in part as the means of change. The government's expectation was that a backward people would, in the fullness of time, abandon their semi-nomadic ways and, with the benefit of the white man's religion, education and agriculture, take their place in the mainstream of the economic and political life of Canada.

The governments of the day did not regard the treaties as anything like a social contract in which different ways of life were accommodated within mutually acceptable limits; they gave little consideration to anything beyond the extinguishment of native claims to the land, once and for all. The native people, by and large, understood the spirit of the treaties differently; they regarded the treaties as the means by which they would be able to retain their own customs and to govern themselves in the future. But they lacked the power to enforce their view.

The native peoples of the North now insist that the settlement of native claims must be seen as a fundamental re-ordering of their relationship with the rest of us. Their claims must be seen as the means to the establishment of a social contract based on a clear understanding that they are distinct peoples in history. They insist upon the right to determine their own future, to ensure their place, but not assimilation, in Canadian life. And the Government of Canada has now accepted the principle of comprehensive claims; it recognizes that any settlement of claims today must embrace the whole range of questions that is outstanding between the Government of Canada and the native peoples.

The settlement of native claims is not a mere transaction. It would be wrong, therefore, to think that signing a piece of paper would put the whole question behind us. One of the mistakes of the past has been to see such settlements as final solutions. The definition and redefinition of the relationship with the native people and their place in Confederation will go on for a generation or more. This is because the relationship has never been properly worked out. Now, for the first time, the federal government is prepared to negotiate with the native people on a comprehensive basis, and the native people of the North are prepared to articulate their interests over a broad range of concerns. Their concerns begin with the land, but are not limited to it: they extend to renewable and non-renewable resources, education, health and social services, public order and, overarching all of these considerations, the future shape and composition of political institutions in the North.

Perhaps a redefinition of the relationship between the Government of Canada and the native people can be worked out in the North better than elsewhere: the native people are a larger proportion of the population there than anywhere else in Canada, and no provincial authority stands in the way of the Government of Canada's fulfilment of its constitutional obligations.

In considering the claims of the native people, I am guided primarily by the testimony that the Inquiry heard at the community hearings in the North. No doubt the native organizations will, in due course, elaborate these claims in their negotiations with the government but, for my own purposes, I have, in assessing these claims, relied upon the evidence of almost a thousand native persons who gave evidence in the Mackenzie Valley and the Western Arctic. Finally, I shall indicate what impact construction of the pipeline would have on the settlement of native claims and the goals that the native people seek through the settlement of these claims.

HISTORY OF NATIVE CLAIMS

THE ISSUE: NO PIPELINE
BEFORE NATIVE CLAIMS ARE SETTLED

All the native organizations that appeared at the hearings insisted that this Inquiry should recommend to the Minister of Indian Affairs and

Northern Development that no right-of-way be granted to build a pipeline until native claims along the route, both in the Yukon and the Northwest Territories, have been settled. The spokesmen for the native organizations and the people themselves insisted upon this point with virtual unanimity.

The claims of the Dene and the Inuit of the North derive from their rights as aboriginal peoples and from their use and occupation of northern lands since time immemorial. They want to live on their land, govern themselves on their land and determine for themselves what use is to be made of it. They are asking us to settle their land claims in quite a different way from the way that government settled native land claims in the past; government's past practice, they say, is inconsistent with its newly declared intention to achieve a comprehensive settlement of native claims.

Arctic Gas suggested that the native people should not be permitted to advance such an argument before the Inquiry because it did not fall within my terms of reference. The Order-in-Council stated that I am "to inquire into and report upon the terms and conditions that should be imposed in respect of any right-of-way that might be granted across Crown lands for the purposes of the proposed Mackenzie Valley pipeline." Those words, they argued, limit the Inquiry to the consideration of only the terms and conditions that must be performed or carried out by whichever pipeline company is granted a right-of-way.

It is true that, according to the Pipeline Guidelines, any terms and conditions that the Minister decides to impose upon any right-of-way must be included in a signed agreement to be made between the Crown and the pipeline company. But the Order-in-Council does not confine this Inquiry to a review of the Pipeline Guidelines nor to the measures that the pipeline companies may be prepared to take to meet them. The Order-in-Council calls upon the Inquiry to consider the social, economic and environmental impact of the construction of a pipeline in the North. The effect of these impacts cannot be disentangled from the whole question of native claims. Indeed, the native organizations argue that no effective terms and conditions could be imposed on a pipeline right-of-way, with a view to ameliorating its social and economic impact, before native claims have been settled. It was essential, therefore, if the Inquiry was to fulfil its mandate, to hear evidence on the native organizations' principal contention: that the settlement of native claims ought to precede any grant of a right-of-way.

Only the Government of Canada and the native people can negotiate a settlement of native claims in the North: only they can be parties to such negotiation, and nothing said in this report can bind either side. Evidence of native claims was heard at the Inquiry to permit me to consider fairly the native organizations' principal contention regarding the pipeline, and to consider the answer of the pipeline companies to that contention.

NATIVE LANDS AND TREATIES
IN NORTH AMERICA

When the first European settlers arrived in North America, independent native societies, diverse in culture and language, already occupied the continent. The European nations asserted dominion over the New World by right of their "discovery." But what of the native peoples who inhabited North America? By what right did Europeans claim jurisdiction over them? Chief Justice John Marshall of the Supreme Court of the United States, in a series of judgments in the 1820s and 1830s, described the Europeans' claim in these words:

> America, separated from Europe by a wide ocean, was inhabited by a distinct people, divided into separate nations, independent of each other and of the rest of the world, having institutions of their own, and governing themselves by their own laws.
>
> It is difficult to comprehend the proposition that the inhabitants of either quarter of the globe could have rightful original claims of dominion over the inhabitants of the other, or over the lands they occupied; or that the discovery of either by the other should give the discoverer rights in the country discovered which annulled the existing rights of its ancient possessors.
>
> Did these adventurers, by sailing along the coast and occasionally landing on it, acquire for the several governments to whom they belonged, or by whom they were commissioned, a rightful property in the soil from the Atlantic to the Pacific; or rightful dominion over the numerous people who occupied it? Or has nature, or the great Creator of all things, conferred these rights over hunters and fishermen, on agriculturists and manufacturers?
>
> To avoid bloody conflicts, which might terminate disastrously to all, it was necessary for the nations of Europe to establish some principle which all would acknowledge and which should decide their respective rights as between themselves. This principle, suggested by the actual state of things, was "that discovery gave title to the government by whose subjects or by whose authority it was made, against all other European governments, which title might be consummated by possession."
>
> This principle, acknowledged by all Europeans, because it was the interest of all to acknowledge it, gave to the nation making the discovery, as its inevitable consequence, the sole right of acquiring the soil and of making settlements upon it. [*Worcester v. Georgia* (1832) 31 U.S. 350 at 369]

The Europeans' assumption of power over the Indians was founded on a supposed moral and economic superiority of European culture and civilization over that of the native people. But it was, nevertheless, acknowledged that the native people retained certain rights. Chief Justice Marshall said:

> [the native people] were admitted to be the rightful occupants of the soil, with a legal as well as just claim to retain possession of it, and to use it according to their own discretion; but their rights to complete sovereignty, as independent nations, were necessarily diminished and their power to dispose of the soil at their own will, to whomsoever they pleased, was denied by the original fundamental principle that discovery gave exclusive title to those who made it. [*Johnson v. McIntosh* (1823) 21 U.S. 543]

The concept of aboriginal rights has a firm basis in international law, and we subscribe to it in Canada. During the last century, the Supreme Court of Canada in the St. Catherines Milling case and this century in the Nishga case affirmed the proposition that the original peoples of our country had a legal right to the use and occupation of their ancestral lands. The courts have had to consider whether, in given cases, the native right has been taken away by competent authority, and sometimes the courts have decided it has been. But original use and occupation of the land is the legal foundation for the assertion of native claims in Northern Canada today.

From the beginning, Great Britain recognized the rights of native people to their traditional lands, and acquired by negotiation and purchase the lands the colonists required for settlement and cultivation. That recognition was based not only on international law, but also upon the realities of the times, for in those early days the native people greatly outnumbered the settlers.

The necessity to maintain good relations with the native people led the British to formulate a more clearly defined colonial policy towards Indian land rights in the mid-18th century. The westward expansion of settlers from New England during this period had given rise to discontent among the Indian tribes and during the Seven Years War (1756–1763), the British were at pains to ensure the continued friendship of the Iroquois Confederacy lest they defect to the French. When the war ended, the British controlled the whole of the Atlantic seaboard, from Newfoundland to Florida, and the government promulgated the Royal Proclamation of 1763. This document reserved to the Indians, as their hunting grounds, all the land west of the Allegheny Mountains, excluding Rupert's Land, the territory granted in 1670 to the Hudson's Bay

Company. The Proclamation stated that, when land was required for further settlement, it should be purchased for the Crown in a public meeting held for that purpose by the governor or commander-in-chief of the several colonies. This procedure for the purchase of Indian land was the basis for the treaties of the 19th and 20th centuries.

THE TREATIES

Following the Proclamation of 1763, the British made a series of treaties with the Indians living in what is now Southern Ontario. Many of these treaties were with small groups of Indians for limited areas of land, but, as settlement moved westward in the mid-19th century, there was a dramatic increase in geographical scale. The Robinson treaties, made in Ontario in 1850, and the "numbered treaties," made following Canada's acquisition from Great Britain in 1870 of Rupert's Land and the North-western Territory, covered much larger tracts of land.

The treaties concluded after 1870 on the prairies cleared the way for the settlement of Western Canada and the construction of the Canadian Pacific Railway. The government's instructions to the Lieutenant-Governor of the Northwest Territories in 1870, after the cession of Rupert's Land, were explicit:

> You will also turn your attention promptly to the condition of the country outside the Province of Manitoba, on the North and West; and while as-suring the Indians of your desire to establish friendly relations with them, you will ascertain and report to His Excellency the course you may think the most advisable to pursue, whether by Treaty or otherwise, for the re-moval of any obstructions that might be presented to the flow of popula-tion into the fertile lands that lie between Manitoba and the Rocky Moun-tains. [Canada, Sessional Papers, 1871, No. 20 p. 8]

Treaties 1 to 7, made between 1870 and 1877, covered the territory between the watershed west of Lake Superior and the Rocky Mountains. In 1899, Treaty 8 covered territory northward to Great Slave Lake. Then, in 1921, Treaty 11 dealt with the land from Great Slave Lake down the Mackenzie River to the Mackenzie Delta. Treaties 8 and 11 to-gether cover the whole of Northern Alberta and the western part of the Northwest Territories, including the Mackenzie Valley.

The treaties conform to a distinct pattern: in exchange for the sur-render of their aboriginal rights, the Indians received annual cash pay-ments. The amount varied with the treaty: under Treaties 1 and 2, each man, woman and child received $3 a year; under Treaty 4, the chiefs re-ceived $25, headmen $15, and other members of the tribe $12. In addi-tion, the government established reserves for the use of the Indian bands: the area in some cases was apportioned on the basis of 160 acres of land for a family of five; in other cases, it was one square mile of land for each family. The treaties also recognized the continued right of the native people to hunt and fish over all the unsettled parts of the territories they had surrendered. Beginning with Treaty 3, the government agreed to supply the Indian bands with farm and agricultural implements, as well as with ammunition and twine for use in hunting and fishing.

The spirit of these clauses, together with the guarantee of hunting and fishing rights and the establishment of reserves was, according to the understanding of the Indians, to support their traditional hunting and fishing economy and to help them to develop a new agricultural economy to supplement the traditional one when it was no longer viable.

White settlers soon occupied the non-reserve land that the Indians had surrendered, and their traditional hunting and fishing economy was undermined. Legislation and game regulations limited traditional activities yet further. The land allocated for reserves was often quite unsuitable for agriculture, and the reserves were often whittled away to provide additional land for white settlement. The government never advanced the capital necessary to develop an agricultural base for the Indians, and when the native population began to expand, the whole concept of developing agriculture on reserve lands became impractical.

These prairie treaties were negotiated in periods of near desperation for the Indian tribes. The decimation of the buffalo herds had ruined their economy, and they suffered from epidemic diseases and periodic starvation. Often they had no alternative to accepting the treaty commissioner's offers.

The recent settlement of native claims in Alaska and the James Bay Agreement follow the tradition of the treaties. The object of the earlier surrenders was to permit agricultural settlement by another race. The objects of the Alaska Native Claims Settlement Act and of the James Bay Agreement are to facilitate resource development by another race. The negotiators for the Province of Quebec stated that, if the native people refused to approve the James Bay Agreement, the project would go ahead anyway, and they would simply lose the benefits offered by the Province. This attitude parallels the position of the treaty commissioners a century ago: they said that if the Indians did not sign the treaties offered them, their lands would be colonized anyway.

TREATIES IN THE NORTHWEST TERRITORIES

Throughout the British Empire, the Crown, not the local legislature, was always responsible for the welfare of the aboriginal people. In 1867, therefore, the British North America Act gave the Parliament of Canada jurisdiction over Indian affairs and Indian lands throughout the new country. This jurisdiction encompasses the Inuit, and the Metis as well, at least to the extent that they are pressing claims based on their Indian ancestry. With Canada's acquisition of Rupert's Land and the North-western Territory, and the entry of British Columbia into Confederation, that jurisdiction extended from the Atlantic to the Pacific, from the 49th Parallel to the Arctic Ocean.

The constitutional documents that effected the transfer to Canada of Rupert's Land and the Northwestern Territory all refer to "aboriginal rights." The Imperial Order-in-Council, signed by Queen Victoria, that assigned Rupert's Land to Canada provided that:

> Any claims of Indians to compensation for lands required for purposes of settlement shall be disposed of by the Canadian Government in com-munication with the Imperial Government; and the [Hudson's Bay] Com-pany shall be relieved of all responsibility in respect of them. [Exhibit F569, p. 42]

It was upon these conditions that Canada achieved sovereignty over the lands that comprise the Northwest Territories and Yukon Territory, in-cluding the lands claimed today by the Dene, Inuit and Metis. After the transfer of these territories, the federal government enacted the Domin-ion Lands Act of 1872, the first statute to deal with the sale and disposi-tion of federal crown lands. It stated:

> 42. None of the provisions of this Act respecting the settlement of agricul-tural lands, or the lease of timber lands, or the purchase and sale of min-eral lands, shall be held to apply to territory the Indian title to which shall not at the time have been extinguished. [Exhibit F569, p. 43]

All of these instruments acknowledge the rights of the native people. They illustrate that the recognition of aboriginal title was deeply em-bedded in both the policy and the law of the new nation.

Treaties 8 and 11, made with the Indians of Northern Alberta and the Northwest Territories, continue both the philosophy and the form of earlier treaties. These two treaties are the subject of a recent book by Father René Fumoleau, *As Long as this Land Shall Last.* I cite his text for many official and historical documents related to these treaties.

In 1888, government surveyors reported that there was oil in the Mackenzie Valley, and that the oil-bearing formations were "almost co-extensive with the [Mackenzie] valley itself." The report of a Select Committee of the Senate on the resources of the Mackenzie Basin, in March 1888, has a familiar ring today:

> . . . the petroleum area is so extensive as to justify the belief that eventu-ally it will supply the larger part of this continent and be shipped from

Churchill or some more northern Hudson's Bay port to England. . . . The evidence . . . points to the existence . . . of the most extensive petroleum field in America, if not in the World. The uses of petroleum and consequently the demand for it by all Nations are increasing at such a rapid ratio, that it is probable this great petroleum field will assume an enormous value in the near future and will rank among the chief assets comprised in the Crown Domain of the Dominion. [cited in Fumoleau, op. cit., p. 40]

A Privy Council Report of 1891 set forth the government's intentions:

. . . the discovery [of] immense quantities of petroleum . . . renders it advisable that a treaty or treaties should be made with the Indians who claim those regions as their hunting grounds, with a view to the extinguishment of the Indian title in such portions of the same, as it may be considered in the interest of the public to open up for settlement. [cited in Fumoleau, op. cit., p. 41]

No treaty was made, however, until the Klondike gold rush of 1898. It was the entry of large numbers of white prospectors into the Mackenzie Valley on their way to the Yukon gold fields and the desire of the government to ensure peaceful occupation of the land that led to the making of Treaty 8. The boundaries of Treaty 8 were drawn to include the area in which geologists thought oil or gold might be found; they did not include the area inhabited by the Indians north of Great Slave Lake because, in the words of the Indian Commissioner, Amédée Forget:

. . . their territory so far as it is at present known is of no particular value and they very rarely come into contact with Whites. [cited in Fumoleau, op. cit., p. 59]

Treaty 8 was signed at various points including Fort Smith in 1899 and Fort Resolution in 1900. While the treaty commissioners negotiated with the Indians, a Halfbreed Commission negotiated with the Metis. Following the procedure established on the prairies, the government gave the Metis the option of coming under the treaty with the Indians or of accepting scrip, which entitled the bearer either to $240 or to 240 acres of land. Many Metis chose to come under the treaty.

Treaty 8, like the prairie treaties, provided for an annual payment of $5 per head, the recognition of hunting and fishing rights, and the allocation of reserve lands. But these lands were not allocated then, and, with the sole exception of a small reserve at Hay River in 1974, none have been allocated to this day.

The Indian people did not see Treaty 8 as a surrender of their aboriginal rights: they considered it to be a treaty of peace and friendship. Native witnesses at the Inquiry recalled the prophetic words that Chief Drygeese spoke when Treaty 8 was signed at Fort Resolution:

> If it is going to change, if you want to change our lives, then it is no use taking treaty, because without treaty we are making a living for ourselves and our families . . . I would like a written promise from you to prove you are not taking our land away from us. . . . There will be no closed season on our land. There will be nothing said about the land. . . . My people will continue to live as they were before and no White man will change that. . . . You will in the future want us to live like White man does and we do not want that. . . . The people are happy as they are. If you try to change their ways of life by treaty, you will destroy their happiness. There will be bitter struggle between your people and my people. [cited in Fumoleau, op. cit., p. 91ff.]

In the years that followed, legislation was enacted restricting native hunting and trapping. In 1917, closed seasons were established on moose, caribou and certain other animals essential to the economy of the native people, and in 1918 the Migratory Birds Convention Act further restricted their hunting. The Indians regarded these regulations as breaches of the promise that they would be free to hunt, fish and trap, and because of them they boycotted the payment of treaty money in 1920 at Fort Resolution.

In 1907, and repeatedly thereafter, Henry Conroy, who accompanied the original treaty party in 1899 and who had charge of the annual payment of treaty money, recommended that Treaty 8 should be extended farther north. But, in 1910, the official position was still that:

> . . . at present there is no necessity for taking that action. The influx of miners and prospectors into that country is very small, and at present there [are] no settlers. [cited in Fumoleau, op. cit., p. 136]

The official position remained unchanged until 1920, when the Imperial Oil Company struck oil on the Mackenzie River below Fort Norman. The government quickly moved to ensure that these oil-rich lands should be legally open for industrial development and free of any Indian interest. F. H. Kitto, Dominion Land Surveyor, wrote:

> The recent discoveries of oil at Norman [Wells] have been made on lands virtually belonging to those tribes [of non-treaty Indians]. Until treaty has been made with them, the right of the Mining Lands and Yukon Branch [of the federal government] to dispose of these oil resources is open to debate. [cited in Fumoleau, op. cit., p. 159]

Treaty 11 was soon signed. During the summer of 1921, the Treaty Commission travelled down the Mackenzie River from Fort Providence to Fort McPherson, then returned to visit Fort Rae. In 1922, the treaty was made with the Dene at Fort Liard. As with Treaty 8, the Metis were given the option of taking treaty or accepting scrip. However, the parliamentary approval necessary to pay the scrip was delayed, and the Metis were not paid until 1924, when 172 Metis took scrip. The payments of $240 to each Metis represent the only settlement made with the Metis of the Northwest Territories who did not take treaty. Rick Hardy, President of the Metis Association, told the Inquiry that the Metis do not consider that these payments extinguished their aboriginal rights.

The Dene do not regard Treaty 11, which followed the pattern of Treaty 8, as a surrender of their land, but consider it to be a treaty of peace and friendship. Father Fumoleau writes of Treaty 11:

> A few basic facts emerge from the evidence of documents and testimonies. These are: treaty negotiations were brief, initial opposition was overcome, specific demands were made by the Indians, promises were given, and agreement was reached. . . .
>
> They saw the white man's treaty as his way of offering them his help and friendship. They were willing to share their land with him in the manner prescribed by their tradition and culture. The two races would live side by side in the North, embarking on a common future. [cited in Fumoleau, op. cit., p. 210ff.]

In 1921, as in 1899, the Dene wanted to retain their traditional way of life and to obtain guarantees against the encroachment of white settlers on their land. In fact Commissioner Conroy did guarantee the Dene full freedom to hunt, trap and fish, because many Dene negotiators were adamant that, unless the guarantee was given, they would not sign the treaty. To the Dene, this guarantee that the government would not interfere with their traditional life on the land was an affirmation, not an extinguishment, of their rights to their homeland.

It is important to understand the Dene's view of the treaty, because it explains the vehemence with which native witnesses told the Inquiry that the land is still theirs, that they have never sold it, and that it is not for sale.

Father Fumoleau has written an account of the Treaty negotiations at Fort Norman, based on the evidence of witnesses to the event:

> Commissioner Conroy promised the people that this was their land. "You can do whatever you want," he said. "We are not going to stop you. . . ." This was the promise he made to the people . . . that we could go hunting and fishing. . . .

Then the Treaty party, Commissioner Conroy . . . said, "As long as the Mackenzie River flows, and as long as the sun always comes around the same direction every day, we will never break our promise." The people and the Bishop said the same thing, so the people thought that it was impossible that this would happen—the river would never reverse and go back up-river, and the sun would never go reverse. This was impossible, so they must be true. That is why we took the Treaty. [cited in Fumoleau, op. cit., p. 180ff.]

Joe Naedzo told the Inquiry at Fort Franklin that, according to the native people's interpretation of the treaty, the government made "a law for themselves that as long as the Mackenzie River flows in one direction, the sun rises and sets, we will not bother you about your land or the animals."(C606)

When the treaty commissioners reached Fort Rae in 1921, the Dogrib people there were well aware that the promises the government had made to the Dogribs and Chipewyans, who had signed the treaty at Fort Resolution in 1900, had not been kept. The native people would not sign Treaty 11 unless the government guaranteed hunting and trapping rights over the whole of their traditional territory. This is Harry Black's account of the negotiations with the Dogribs:

Chief Monfwi stated that if his terms were met and agreed upon, then there will be a treaty, but if his terms were not met, then "there will be no treaty since you [Treaty Officials] are on my land." . . . The Indian agent asked Chief Monfwi . . . what size of land he wanted for the band. Monfwi stated . . . "The size of land has to be large enough for all of my people." . . . Chief Monfwi asked for a land boundary starting from Fort Providence, all along the Mackenzie River, right up to Great Bear Lake, then across to Contwoyto Lake . . . Snowdrift, along the Great Slave Lake, back to Fort Providence.

The next day we crowded into the meeting tent again and began the big discussion about the land boundary again. Finally they came to an agreement and a land boundary was drawn up. Chief Monfwi said that within this land boundary there will be no closed season on game so long as the sun rises and the great river flows and only upon these terms I will accept the treaty money. [cited in Fumoleau, op. cit., p. 192ff.]

The Government of the Northwest Territories had, by this time, begun to take shape. The first territorial government headquarters opened in Fort Smith in 1921, and its first session was the same year, with oil the main item on the agenda. The duties of the new administration included inspection of the oil well and of the country to see if it was suitable for a pipeline.

The Dene had signed Treaties 8 and 11 on the understanding that they would be free to hunt and fish over their traditional territory, and that the government would protect them from the competition and intrusion of white trappers. Yet, contrary to treaty promises, an influx of white trappers and traders into the country was permitted to exploit the game resources almost at will, and soon strict game laws were necessary to save certain animal populations from extinction. The enforcement of these game laws caused hardship to the native people who depended on the animals for survival.

The encroachment of white trappers on lands that the native people regarded as their own led them to demand the establishment of game preserves in which only they would be permitted to hunt and trap. Frank T'Seleie told of such a request made by Father Antoine Binamé on behalf of the people of Fort Good Hope in 1928:

> At the present time the Indians are in fear of too many outside trappers getting into the districts outlined ... and should these preserves be granted ... the Indians would be more likely to endeavour to preserve the game in their own way. They at present are afraid of leaving the beaver colonies to breed up as the white man would in all likelihood come in and hunt them. [C1773]

The request was never granted, although some game preserves were established in other areas.

Wood Buffalo National Park was established in 1922 and enlarged in 1926. Shooting buffalo was strictly forbidden, although Treaty Indians were allowed to hunt other game and to trap furbearing animals in the park. These regulations were strictly enforced, and the protection of buffalo took precedence over the protection of Indian hunting rights.

In 1928, the government imposed a three-year closed season on beaver in the Mackenzie District. This regulation came at the worst possible time for the Dene, for that year they were decimated by an influenza epidemic. Other furbearing animals were scarce, and without beaver they were short of meat. The Dene at Fort Rae protested and refused to accept treaty payment until they had been assured that they could kill beaver. Bishop Breynat had appealed to the government on their behalf, and some modifications to the closed season were made. Despite continuing protests about the activities of white trappers, they received no protection from this threat. In 1937, the Indians of Fort Resolution again refused, as they had in 1920, to accept treaty payment in protest against their treatment by the government.

Finally, in 1938, legislation was passed to regulate the activity of white trappers and to restrict hunting and trapping licences only to those white persons who already held them. But, as Father Fumoleau told us, by this time most of the white trappers had turned from trapping to mining. At the same time that the native people had been restricted in their traditional activities, oil and mineral exploration and development had proceeded apace. In 1932, the richest uranium mine in the world began operation at Port Radium on Great Bear Lake. Gold was discovered in Yellowknife in 1933. In 1938, Norman Wells produced 22,000 barrels of oil, and in 1938–1939 the value of gold mined in the Northwest Territories exceeded for the first time the total value of raw furs produced.

The Dene insist the history of broken promises continues today. Jim Sittichinli, at the very first community hearing, held in Aklavik, related the recent experience of the native people:

> Now, at the time of the treaty . . . 55 years ago . . . they said, "As long as the river runs, as long as the sun goes up and down, and as long as you see that black mountain up there, well, you are entitled to your land."
>
> The river is still running. The sun still goes up and down and the black mountain is still up there, but today it seems that, the way our people understand, the government is giving up our land. It is giving [it up] to the seismic people and the other people coming up here, selling . . . our land. The government is not keeping its word, at least as some of us see it.
>
> Now, there has been lots of damage done already to this part of the northland, and if we don't say anything, it will get worse. . . .
>
> The other day I was taking a walk in Yellowknife . . . and I passed a house there with a dog tied outside. I didn't notice it and all of a sudden this dog jumped up and gave me a big bark, and then, after I passed through there, I was saying to myself, "Well, that dog taught me a lesson." You know, so often you [don't] see the native people, they are tied down too much, I think, by the government. We never go and bark, therefore nobody takes notice of us, and it is about time that we the people of this northland should get up sometime and bark and then we would be noticed. [C87ff.]

So far I have been describing treaties made with the Indians and Metis. No treaties were ever made with the Inuit, although the boundaries of Treaty 11 include part of the Mackenzie Delta that was occupied and used by the Inuit. They were not asked to sign the treaty in 1921 and, when they were invited to do so in 1929, they refused.

The absence of a treaty has made little difference to the Inuit, although they have been spared the invidious legal distinctions introduced among the Dene by treaty and non-treaty status. The Inuit witnesses who spoke to the Inquiry made clear that they, no less than the Dene, regard their traditional lands as their homeland. They also demand recognition of their rights to the land and their right to self-determination as a people. At Tuktoyaktuk, Vince Steen summarized the historical experience of the Inuit:

A lot of people seem to wonder why the Eskimos don't take the white man's word at face value any more. . . . Well, from my point of view, it goes way back, right back to when the Eskimos first saw the white man.

Most of them were whalers, and the whaler wasn't very nice to the Eskimo. He just took all the whales he could get and never mind the results. Who is paying for it now? The Eskimo. There is a quota on how many whales he can kill now.

Then next, following the whales, the white traders and the white trappers. The white traders took them for every cent they could get. You know the stories in every history book where they had a pile of fur as high as your gun. Those things were not fair. The natives lived with it—damn well had to—to get that gun, to make life easier for himself.

Then there was the white trapper. He came along and he showed the Eskimo how to use the traps, steel-jawed traps, leg-hold traps. They used them, well they're still using them today, but for the first 70 years when they were being used, there were no complaints down south about how cruel those traps are—as long as there was white trappers using them. Now for the last five years they are even thinking of cutting us off, but they haven't showed us a new way of how to catch those foxes for their wives though.

After them, after the white trappers and the fur traders, we have all the settlements, all the government people coming in and making settlements all over, and telling the people what to do, what is best for them. Live here. Live there. That place is no good for you. Right here is your school. So they did—they all moved into settlements, and for the 1950s and 1960s they damn near starved. Most of them were on rations because they were not going out into the country any more. Their kids had to go to school.

Then came the oil companies. First the seismographic outfits, and like the Eskimo did for the last 50 or 60 years, he sat back and watched them. Couldn't do anything about it anyway, and he watched them plough up their land in the summertime, plough up their traps in the wintertime. What are you going to do about it? A cat [caterpillar tractor] is bigger than your skidoo or your dog team.

Then the oil companies. Well, the oil companies, I must say, of all of them so far that I have mentioned, seem to . . . have the most respect for the people and their ways; but it is too late. The people won't take a white man's word at face value any more because you fooled them too many times. You took everything they had and you gave them nothing. You took all the fur, took all the whales, killed all the polar bear with aircraft and everything, and put a quota on top of that, so we can't have polar bear when we feel like it any more. All that we pay for. Same thing with the seismic outfits. . . .

Now they want to drill out there. Now they want to build a pipeline and they say they're not going to hurt the country while they do it. They're going to let the Eskimo live his way, but he can't because . . . the white man has not only gotten so that he's taken over, taken everything out of the country . . . but he's also taken the culture, half of it anyway. . . .

For the Eskimo to believe now that the white man is not going to do any damage out there . . . is just about impossible, because he hasn't proven himself. As far as I'm concerned he hasn't proven himself worthy of being believed any more. . . .

The Eskimo is asking for a land settlement because he doesn't trust the white man any more to handle the land that he owns, and he figures he's owned for years and years. [C4199ff.]

Because the native people of the North believe the pipeline and the developments that will follow it will undermine their use of the land and indelibly shape the future of their lives in a way that is not of their choosing, they insist that, before any such development takes place, their right to their land and their right to self-determination as a people must be recognized. They have always held these beliefs, but their articulation of them has seldom been heard or understood.

ENTRENCHMENT, NOT EXTINGUISHMENT

Canadian policy has always contemplated the eventual extinguishment of native title to the land. The native people had to make way for the settlement of agricultural lands in the West, and now they are told they must make way for the industrial development of the North. But the native people of the North do not want to repeat the history of the native peoples of the West. They say that, in the North, Canadian policy should take a new direction.

Throughout Canada, we have assumed that the advance of western civilization would lead the native people to join the mainstream of Canadian life. On this assumption, the treaties promised the Indians education and agricultural training. On this assumption, the federal government has introduced programs for education, housing, job training and welfare to both treaty and non-treaty Indians. Historical experience has clearly shown that this assumption is ill-founded, and that such programs do not work. The statistics for unemployment, school drop-outs, inadequate housing, prison inmates, infant mortality and violent death bespeak the failure of these programs. George Manuel, President of the National Indian Brotherhood, told the Inquiry that the programs failed because the native people were never given the political and constitutional authority to enforce the treaty commitments or to implement the programs. Every program has assumed, and eventually has produced, greater dependency on the government. Manuel told the Inquiry:

> We, the aboriginal peoples of Southern Canada, have already experienced our Mackenzie Valley pipeline. Such projects have occurred time and time again in our history. They were, and are, the beginnings of the type of developments which destroy the way of life of aboriginal peoples and rob us of our economic, cultural and political independence. . . .
>
> Developments of this kind can only be supported on the condition that the [native] people must first be assured economic, political and cultural self-reliance. [F21761]

Manuel argued that the settlement of native claims in the North must recognize the native people's rights to land and to political authority over the land, as opposed to cash compensation for the purchase of their land. The object of negotiations, he said, should be the enhancement of aboriginal rights, not their extinguishment. Only through transfer to them of real economic and political power can the native people of the North play a major role in determining the course of events in their homeland and avoid the demoralization that has overtaken so many Indian communities in the South. The determination to arrest this historical process, which is already underway in some northern communities, explains the native people's insistence on a settlement that entrenches their right to the land and offers them self-determination.

The demand for entrenchment of native rights is not unique to the native people of the North. Indians in Southern Canada, and aboriginal peoples in many other parts of the world, are urging upon the dominant society their own right to self-determination. As Manuel said:

> Aboriginal people everywhere share a common attachment to the land, a common experience and a common struggle. [F21760]

James Wah-Shee, voicing a sentiment shared by virtually all of the native people in the North, said:

> The general public has been misinformed on the question of land settlement in the North. What is at issue is land not money.
>
> A land settlement in the Northwest Territories requires a new approach, a break in a historical pattern. A "once-and-for-all" settlement in the tradition of the treaties and Alaska will not work in the Northwest Territories. What we are seriously considering is not the surrender of our rights "once and for all" but the formalization of our rights and ongoing negotiation and dialogue. We are investigating a solution which could be a source of pride to all Canadians and not an expensive tax bur-

den, for ours is a truly "developmental" model in the widest and most human sense of the word. It allows for the preservation of our people and our culture and secures our participation as equals in the economy and society of Canada. [*Delta Gas: Now or Later,* speech presented in Ottawa, May 24, 1974, p. 14]

The treaties already made with the Dene do not stand in the way of a new settlement. The Dene maintain that Treaties 8 and 11 did not extinguish their aboriginal rights, and the government, for its part, has agreed to negotiate settlement of native claims without insisting on whatever rights it may claim under the treaties. Since no reserves were ever set aside under the treaties (except one at Hay River), federal policy, therefore, is not impeded by the Indian Act, the provisions of which relate primarily to the administration of reserve lands.

In the case of the non-status Indians—treaty Indians who for one reason or another have lost their treaty status—the Indian Act has no application, and the federal government has agreed to negotiate with them on the footing that they are entitled to participate in a settlement in the same way as treaty Indians. The government has made the same undertaking to the Metis. The government is not, therefore, arguing that the payment of scrip by the Halfbreed Commissions in the past extinguished the aboriginal rights of the Metis. In the case of the Inuit, there are neither treaties nor reserves, and the provisions of the Indian Act have never been applied to them.

There is, therefore, no legal or constitutional impediment to the adoption of a new policy in the settlement of native claims. The federal government, in dealing with the claims of the northern people, has recognized both that there are new opportunities for the settlement of claims and that such claims must be treated as comprehensive claims.

The native people, like the federal government, see their claims as the means of opening up new possibilities. Robert Andre, at Arctic Red River, articulated for the Inquiry the native people's view of the objectives of their claims:

We are saying we have the right to determine our own lives. This right derives from the fact that we were here first. We are saying we are a distinct people, a nation of people, and we must have a special right within Canada. We are distinct in that it will not be an easy matter for us to be brought into your system because we are different. We have our own system, our own way of life, our own cultures and traditions. We have our own languages, our own laws, and a system of justice. . . .

Land claims . . . [mean] our survival as a distinct people. We are a people with a long history and a whole culture, a culture which has survived. . . . We want to survive as a people, [hence] our stand for maximum independence within your society. We want to develop our own economy. We want to acquire political independence for our people, within the Canadian constitution. We want to govern our own lives and our own lands and its resources. We want to have our own system of government, by which we can control and develop our land for our benefit. We want to have the exclusive right to hunt, to fish and to trap. [C4536ff.]

We are saying that on the basis of our [aboriginal] land rights, we have an ownership and the right to participate directly in resource development. [C4536]

We want, as the original owners of this land, to receive royalties from [past] developments and for future developments, which we are prepared to allow. These royalties will be used to fund local economic development, which we are sure will last long after the companies have exhausted the non-renewable resources of our land. The present system attempts to put us into a wage economy as employees of companies and governments over which we have no control. We want to strengthen the economy at the community level, under the collective control of our people. In this way many of our young people will be able to participate directly in the community and not have to move elsewhere to find employment.

We want to become involved in the education of our children in the communities where we are in the majority. We want to be able to control the local schools. We want to start our own schools in the larger centres in the North where we are in the minority. . . .

Where the governments have a continuing role after the land settlement, we want to have a clear recognition as a distinct people, especially at the community level. Also at the community level, powers and control should lie with the chief and band council. To achieve all this is not easy. Much work lies ahead of us. . . .

We must again become a people making our own history. To be able to make our own history is to be able to mould our own future, to build our society that preserves the best of our past and our traditions, while enabling us to grow and develop as a whole people.

We want a society where all are equal, where people do not exploit others. We are not against change, but it must be under our terms and under our control. . . . We ask that our rights as a people for self-determination be respected. [C4539ff.]

SELF-DETERMINATION AND CONFEDERATION

THE CLAIM TO SELF-DETERMINATION

Why do the native people in the North insist upon their right to self-determination? Why cannot they be governed by the same political institutions as other Canadians? Many white people in the North raised these questions at the Inquiry. Ross Laycock at Norman Wells put it this way:

> I don't see why . . . we say Dene nation, why not a Canadian nation? The Americans in coping with racial prejudice have a melting pot where all races become Americans. We have a patchwork quilt, so let us sew it together and become Canadians, not white and Indians. [C2149]

But all of our experience has shown that the native people are not prepared to assimilate into our society. The fact is, they are distinct from the mass of the Canadian people racially, culturally and linguistically. The people living in the far-flung villages of the Canadian North may be remote from the metropolis, but they are not ignorant. They sense that their determination to be themselves is the only foundation on which they can rebuild their society. They are seeking—and discovering — insights of their own into the nature of the dominant white society and into the relationship between that society and their own. They believe they must formulate their claims for the future on that basis.

Native leadership can come only from the native people, and the reasons for this lie deep within man's soul. We all sense that people must do what they can for themselves. No one else, no matter how well-meaning, can do it for them. The native people are, therefore, seeking a fundamental reordering of the relations between themselves and the rest of Canada. They are seeking a new Confederation in the North.

The concept of native self-determination must be understood in the context of native claims. When the Dene people refer to themselves as a nation, as many of them have, they are not renouncing Canada or Confederation. Rather they are proclaiming that they are a distinct people, who share a common historical experience, a common set of values, and a common world view. They want their children and their children's children to be secure in that same knowledge of who they are and where they come from. They want their own experience, traditions and values to occupy an honourable place in the contemporary life of our country. Seen in this light, they say their claims will lead to the enhancement of Confederation—not to its renunciation.

It is a disservice to the Dene to suggest that they—or, for that matter, the Inuit or the Metis—are separatists. They see their future as lying with and within Canada, and they look to the Government of Canada, to the Parliament of Canada, and to the Crown itself to safeguard their rights and their future. Indeed it is this Inquiry, established by the Government of Canada under the Territorial Lands Act, a statute enacted by the Parliament of Canada, which they have chosen to be a forum for the presentation of their case before the people of Southern Canada.

SELF-DETERMINATION
AND THE CANADIAN CONSTITUTION

Can a settlement that embraces the native people's claim to self-determination be accommodated within our constitutional tradition and framework?

The roots of most Canadians lie in Europe, but the cultures of the native peoples have a different origin: they are indigenous to North America. The Fathers of Confederation provided in the constitution that the Parliament of Canada should protect the native people of our country. There is no such provision in the constitution for any other people.

Parliament has exclusive legislative jurisdiction in relation to the native peoples of Canada, but the British North America Act does not prescribe any particular legislative arrangements for them. There is nothing in the constitution that would preclude the kind of settlement the native people of the North are seeking.

Under the constitutional authority of Parliament to legislate for the peace, order and good government of Canada, there has been a wide range of administrative arrangements in the Northwest Territories, beginning with the Act of 1869 (S.C. 32–33 Victoria, Ch.3), which established a temporary system of administrative control for Rupert's Land and the Northwestern Territory, right up to 1970 with the establishment of the contemporary Territorial Council under the Northwest Territories Act (R.S.C. 1970, Ch. N-22). It is certainly within Parliament's power to reorganize the territorial government to permit a devolution of self-government to Dene and Inuit institutions. Parliament is competent, in the exercise of its jurisdiction under Section 91(24) of the British North America Act, to restrict participation in such institutions to persons of a certain racial heritage.

Could the native people's claims to self-determination, to the land, and to self-governing institutions be accommodated constitutionally within any future legislation that might establish a province in the Territories? Under our constitution, specific limitations and conditions could be attached to the powers of a new province. Constitutionally, there is no bar to the native ownership of land nor to a guarantee of native institutions of self-government in a new province.

I think such special guarantees would be in keeping with the Canadian tradition. Lord Durham, in his report of 1839, looked toward the assimilation of all Canadians into the British culture. The Act of Union in 1840 established a framework of government designed to promote this solution: one province and one legislature for both the French-speaking people of Lower Canada and the English-speaking people of Upper Canada. But the people of Quebec would not be assimilated. Thus, in 1867, as Dr. Peter Russell wrote, "it was Cartier's ideal of a pluralistic nation, not Durham's ideal of a British nation in North America, that prevailed." The Dene, the Inuit and the Metis call for the extension to Canada's native people of the original spirit of Confederation.

Canada has not been an easy nation to govern, but over the years we have tried to remain true to the ideal that underlies Confederation, an ideal that Canada and Canadians have had to affirm again and again in the face of continuing challenges to their tolerance and sense of diversity. Why should the native people of Canada be given special consideration? No such consideration has been offered to the Ukrainians, the Swedes, the Italians, or any other race, ethnic group or nationality since Confederation. Why should the native people be allowed political institutions of their own under the Constitution of Canada, when other groups are not?

The answer is simple enough: the native people of the North did not immigrate to Canada as individuals or families expecting to assimilate. Immigrants chose to come and to submit to the Canadian polity; their choices were individual choices. The Dene and the Inuit were already here, and were forced to submit to the polity imposed upon them. They were here and had their own languages, cultures and histories before the arrival of the French or English. They are the original peoples of Northern Canada. The North was—and is—their homeland.

EVOLUTION OF GOVERNMENT
IN THE NORTHWEST TERRITORIES

The concept of native self-determination is antithetical to the vision of the future held by many white people in the Northwest Territories, who believe that, in due course, the Territories should become a province like the other provinces. They see no place for native self-determination in such a future. It is not surprising they should feel this way, because their vision of the future is a reflection of what occurred during the settlement of the West. Agricultural settlers moved into Indian country, and when they were well enough established, they sought admittance to Confederation as a province. In 1870 Manitoba was carved out of the Northwestern Territory; in 1880 a large area of the Northwestern Territory was transferred to Ontario; in 1905 Alberta and Saskatchewan were created; and in 1912 a large area was added to the Province of Quebec. Many white northerners expected the Northwest Territories, following this process, to become a province like the others; a province in which white men govern a land that once belonged to others. Some witnesses have urged me to recommend to the federal government the granting of additional powers to the Territorial Council in order to bring the Northwest Territories closer to provincial status.

In fact, the evolution of political institutions in the Northwest Territories since 1905 has followed the pattern of the provinces. The Territorial Council is modelled after the provincial legislatures, although because it is the creation of Parliament, it has no standing under the constitution.

In 1966, the Carrothers Commission recommended that local municipal bodies should be the basis for the development of self-government in the Northwest Territories. As a result, institutions of local government were established following the model of municipal institutions as they exist in Southern Canada. In the larger centres, local government has a tax base founded on private property. The same system, whereby increased responsibility for local affairs is tied to the evolution of a tax base, was established in native communities. Even though there is virtually no private property in these communities, the assumption seems to have been that they would progress in time from settlements and hamlets—the most limited forms of local government—to the status of villages, towns and cities, like Fort Simpson, Inuvik and Yellowknife.

Settlements and hamlets, the highest levels of local government that the native communities have so far achieved, have very limited authority. In practice, this authority relates only to the day-to-day operations of the community, such as roads, water, sewage and garbage. In the native communities, most members of the local council are natives, but the native people made it quite clear to me that these councils have no power to deal with their vital concerns, such as the protection of their land and the education of their children. These important decisions are still made in Yellowknife and Ottawa. The native people regard local government, as it exists at present, as an extension of the territorial government, not a political institution of the community itself. Paul Andrew, Chief of the Fort Norman Band, had formerly worked as settlement secretary at Fort Norman. He described local government in this way:

> It was quite obvious that this whole Settlement Council system has never worked and never will work because it is a form of tokenism to the territorial government. . . . [It is] an Advisory Board whose advice [is] not usually taken. . . .
>
> The frustrations that I found for the position was that I was told that I was working for the people. But I was continuously getting orders from the regional office. They were the ones that finally decided what would happen and what would not happen. [C875ff.]

Though there is a majority of native people on the Territorial Council, it is not regarded as a native institution. The bureaucracy of the territorial government, concentrated in Yellowknife and the other large centres, plays a far more important part than the Territorial Council in shaping the lives of the native people and their communities. The native people see the Government of the Northwest Territories as a white institution; indeed, of the persons who hold the position of director in the Government of the Northwest Territories, all are white. For the most part, native employees hold clerical and janitorial positions. Noel Kakfwi expressed to the Inquiry at Fort Good Hope the native people's sense of non-participation in the existing government:

> In Yellowknife last week I spent about eight days. Out of curiosity I went into the offices and I was exploring the building in different places. All I seen was those white people with the brown hair, white collar, neckties, sitting on the desk. I looked around if I could see one native fellow, one Dene. Nothing doing. [C1923ff.]

In developing institutions of government in the North, we have sought to impose our own system, to persuade the native people to conform to our political models. We have not tried to fashion a system of government based on the Dene and Inuit models of consensus, or to build on their traditional forms of local decision-making. So long as the native people are obliged to participate in political institutions that are not of their making or of their choosing, it seems to me their participation will be half-hearted. Indeed, two Dene members withdrew from the Territorial Council last year on the ground that such membership was inconsistent with the furtherance of the claims of the Dene.

To understand why Dene and Inuit models have not been used to develop local and regional government in the North, we have to look closely at our own assumptions about the native people. During the past few years, the native people have challenged the validity of these assumptions.

We have assumed that native culture is static and unchanging, and we have not seriously considered the possibility that the native people could adapt their traditional social, economic and political organization to deal with present realities. The native people are seen as a people locked into the past. Such an assumption becomes self-fulfilling. But not allowing them the means to deal with their present problems on their own terms, their culture does, in fact, tend to become degraded and static. Their challenges to our assumptions and their assertion of their rights have made many white people in the Northwest Territories uneasy. Native organizations are resented, and the federal government is criticized for providing funds to them. A world in which the native people could not assert their rights is changing into a world in which they can insist and are insisting upon them.

Many white people in the North are convinced that it is wrong to concede that differences based on racial identity, cultural values and economic opportunities even exist. But it is better to articulate and understand these differences than it is to ignore them. The differences are real. They have always existed, but they have been suppressed. Now the native people are proclaiming their right to shape their world in their own image and not in the shadow of ours. As a result, some white people now resent what they regard as an attempt to alter the political, economic and social order of the Northwest Territories. They are right to regard this as an attempt to change the existing order. But they should not resent it, because a growing native consciousness is a fact of life in the North. It was bound to come. It is not going to go away, even if we impose political institutions in which it has no place.

Both the white and the native people in the North realize that the government's decision on the pipeline and on the way in which native claims are settled, will determine whether the political evolution of the North will follow the pattern of the history of the West or whether it will find a place for native ideas of self-determination. The settlement of native claims must be the point of departure for any political reorganization in the Northwest Territories. That is why the decision on the pipeline is really a decision about the political future of the Northwest Territories. It is the highest obligation of the Government of Canada, now as it was a century ago in the West, to settle the native people's claims to their northern homeland.

The pipeline project represents a far greater advance of the industrial system into the North than anything that has gone before it. The native people throughout the Mackenzie Valley and the Western Arctic sense that the decision on the pipeline is the turning point in their history.

NATIVE CLAIMS: THEIR NATURE AND EXTENT

THE LAND

The native people presented extensive evidence to the Inquiry to show that they have used and occupied vast tracts of the Mackenzie Valley and the Western Arctic since time immemorial, and they now seek recognition of their right as a people to their homeland.

The special character of native land use explains why they seek title to areas of land that are, by southern standards, immense. Within living memory, the Inuit of the Western Arctic have used nearly 100,000 square miles of land and water to support themselves. The Dene presented evidence to show that they have used and occupied 450,000 square miles of land in the Northwest Territories. The native people rely not only on the areas in which they actually hunt, fish and trap, but they also need the areas that are of critical importance to the animal populations. At Sachs Harbour, David Nasogaluak explained to the Inquiry how the Bankslanders rely upon the whole of Banks Island, an area of 25,000 square miles, even though they do not hunt or trap in the northern part of the island. Andy Carpenter added, "We are saving the north end of Banks Island for breeding areas. That's for foxes, caribou, musk-oxen." [C4120]

Daniel Sonfrere, Chief of the Hay River Indian Band, emphasized how his people saved some areas:

> . . . just like they are keeping it for the future because they don't want to clean everything out at once. So they are kind of saving that area out there. [C522]

The native people maintain that the use they make of the land requires them to control vast tracts of it. They reject a land settlement that would give them title only to discrete blocks of land around their villages. They reject any suggestion, therefore, of an extension of the reserve system to Northern Canada.

REGULATION OF LAND USE

The native people want to entrench their rights to the land, not only to preserve the native economy, but also to enable them to achieve a measure of control over alternative uses of land, particularly the development of non-renewable resources. With such control, they can influence the rate of advance of industrial development in the North. Alizette Potfighter of Detah, the Dene village across the bay from Yellowknife, explained why the native people regard such control as essential:

> Yellowknife . . . is in the process of becoming as large and as organized as the large towns down south. In the past, people here used to hunt moose and fish right by the Yellowknife Bay and used to hunt caribou. They used to go berry picking practically right in their back yards. Now the people have to travel miles and miles from home to hunt and trap, the fish are no longer good to eat, and [the people] have to go to the Big Lake if they want fish, which again means that we have to travel far.
>
> The mines have polluted our waters and the fish. . . . The arsenic has caused this; it also affects the greenery around us. The people who live right in town are warned beforehand about planting gardens and how they may be affected by high arsenic levels. . . .
>
> The wildlife has been driven further into the bush. The coming of the white man and the development he brought with him has only served to take away our way of life. [C8426ff.]

In light of their experience of the treaties, the native people insist that their hunting, fishing and trapping rights cannot be protected merely by just incorporating them in a settlement. They see ownership and control of the land itself as the only means of safeguarding their traditional economy.

There are other reasons why the native people of the North seek recognition of their right to ownership of the land. Not only will such ownership give them the legal basis from which they can negotiate with government and industry to ensure that any proposed developments are environmentally acceptable, it will also enable them to share in the benefits of economic development. Royalties from the development of non-renewable resources could be used to modernize the native economy and to promote development of renewable resources. There may be other benefits from joint-venture arrangements with outside developers, by which the native people who wish to participate in various forms of development may do so, not merely as employees at the lowest level—which has been the experience of the past—but also as managers and contractors.

SELF-GOVERNMENT

The native people have proposed a restructuring of political institutions in the Northwest Territories. This restructuring, which is the overarching feature of their claims, would reflect both in law and in fact the principle that the North is their homeland and that they have the right, under the constitution and within Confederation, to shape their future. The proposal of the Inuit Tapirisat of Canada called for the establishment of a new political entity comprising the land north of the tree line. Political control of that territory would lie with the Inuit, at least for the foreseeable future, by a 10-year residency requirement for voting.

The Dene, in their proposal to the federal government, stated:

The Dene have the right to develop their own institutions and enjoy their rights as a people in the framework of their own institutions.

There will therefore be *within* Confederation, a Dene government with jurisdiction over a geographical area and over subject matters now within the jurisdiction of the Government of Canada or the Government of the Northwest Territories, [para. 7 of the proposed Agreement in Principle]

The native people seek a measure of control over land use, and they see that the ownership of the land and political control of land use are intimately linked. They also seek control over the education of their children, and control over the delivery of community services, such as housing, health and social services. The native people acknowledge that these services have made important contributions to their material and physical well-being, but they reject the idea that they should continue to be passive recipients of these services.

These claims must be regarded together, for they are closely integrated. Many people in the native communities told the Inquiry that they want to continue living off the land. This would require changes in the present school curriculum and school year that would allow the children to accompany their parents into the bush without disrupting their education. Some families wish to move back into the bush more or less permanently. However, this option would require a change in not only educational policy, but also in housing policy to provide loans to build permanent log houses outside of the communities. Communications policy must be formulated to ensure an effective radio service between the bush and the communities. Transportation policy must be formulated to ensure the means of travel to and from bush camps. Land use and economic development policy must be formulated to ensure that the areas within which families are living the traditional life are not damaged by exploration for or development of non-renewable resources and to ensure that financial support is given to the native economy.

These claims leave unanswered many questions that will have to be clarified and resolved through negotiations between the Government of Canada and the native organizations. A vital question, one of great concern to white northerners, is how Yellowknife, Hay River and other communities with white majorities would fit into this scheme. Would they be part of the new territory? Or would they become enclaves within it? It is not my task to try to resolve these difficult questions. Whether native self-determination requires native hegemony over a geographical area, or whether it can be achieved through the transfer of political control over specific matters to the native people, remain questions to be resolved by negotiations.

THE CLAIM TO
RENEWABLE RESOURCES

The game, fish and fur, and the other renewable resources of the land are the foundation upon which the native people believe their economic future can and should be established. They seek to defend what is for many of them a way of life, and at the same time to modernize and expand the native economy.

A mixture of hunting and fishing and of trapping-for-trade is widely regarded by the Dene and Inuit as their traditional life. This economy is based on primary production at the individual or family level and, because it relies on traditional skills and a detailed knowledge of animal life and the land, this way of life is basic to native culture and gives meaning to the values that the native people still hold today.

If the economic future of the native people is to correspond with their declared preferences, the native economy of the bush and the barrens must be fortified. Small-scale harvesting of renewable resources must cease to be economically uncertain and insecure. The close links between primary production and the collective well-being of the native people should find a prominent place in planning for northern development.

The native people and the native organizations spoke to the Inquiry of the need for innovation in the use of renewable resources. Among their suggestions were the development of a fishery in the Mackenzie River, the systematic harvesting of caribou, the provision of incentives to fur trappers, and an orderly system for marketing fur.

VIABILITY OF THE RENEWABLE RESOURCE SECTOR

The argument against too heavy reliance on traditional, small-scale primary production centres on the question: how many people can the land ultimately support even when the renewable resources of the North are fully utilized? There are now some 15,000 native people living in the Mackenzie Valley and the Western Arctic, and the population is increasing. It is argued, therefore, that the increase of the native people themselves will threaten the viability of their own resource base.

In the past, policies for the North have been influenced, if not determined, by the belief that the available renewable resources cannot support native populations. The conventional wisdom since the decline of the fur trade has insisted that economic development in the North ought to consist of mines, roads, oil and gas, and pipelines. This wisdom so overwhelmed any contrary suggestions that some of the native people themselves have been inclined to doubt the worth of their own economy. Such doubts tended to be confirmed by the consequences of the government policy of concentrating activity in the non-renewable resource sector, which of course increased the vulnerability of the traditional native economy. The prophecies of conventional wisdom thus tended toward self-fulfilment. The conviction that there was no hope for the old way made that way indeed hopeless.

Can the land support a larger native population? The native people testified that industrial development has driven the animals away from many places they used to inhabit. But despite this fact—which is very important from the hunter's and trapper's perspective because it makes his activities more arduous—animal populations appear to be thriving throughout the Mackenzie Valley and the Western Arctic. It should also be remembered that in aboriginal times the land supported a larger native population than it does today. In fact, there is little evidence that native people are over-exploiting their resources at present, and there is much evidence that overall yields could be increased. I shall deal with this evidence when I turn to the proposals made to the Inquiry for the modernization of renewable resource harvesting.

Northerners point to many animal species that may have some potential for commercial or domestic use and that are not being harvested at the present time. Consider the Western Arctic, where you will find white whale, seal, char, herring, whitefish, trout, moose, caribou, bear, wolf, fox, numerous bird species, edible plants and berries. Consider the strong economy of the people of Banks Island, which is based on white fox trapping. Look at the Mackenzie Valley with its moose, caribou, beaver, muskrat, marten, mink, wolverine, lynx and coloured fox populations, river and lake fisheries, timber stands along the Liard River and the south shore of Great Slave Lake.

I do not want to be misunderstood here: the North is, in fact, a region of limited biological productivity. Its renewable resources will not support a large population. But through a long history the region has been productive enough for the native people, and they believe it could be made to be yet more productive in the years to come.

There has been a dearth of research into the means of improving productivity in the North. Assertions about the impossibility of strengthening the native economy have often been just that—assertions. We do not have adequate inventories of the various species available there—not even for the Mackenzie River. Nor for that matter do we know very much about the present intensity of renewable resource use. We do not know enough about food chains and ecological relationships in the North to be able to predict what effect an increased harvest of one species may have on other species. We have not considered whether or not new systems of marketing and price support might strengthen the native economy.

PROPOSALS MADE TO THE INQUIRY

The native organizations offered some ideas for strengthening the native economy by development of renewable game, fish and fur resources.

Dr. Robert Ruttan and John T'Seleie discussed the fishery potential of the Mackenzie Valley. They emphasized that the Mackenzie, Liard, Hay and Slave Rivers contain at least ten species of fish. Lake trout also occur in harvestable numbers in Great Slave Lake, and arctic char are found in certain tributaries of the Mackenzie River west of the Delta. They reminded the Inquiry that each community along the Mackenzie River makes extensive use of the river fishery during the summer months, and that the fish of many large lakes along the Valley are a relatively untouched resource. The primary species available are lake trout, whitefish, grayling, pickerel, inconnu (coney), cisco (herring) and northern pike. Although many of these lakes have low temperatures and relatively low productivity, they have sustained for a long time fairly high levels of subsistence fishing. The people of Fort Good Hope and Colville Lake fish more than 50 lakes: in 1975, during a six-month period, the Fort Good Hope people harvested an estimated 127,000 to 186,000 pounds of fish.

The total value of the fishery resource of the Mackenzie River region has never been calculated. Ruttan and T'Seleie reckon the replacement value of the fish taken at Fort Good Hope over the six-month period in 1975 was between $143,000 and $209,000, and said that a potential annual production of 500,000 to 1,000,000 pounds of fish would not be unreasonable. They argued that, with a long-range fish management program, the economic value of the fishery could be maximized by the establishment of community and regional markets and by processing for domestic and commercial use or for resale. Certain lakes and streams could be used for sport-fishing camps. At present, several tourist lodges operate on Great Bear and Great Slave Lakes. However, the role of the native people in them is limited to that of guides; they have no control over the management of the lodges nor of the resource base.

Similarly, evidence was given on the possibilities for increased utilization of caribou. Three major herds range within or very near the Mackenzie drainage basin. The population of the Bathurst herd may be approaching 200,000 animals, and the potential annual harvest for this herd alone may well be 10,000 animals. The Bluenose herd, which ranges in winter along the north shore of Great Bear Lake, is expanding at present and may now number as many as 50,000. In the chapter on the Northern Yukon, I have discussed the importance of the Porcupine caribou herd to the people of Old Crow. But the herd is utilized by native people in the Northwest Territories too. It is an important resource in spring and autumn for the native hunters from Fort McPherson and Aklavik.

These three herds now supply hundreds of thousands of pounds of meat to the native people of the Mackenzie Valley and the Western Arctic. With systematic management, they could constitute an even more important domestic resource and perhaps a commercial resource as well, but the potential harvest limits of this species cannot safely be determined without accurate estimates of their total populations, annual increments and long-term cycles.

From the beginning of the fur trade, furbearers have been a major source of income for native people. Although trapping has declined over the last 20 years, it still remains an important part of the native economy. Beaver, muskrat, marten, mink, fox, lynx and wolverine are the most important animals in the trapping economy. Even though, during the past few years, there has been some increase in trapping owing to higher fur prices, there is evidence to show that much higher levels of trapping could be sustained. A report entitled *Development Agencies for the*

Northwest Territories prepared in 1973 by Edward Weick for a Special Staff Group of the Department of Indian Affairs and Northern Development under the chairmanship of Kalmen Kaplansky stated:

> The number of pelts taken in 1970–71 as shown in Statistics Canada's data on fur production is well below the optimum. Estimates suggest that muskrat production could be increased from 74,450 to 250,000 pelts; white fox, from 25,584 to 100,000 pelts; ermine, from 1,844 to 10,000 pelts; mink, from 4,021 to 10,000 pelts and beaver, from 6,888 to 12,000 pelts. Since Northwest Territories production is a small part of total international production, an increase in exploitation would not likely have a depressive effect on prices except, perhaps, in the case of distinctive species such as the white fox. [p. 20–21]

Ruttan and T'Seleie told the Inquiry that potential fur yields could readily be increased by more effective management. Values could also be increased by an improved marketing system, including public auctions and the development of trapper-owned trading stores to ensure the lines of credit so essential to trapping, sales to handicraft centres, and further development of a fur-garment industry within the Northwest Territories. The Special Staff Group report indicated what would be required to modernize the trapping industry. It would have to include:

> ... better information on resource availability, restrictive licensing, improved equipment and access to remote, underexploited areas, adjustment of trapping, wage work and school term seasons, to avoid conflicts. It could also include more rational marketing mechanisms to minimize currently excessive control by middlemen, of both the primary production and the manufacturing-retailing markets. Standards of size and quality should be established and enforced. [ibid., p. 22–23]

At Fort Liard, Chief Harry Deneron explained that many trappers, who had no established lines of credit, were forced to sell their furs to local traders at prices much lower than the furs ultimately fetched at auctions in the South. He argued that a settlement of native claims that gave the native people control of the renewable resources of their land and access to capital would enable trappers to maximize their returns.

Ruttan and T'Seleie also gave evidence on the forest resources of the Mackenzie River basin. The most extensive stands of commercially valuable timber occur along the Liard River and on the alluvial flood plains and islands along the Mackenzie River and its tributaries. The Special Staff Group report expressed some doubt on whether or not the forests of the Mackenzie Valley could support a pulp-and-paper industry, and it emphasized that the forest resource is better suited to supply the local and regional market and that forest products should be especially developed for use in the North. The report suggested:

It should be possible to integrate the northern forest resource into the construction industry by planning in advance to use regional materials in housing programs and thus provide a basis for local development. It might be more expensive initially to supply northern lumber needs from territorial forest stands. Yet, when one considers the jobs that might be created in logging, sawmilling, perhaps transportation and prefabrication, probable reduction in welfare costs, the development of useful skills and competence, and the possible growth of a viable forest industry, these positive factors might offset the somewhat higher initial costs. [ibid.,p. 40]

This view accords with what many native people in the villages told me. They maintained that housing constructed out of logs and designed locally would provide them with shelter that is better suited to their needs, and would permit them to use local materials and develop native skills.

If renewable resources are to be the basis of an economy, perhaps the native people will have to be subsidized. We already subsidize wheat farmers by price supports because we regard the production of wheat and the stability of farm families as an important goal. We subsidize fishermen on the Atlantic and Pacific coasts by the payment of extended unemployment insurance benefits in the off-season. But, until now, we have never regarded hunting and trapping in the same light. In the North, hunters and trappers have been subsidized—and stigmatized — by welfare. It should now be recognized that people who hunt and trap for a living are self-employed in the same way that commercial fishermen or farmers are.

There should be a reassessment of the goals of educational and social policy as they relate to the traditional sector and to wage employment. There are many young people today who want to participate in the renewable resource sector, not necessarily to the exclusion of other employment, and not necessarily as a lifetime career. They wish to choose and, perhaps, to alternate choices. The teaching of skills that are necessary to participate in a modernized renewable resource economy must therefore be integrated into the educational program, and the importance of these skills must be properly recognized in economic and social policies.

The native economy of the Western Arctic and the Mackenzie Valley is unfamiliar to urban southerners, and policy-makers are generally uncomfortable in thinking about it. They may regard the native economy as unspecialized, inefficient and unproductive. It is true that such economies have not historically generated much surplus, nor have they produced a labour force that is easily adaptable to large-scale industrial enterprise. They can provide, however, for the needs of those who participate in them. The ways in which we measure economic performance in a modern industrial setting do not necessarily apply in other settings. Nevertheless, other economies can change and modernize in their own way, just as an industrial economy does.

It is increasingly recognized that the economic development of the Third World hinges on agrarian reform, on the modernization of existing agriculture to serve domestic needs; in the same way, and to a greater extent than we have been prepared to concede, the economic development of the North hinges on the modernization of the existing native economy, based as it is on the ability of the native people to use renewable resources to serve their own needs. Productivity must be improved and the native economy must be expanded so that more people can be gainfully employed in it. In my judgment, therefore, the renewable resource sector must have priority in the economic development of the North.

NATIVE MANAGEMENT OF RENEWABLE RESOURCES

The idea of modernizing the native economy is not new. It has been adumbrated in many reports bearing the imprimatur of the Department of Indian Affairs and Northern Development. But nothing has been done about it. Why? Because it was not important to us, whereas large-scale industrial development was. Indeed, such large-scale projects hold great attraction for policy-makers and planners in Ottawa and Yellowknife. Small-scale projects, amenable to local control, do not.

The remarkable thing is that, despite two decades of almost missionary zeal by government and industry, the native people of the North still wish to see their economic future based on renewable resource development. They have argued that the renewable resource sector must take priority over the non-renewable resource sector. This was said in every native village, in every native settlement.

The native people claim the right to the renewable resources of the North. This claim implies that all hunting, trapping, and fishing rights throughout the Mackenzie Valley and the Western Arctic, along with the control of licensing and other functions of game management, should be given to the native communities, and that, for matters affecting all native communities, the control should be vested in larger native institutions at the regional or territorial level. The native people seek the means to manage, harvest, process and market the fur, fish and game of the Northwest Territories.

It is worth bearing in mind that modernization of the renewable resource sector can be achieved with a comparatively small capital outlay. A reasonable share of the royalties from existing industries based on non-renewable resources in the Mackenzie Valley and the Western Arctic would suffice. Huge subsidies of the magnitude provided to the non-renewable resource industries would not be necessary. And the possibilities for native management and control would be greater.

The question of scale, however, suggests that we may consider some resources that, although they are not renewable, are nonetheless amenable to the kind of development that is consistent with local interest and local control. I have in mind here certain accessible surface resources, such as gravel. These and other resources will no doubt be of importance in the claims negotiations and in land selection. The native people will, in time, judge this matter for themselves, but they should not be constrained or limited by any narrow meaning of the word "renewable."

I do not mean to say that industrial development should not take place. It has taken place, and it is taking place. But unless we decide that, as a matter of priority, a firmly strengthened renewable resource sector must be established in the Mackenzie Valley and the Western Arctic, we shall not see a diversified economy in the North.

NATIVE CLAIMS AND THE PIPELINE

We must now address the central question, can we build the pipeline and, at the same time, do justice to native claims?

The case made by the native people is that the pipeline will bring an influx of construction workers from the South, that it will bring large-scale in-migration, that it will entail a commitment by the Governments of Canada and of the Northwest Territories to a program of large-scale frontier development that, once begun, cannot be diverted in its course. They say it will mean enhanced oil and gas exploration and development throughout the Mackenzie Valley and the Western Arctic. They say that, to the extent that there is a substantial in-migration of white people to the North, there will be a still greater tendency to persist with southern patterns of political, social and industrial development, and it will become less and less likely that the native people will gain any measure of self-determination.

The native people say that the construction of a pipeline and the establishment of an energy corridor will lead to greater demand for industrial sites, roads and seismic lines, with ever greater loss or fragmentation of productive areas of land. Industrial users of land, urban centres, and a growing non-native population will make ever greater demands on water for hydro-electricity and for other industrial and domestic uses. The threats to the fishery will be increased. And last, but by no means least, the emphasis the Governments of Canada and the Northwest Territories have placed on non-renewable resources will become even greater than it is now, and the two governments will be less and less inclined to support the development of renewable resources.

Others argue that these developments are inevitable, and that there really is no choice. The industrialization of the North has already begun, and it will continue and will force further changes upon the native people. The power of technology to effect such changes cannot be diminished, nor can its impact be arrested. Rather than postponing the pipeline, we should help the native people to make as easy a transition as possible to the industrial system. This is the law of life, and it must prevail in the North, too.

The native people insist that a settlement of their claims must precede any large-scale industrial development. That, they say, is the essential condition of such development. They say that, notwithstanding any undertakings industry may give, and notwithstanding any recommendations this Inquiry may make, they will never have any control over what will happen to them, to their villages and to the land they claim, unless they have some measure of control over the development of the North. The only way they will acquire that measure of control, they say, is through a settlement of their land claims.

The native people do not believe that any recommendations this Inquiry may make for the pipeline project will be carried out, even if the government finds them acceptable, and even if industry says they are acceptable, unless they are in a position to insist upon them. And they will be in that position only if their claims are settled, if their rights to their land are entrenched, and if institutions are established that enable them to enforce the recommendations. They say the experience of the treaties proves this.

Let us consider, then, whether construction of the pipeline and establishment of the energy corridor before native claims are settled, will retard achievement of the goals of the native people or indeed render them impossible of achievement?

LAND AND CONTROL OF LAND USE

In many villages along the Mackenzie River, the native people expressed great concern over the proximity of the proposed pipeline to their villages. These small villages are the hearth of native life, and the people in them can be expected to seek special protection for the lands near them. Inuit Tapirisat of Canada, in their submission to the federal government, asked for the native communities' right to select any lands within a 25-mile radius, and the Dene may well seek similar protection for their villages. Acceptance by the government of the proposed route and the designation of an energy corridor along that route before native claims are settled would certainly prejudice those claims. The proposed pipeline route at present passes within 25 miles of Fort Good Hope, Fort Norman, Wrigley, Fort Simpson and Jean Marie River.

Of course, the Dene and Inuit claims are not limited to the vicinity of their villages. They seek ownership and control of the use of vast tracts of land to achieve a number of objectives. They seek to strengthen the renewable resource sector of the northern economy. This, they insist, must take place before a pipeline is built. Their reasoning is simple: once the pipeline is underway, the primary flow of capital will be to the non-renewable resource sector. Once the gas pipeline is built and the corridor is established, the gas pipeline will probably be looped, and after that, an oil pipeline may be constructed, and, of course, gas and oil exploration will be intensified all along the corridor. Given the fact that over the past decade, in the pre-pipeline period, there has been a concentration on the non-renewable resource sector of the economy, the shift to that sector, and away from the renewable resource sector, once the construction of the pipeline is begun, will become complete.

A second objective of the claims to land and control of land use relates to non-renewable resources. The native people seek to exercise a measure of control over projects such as the pipeline to protect the renewable resource base and environment upon which they depend. If we build the pipeline now, the federal government will establish a regulatory authority to supervise its construction and enforce, among other matters, environmental protection measures. The authority will employ a large number of inspectors, monitors and other personnel. The public service population in the Northwest Territories, mainly white, will further increase. The necessity, acknowledged on all sides, for a regulatory authority will mean that its staff will have extensive power over land use all along the corridor. There is little likelihood of the native people having any control over land use, whether it be access roads to the pipeline, or seismic exploration, or extensions of the corridor. The machinery for regulating the pipeline will entrench and reinforce the existing federal and territorial bureaucracies.

The native people, through their claims, seek benefits from those industrial developments by which they are prepared to give their consent and which the government deems necessary in the national interest. Would they be in a position to take advantage of any benefits that might accrue from a pipeline, prior to a claims settlement? The native people, with some few exceptions, do not have the necessary capital or the experience to participate effectively in joint ventures on projects such as the pipeline. But a claims settlement would be the means of supplying capital to native development corporations so they could participate in such ventures.

SELF-GOVERNMENT

The native people believe that, with a new wave of white in-migration in the wake of a pipeline, they will see repeated in the North the experience of native people throughout the rest of North America. An increase in the white population would not only reinforce the existing structure of government; it would reduce the native people to a minority position within that structure, thereby undermining their constitutional claim to self-determination.

We know there was virtually uncontrolled in-migration to Alaska of non-Alaskan residents as a result of the construction of the trans-Alaska pipeline. Arctic Gas says that measures can be taken to restrict such in-migration to the Northwest Territories. It is also said that stringent measures can be imposed to regulate housing, land use—indeed, the whole of northern life—in a way that was not possible in Alaska. But a proposal to use the power of the state in that way confirms the very fear that the native people have: a large-scale project such as the pipeline would lead to the further entrenchment of the existing, and largely white, bureaucracy in the North, and the chances of achieving a transfer of power to native institutions—one of the major objectives of native claims—would be made so difficult as to be impossible.

Since the Carrothers Commission in 1966, the development of municipal government has been the focus for the evolution of local self-government in the Northwest Territories. If this policy is to continue, then there is nothing further to be said. If it is to be changed—and the claims of the native people may require change in the existing institutions of local government—the change should be effected before construction of the pipeline is underway and before existing government structures become further entrenched. To the extent that the Dene and Inuit proposals call for the restriction of the franchise in local, regional and territorial political entities to long-term residents of the North, the effect of the construction of the pipeline, swelling the population of white southerners, would render the prospect of agreement on such a limitation that much more unlikely.

The native people seek control over social services so that they themselves can deal with the problems that already exist in the North. It would not be possible to achieve the same objective merely by pursuing a crash program making funds available to support existing local native rehabilitation programs and to establish new ones to deal with the problems associated with the pipeline. The sheer scale of the pipeline's impact on the social fabric of the small communities is likely to overwhelm the capabilities of such native programs as the Koe Go Cho Society at Fort Simpson and Peel River Alcoholics Anonymous at Fort McPherson.

At the same time, if the pipeline precedes a settlement of claims, the process of bureaucratic entrenchment will also take place in the social services. The services themselves will have to be expanded to deal with the anticipated increases in alcoholism, crime, family breakdowns, and other forms of social disorganization that experience in the North, and elsewhere, has shown to be associated with large-scale frontier development. This expansion will mean more social workers, more police, more alcohol rehabilitation workers and a corresponding increase in the size of the bureaucracy.

The idea that new programs, more planning and an increase in social service personnel will solve these problems misconstrues their real nature and cause. The high rates of social and personal breakdown in the North are, in good measure, the responses of individuals and families who have suffered the loss of meaning in their lives and control over their destiny. A pipeline before a settlement would confirm their belief that they have no control over their land or their lives. Whether that conviction is true or not, that will be their perception. These problems are beyond the competence of social workers, priests and psychiatrists. They cannot be counselled away.

Of course, a settlement of native claims will not be a panacea for all of the social ills of the North, but it would permit the native people to begin to solve these problems themselves. That would take time. But it is worth taking the time, because to build a pipeline before native claims are settled would compound existing problems and undermine the possibility of their solution.

I have said that control of education and the preservation of the native languages are central to the issue of cultural survival. The effects that prior construction of a pipeline would have on education and language could be regarded as a litmus test of prejudice to native claims.

The educational system in the North already reflects the demands of white families, who, although they stay only a year or two in the North, insist upon a curriculum similar to that of Ottawa, Edmonton or Vancouver because they intend to return south. They do not want their children to lose a year or to have to adjust to a different school system in the North.

Pipeline construction would bring yet more white families north, and it would therefore entrench the present system and its curriculum. At the same time as the native people find themselves part of an industrial labour force, without having had a chance to build up and develop their own forms of economic development, they would find increasing difficulty in making their case that the curriculum does not meet the needs of their children.

If the native peoples' claim to run their own schools is to be recognized, it must be done now.

THE LESSONS OF HISTORY

The native people of the North seek in their claims to fulfil their hope for the future. The settlement of their claims would therefore be an event of both real and symbolic importance in their relationship to the rest of Canada. The native people want to follow a path of their own. To them, a decision that their claims must be settled before the pipeline is built will be an affirmation of their right to choose that path. On the other hand, if the pipeline is built before native claims are settled, that will be a demonstration to the native people of the North that the Government of Canada is not prepared to give them the right to govern their own lives; for if they are not to be granted that right in relation to the decision which more than anything else will affect their lives and the lives of their children, then what is left of that right thereafter?

What are the implications of not recognizing that right and proceeding with the pipeline before settlement? Feelings of frustration and disappointment among the native people of the North would be transformed into bitterness and rage. There is a real possibility of civil disobedience and civil disorder.

These things are possibilities. But I can predict with certainty that if the pipeline is built before a settlement is achieved, the communities that are already struggling with the negative effects of industrial development will be still further demoralized. To the extent that the process of marginalization—the sense of being made irrelevant in your own land—is a principal cause of social pathology, the native people will suffer its effects in ever greater measure.

Can we learn anything from our own history? I hope we can, if we examine the settlement of the West and the events that led to the Red River Rebellion of 1869 and the Northwest Rebellion of 1885. Let me make it plain that, while I believe there is a real possibility of civil disobedience and civil disorder in the North if we build the pipeline without a settlement of native claims, I do not believe that there is likely to be a rebellion. Nevertheless the events of 1869–1870 and 1885 offer us an insight into the consequences of similar policies today. These events, and their aftermath, make it impossible to reconcile native claims with the demands of white advance to the frontier.

The establishment of a Provisional Government by Louis Riel and his followers in 1869 in the Red River Valley was a consequence of Canada's having acquired Rupert's Land from the Hudson's Bay Company without recognition of the rights of the Metis, Indians and whites living there. The List of Rights drawn up by the Provisional Government called for the settlement of the land claims of the Metis and the signing of treaties with the Indians. In the Manitoba Act of 1870, the claims of the Metis were recognized, and 1,400,000 acres were set aside for their benefit. But their claims were processed very slowly, and, with their lands in doubt and their hunting opportunities continually declining, many Metis migrated north and west to the Valley of the Saskatchewan. There they built a prosperous and stable society that was a product of both the old and new ways. In 1873 they established their own government in the unorganized territory of the Northwest with Gabriel Dumont as president. But the advance of white settlement soon reached them even there.

Manitoba entered Confederation in 1870, and the following year the Canadian Pacific Railway was incorporated. Between 1871 and 1877, the government signed seven treaties with the Indians to enable rail construction to proceed, and by the mid-1870s railway survey crews reached the Saskatchewan.

The CPR, built across the prairies in 1882 and 1883, with the labour of five thousand men, completed the displacement of Indian society that had begun with the treaty negotiations. The settlers who followed the laying of the track soon spread out across the hunting grounds of the Cree and the Blackfoot. The Indians, demoralized and racked by disease, watched from their newly established reserves as their lands were divided.

The construction of the railway was not without serious incident. In 1882, Chief Piapot's Cree pulled up some 40 miles of CPR survey stakes, and camped directly in the path of construction crews. Only the intervention of the Northwest Mounted Police averted violence then. When the railway crossed the Blackfoot reserve, the Indians again confronted the construction crews. Father Lacombe succeeded in persuading them to give up that land for a new reserve elsewhere.

The Northwest Rebellion of 1885 arose from the grievances and frustrations of the Metis and Indians. Dr. Robert Page, an historian from Trent University, told the Inquiry that, although the CPR acted as a catalyst to bring these tensions to a head, it was not the sole issue. In 1884, serious political agitation led the people in Saskatchewan to ask Riel to return. They sent a petition of rights and grievances to Ottawa which cited the government's failure to provide the Metis with patents to the land they already occupied, and the destitution of the Indians.

The government procrastinated in dealing with the claims despite official entreaties of Inspector Crozier of the Northwest Mounted Police urging that the claims should be settled immediately. In March 1885, the Metis rose in rebellion. The Cree, under Poundmaker and Big Bear, also took up arms. A military operation was organized, and the militia was sent to the west on the CPR. The Metis and Indians were defeated.

On November 7, 1885, the last spike was driven at Craigellachie. Nine days later, Louis Riel was hanged at the police barracks in Regina. Eight Indians were also hanged. The Metis were dispersed, and the Indians were confined to their reserves. Some Metis fled to the United States, some to Indian reserves and some to the Mackenzie Valley. In the years after the rebellion, some Metis were granted land or scrip, but the final settlement of their claims dragged on for years. Their scrip was often bought up by white speculators and, under the impact of advancing settlement, some of them retreated to the North.

The historical record shows that if the land claims of the Metis had been settled, there would have been no Northwest Rebellion. It is equally plain that the opening of the West to white settlers made it difficult, if not impossible, for the Government of Canada to recognize the land claims of the native people, who had lived on the plains before the coming of the railway.

There is a direct parallel between what happened on the prairies after 1869 and the situation in the Northwest Territories today. Then, as now, the native people were faced with a vast influx of whites on the frontier. Then, as now, the basic provisions for native land rights had not been agreed. Then, as now, a large-scale frontier development project was in its initial stages, and a major reordering of the constitutional status of the area was in the making.

The lesson to be learned from the events of that century is not simply that the failure to recognize native claims may lead to violence, but that the claims of the white settlers, and the railway, once acknowledged, soon made it impossible to carry out the promises made to the native peoples.

The Government of Canada was then and is now committed to settling the claims of the native people. White settlement of the West made it impossible for the government to settle native claims. Today, the Government of Canada is pledged to settle native claims in the North, and the pledge is for a comprehensive settlement. It is my conviction that, if the pipeline is built before a settlement of native claims is made and implemented, that pledge will not and, in the nature of things, cannot be fulfilled.

POSTPONEMENT OF THE PIPELINE

In my judgment, we must settle native claims before we build a Mackenzie Valley pipeline. Such a settlement will not be simply the signing of an agreement, after which pipeline construction can then immediately proceed. Intrinsic to the settlement of native land claims is the establishment of new institutions and programs that will form the basis for native self-determination.

The native people of the North reject the model of the James Bay Agreement. They seek new institutions of local, regional and indeed territorial government. John Ciaccia, speaking to the Parliamentary Committee convened to examine the James Bay Agreement, said that the Government of Quebec was "taking the opportunity to extend its administration, its laws, its services, its governmental structures through the entirety of Québec." [*The James Bay and Northern Québec Agreement,* p. xvi] The Dene and the Inuit seek a very different kind of settlement.

They also reject the Alaskan model. The Alaskan settlement was designed to provide the native people with land, capital and corporate structures to enable them to participate in what has become the dominant mode of economic development in Alaska, the non-renewable resource sector. This model is only relevant if we decide against the strengthening of the renewable resource sector in the Canadian North.

The Alaskan settlement also rejects the idea that there should be any special status for native people. That is a policy quite different from the policy formulated by the Government of Canada. In Alaska the settlement was designed to do away with special status by 1991 and to assimilate Alaskan natives. The Government of Canada faced that issue between 1969 and 1976 and decided against it.

The issue comes down to this: will native claims be rendered more difficult or even impossible of achievement if we build a pipeline without first settling those claims? Must we establish the political, social and economic institutions and programs embodied in the settlement before building a pipeline? Unless we do, will the progress of the native people toward realization of their goals be irremedially retarded? I think the answer clearly is yes. The progress of events, once a pipeline is under construction, will place the native people at a grave disadvantage, and will place the government itself in an increasingly difficult position.

In my opinion a period of ten years will be required in the Mackenzie Valley and Western Arctic to settle native claims, and to establish the new institutions and new programs that a settlement will entail. No pipeline should be built until these things have been achieved.

It might be possible to make a settlement within the year with the Metis, and perhaps to force a settlement upon the Inuit. It would, however, be impossible, I think, to coerce the Dene to agree to such a settlement. It would have to be an imposed settlement.

You can sign an agreement or you can impose one; you can proceed with land selection; you can promise the native people that no encroachments will be made upon their lands. Yet you will discover before long that such encroachments are necessary. You can, in an agreement, promise the native people the right to rebuild the native economy. The influx of whites, the divisions created among the native people, the preoccupations of the federal and territorial governments, faced with the problems of pipeline construction and the development of the corridor, would make fulfilment of such a promise impossible. That is why the pipeline should be postponed for 10 years.

A decision to build the pipeline now would imply a decision to bring to production now the gas and oil resources of the Mackenzie Delta and the Beaufort Sea. The industrial activity that would follow this decision would be on a scale such as to require the full attention of the government, and entrench its commitment to non-renewable resource development in the North. The drive to bring the native people into the industrial system would intensify, and there would be little likelihood of the native people receiving any support in their desire to expand the renewable resource sector.

If we believe that the industrial system must advance now into the Mackenzie Valley and the Western Arctic, then we must not delude ourselves or the native people about what a settlement of their claims will mean in such circumstances.

It would be dishonest to impose a settlement that we know now—and that the native people will know before the ink is dry on it—will not achieve their goals. They will soon realize—just as the native people on the prairies realized a century ago as the settlers poured in—that the actual course of events on the ground will deny the promises that appear on paper. The advance of the industrial system would determine the course of events, no matter what Parliament, the courts, this Inquiry or anyone else may say.

If we think back to the days when the treaties were signed on the prairies, we can predict what will happen in the North if a settlement is forced upon the native people. We shall soon see that we cannot keep the promises we have made.

XI

EPILOGUE: THEMES FOR THE NATIONAL INTEREST

PRIME MINISTER TRUDEAU HAS SAID THAT CANADA IS A PRODUCT of the providential encounter between the French and the English on this continent. Canada takes its identity from the evolution of that encounter. The contours of that meeting between the French and the English in North America define the political institutions of the nation, and constitute Canada's unique contribution to the search by man for a rational polity.

But there was an earlier encounter on this continent that made possible the very existence of the nation—between the Europeans and the indigenous peoples of the Americas. Here, in what is now Canada, it was an encounter first between the French and the native people, then between the English and the native people. It was an encounter which has ramified throughout our history, and the consequences of which are with us today. This encounter may be as important to us all, in the long sweep of history, as any other on this continent. And it is taking place in its most intense and contemporary form on our northern frontier.

It is for this reason that so many eyes are drawn to the North. As André Siegfried, the de Tocqueville of Canada, said:

> Many countries—and they are to be envied—possess in one direction or
> another a window which opens out on to the infinite—on to the potential
> future. . . . The North is always there like a presence, it is the background
> of the picture, without which Canada would not be Canadian. [*Canada*,
> p. 28–29]

It may be that, through this window, we shall discover something of the shape that our future relations with the native people of our country must assume.

The English and French are the inheritors of two great streams of western civilization. They hold far more in common than divides them: they have similar linguistic and literary traditions and rivalry and commonality of interests that have caused their histories repeatedly to overlap. What is more, the industrial system is the foundation for the material well-being they both enjoy.

Now the industrial system beckons to the native people. But it does not merely beckon: it has intruded into their culture, economy and society, now pulling, now pushing them towards another, and in many ways an alien, way of life. In the North today, the native people are being urged to give up their life on the land; they are being told that their days and their lives should become partitioned like our own. We have often urged that their commitment to the industrial system be entire and complete. Native people have even been told that they cannot compromise: they must become industrial workers, or go naked back to the bush.

Yet many of them refuse. They say they have a past of their own; they see that complete dependence on the industrial system entails a future that has no place for the values they cherish. Their refusal to make the commitment asked of them is one of the points of recurring tension in the North today. They acknowledge the benefits we have brought to them. They say that they are, in some respects, more comfortable now than they were in the old days. The industrial system has provided many things that they value, such as rifles, radios, outboard motors and snowmobiles. But they know that, in the old days, the land was their own. Even in the days of the fur trade, they and the land were essential to it. Now they recognize they are not essential. If it is in the national interest, a pipeline can and will be built across their land. They fear that they will become strangers in their own land. The native people know that somehow they must gain a measure of control over their lives and over the political institutions that shape their lives, and that they must do this before the industrial system overtakes and, it may be, overwhelms them. This is what their claims are about, and this is why they say their claims must be settled before a pipeline is built.

The native people know their land is important to us as a source of oil and gas and mineral wealth, but that its preservation is not essential to us. They know that above all else we have wanted to subdue the land and extract its resources. They recognize that we do not regard their hunting, trapping and fishing as essential, that it is something we often regard in a patronizing way. They say that we reject the things that are valuable to them in life: that we do so explicitly and implicitly.

We have sought to make over these people in our own image, but this pronounced, consistent and well-intentioned effort at assimilation has failed. The use of the bush and the barrens, and the values associated with them, have persisted. The native economy refuses to die. The Dene,

Inuit and Metis survive, determined to be themselves. In the past their refusal to be assimilated has usually been passive, even covert. Today it is plain and unmistakable, a fact of northern life that must be understood.

The native people have had some hard things to say about the government, about the oil and gas industry and about the white man and his institutions. The allegation has been made that what the leaders of native organizations in Northern Canada are saying is not representative of the attitudes and thinking of northern native peoples. But this Inquiry not only has sought the views of the native organizations, but has obtained the views of the native people who live in every settlement and village of the Mackenzie Valley and the Western Arctic. There the native people, speaking in their own villages, in their own languages and in their own way, expressed their real views. About that I am in no doubt.

It would be a mistake to think that the native people are being manipulated by sinister forces, unseen by them, yet discernible to us. It is demeaning and degrading to tell someone that he does not mean or does not know what he is saying, that someone has told him to say it. It would be wrong to dismiss what they have said because we would rather believe that they are not capable of expressing their own opinions.

It may be uncomfortable to have to listen, when we have never listened in the past. But we must listen now. If we do not understand what is in the minds of the native people, what their attitudes really are toward industrial development, we shall have no way of knowing what impact a pipeline and an energy corridor will have on the people of the North.

We all have different ideas of progress and our own definitions of the national interest. It is commonplace for people in Southern Canada to dismiss the notion that a few thousand native people have a right to stand in the way of industrial imperatives. But many of the Dene intend to do just that. Philip Blake told the Inquiry at Fort McPherson:

> If your nation chooses . . . to continue to try and destroy our nation, then I hope you will understand why we are willing to fight so that our nation can survive. It is our world.
>
> We do not wish to push our world onto you. But we are willing to defend it for ourselves, our children, and our grandchildren. If your nation becomes so violent that it would tear up our land, destroy our society and our future, and occupy our homeland, by trying to impose this pipeline against our will, then of course we will have no choice but to react with violence.
>
> I hope we do not have to do that. For it is not the way we would choose. However, if we are forced to blow up the pipeline . . . I hope you will not only look on the violence of Indian action, but also on the violence of your own nation which would force us to take such a course.

We will never initiate violence. But if your nation threatens by its own violent action to destroy our nation, you will have given us no choice. Please do not force us into this position. For we would all lose too much. [C1085ff.]

Chief Fred Greenland said to the Inquiry at Aklavik:

It's clear to me what the native people are saying today. They're discussing not their future but the future of their children and grandchildren, and if the government continues to refuse or neglect [us] . . . I think the natives would just stop their effort and discussions and the opportunities for a peaceful settlement would be lost. We must choose wisely and carefully because there will be a future generation of Canadians who will live with the results. [C3863]

Frank T'Seleie, then Chief at Fort Good Hope, also spoke of the future generations, of the children yet unborn. He told the Inquiry:

It is for this unborn child, Mr. Berger, that my nation will stop the pipeline. It is so that this unborn child can know the freedom of this land that I am willing to lay down my life. [C1778ff.]

Chief Jim Antoine of Fort Simpson:

. . . every time we try to do something, within the system . . . it doesn't seem to work for us, as Indian people. We tried it, we tried to use it, it doesn't work for us. . . . We're going to keep on trying to use the system until we get frustrated enough that we're going to try changing it. I think that's where it's directed, that's where it's going. I would stand with my brother from Good Hope that he would lay down his life for what he believes in, and I feel the same way. There's a lot of us young people who feel the same way. [C2625]

Raymond Yakaleya, speaking at Norman Wells:

Our backs are turned to the corners. This is our last stand.

I ask each and every one of you in this room what would you do if you were in our shoes? How would you feel if you had these conditions on you? I ask you one more time, let us negotiate, there's still time, but don't force us, because this time we have nothing to lose. When I ask for the lives of my people, am I asking you for too much? [C2177]

I have given the most anxious consideration to whether or not I should make any reference in this report to these statements. It may be said that merely reciting them would be to invite a violent reaction to the pipeline, if it were built without a just settlement of native claims. Yet these statements were not lightly made. No one who heard them could doubt that they were said in earnest. So I have concluded that they cannot be ignored. They illustrate the depth of feeling among the native people.

I want to emphasize that my recommendation that the construction of a Mackenzie Valley pipeline should be postponed until native claims are settled is not dependent upon this evidence. That recommendation is based upon the social and economic impact of a pipeline, and upon the impact it would have on native claims. I would be remiss in my duty, however, if I did not remind the Government of Canada that these things were said. I do not want anyone to think I am predicting an insurrection. But I am saying there is a real possibility of civil disobedience and civil disorder that—if they did occur—might well render orderly political evolution of the North impossible, and could poison relations between the Government of Canada and the native people for many years to come.

We ought not to be surprised that native people should express themselves so strongly. Julius Nyerere, President of Tanzania, said at a meeting commemorating the twenty-fifth anniversary of the United Nations on October 15, 1970:

> A man can change his religion if he wishes; he can accept a different political belief—or in both cases give the appearance of doing so—if this would relieve him of intolerable circumstances. But no man can change his colour or his race. And if he suffers because of it, he must either become less than a man, or he must fight. And for good or evil, mankind has been so created that many will refuse to acquiesce in their own degradation; they will destroy peace rather than suffer under it. [p. 4, no. 42]

It has been said that the native people have not articulated their claims, that they are taking too long over it. Yet, when you realize that we have tried to suppress systematically their own institutions, traditions and aspirations, why should we expect them to develop a blueprint for the future in haste?

It has also been suggested that the native people would not be able to manage their own affairs. In fact, they have brought before this Inquiry their own scheme for self-government and for the economic development of the North. And it would be wrong to dismiss this scheme out of hand. They have offered a first, not a final, draft. But it is founded on their own past and their own experience, on their own preferences and aspirations; they wish to see it realized in a future that is of their fashioning. The modernization of the native economy, the development of the renewable resource sector, constitutes as rational a program for the development of the North as we have so far been able to devise.

All that has been said in this report should make it plain that the great agency of change in the North is the presence of industrial man. He and his technology, armed with immense political and administrative power and prepared to transform the social and natural landscape in the interests of a particular kind of society and economy, have a way of soon becoming pervasive. It is not just a question of a seismic trail being cleared across their hunting grounds, or of a drilling rig outside their village that troubles the native people. It is the knowledge that they could be overwhelmed by economic and political strength, and that the resources of their land—indeed the land itself—could be taken from them.

In each native village there is a network of social relationships established over many generations. If there were a pipeline, would all those threads linking family to family, and generation to generation, be snapped?

The native people are raising profound questions. They are challenging the economic religion of our time, the belief in an ever-expanding cycle of growth and consumption. It is a faith shared equally by capitalist and communist.

Dr. Ian McTaggart-Cowan has said:

> Is the only way to improve the lot of a country's citizens the way of industrialization, whether it be the western way or the forced march of the USSR? . . .
>
> Almost inevitably, diversity is sacrificed to a spurious efficiency. The loss of diversity is not merely a matter for sentimental regret. It is a direct reduction in the number of opportunities open to future generations.
>
> As we look toward the end of the twentieth century . . . we see . . . this diversity threatened by dominant societies pursuing goals that, though they have produced a rich material culture, are already eroding the sources of their original stimulus. [In an address to the Pacific Science Congress, August 26, 1975]

The native people take an historical point of view. They argue that their own culture should not be discarded, that it has served them well for many years, and that the industrial system of the white man may not, here in the North, serve them as well for anything like so long a time. They do not wish to set themselves up as a living folk museum, nor do they wish to be the objects of mere sentimentality. Rather, with the guarantees that can be provided only by a settlement of their claims, and with the strengthening of their own economy, they wish to ensure that their cultures can continue to grow and change—in directions they choose for themselves.

Here on our last frontier we have a chance to protect the environment and to deal justly with some of the native people of Canada. If we postpone the pipeline, there will be an opportunity for the native people of the North to build a future for themselves. But if we build the pipeline now, there is every reason to believe that the history of the northern native people will proceed along the same lamentable course as that of native people in so many other places.

Now it has been said that, without the industry's drive to build a pipeline, there is unlikely to be a settlement of native claims. Why should this be so? The Government of Canada has an obligation to settle these claims, pipeline or no pipeline: a solemn assurance has been given. Postponement of pipeline construction will be no reason to turn away from the other issues that confront us in the North.

A settlement of native claims that does no more than extinguish the native interest in land will get us nowhere so far as the social and economic advancement of the native people are concerned. Those social and economic gains will follow from the achievement of a sense of collective pride and initiative by the Dene, Inuit and Metis, and not simply from a clearing away of legal complications to enable industrial development to proceed.

If the pipeline is not built now, an orderly program of exploration can still proceed in the Mackenzie Delta and the Beaufort Sea. And, even if the oil and gas industry withdraws from its exploration activities because of a decision to postpone the pipeline, the Government of Canada has the means to ensure the continuation of exploratory drilling if it were held to be in the national interest. Postponement of the pipeline would mean that, if continued drilling in the Mackenzie Delta and the Beaufort Sea reveals sufficient reserves, Canada can proceed to build a pipeline at a time of its own choosing, along a route of its own choice, by means it has decided upon, and with the cooperation of the native people of the North.

Let me make it clear that if we decide to postpone the pipeline, we shall not be renouncing our northern energy supplies. They will still be there. No one is going to take them away. In years to come, it will still be available as fuel or as industrial feedstocks.

We have never had to determine what is the most intelligent use to make of our resources. We have never had to consider restraint. Will we continue, driven by technology and egregious patterns of consumption, to deplete our energy resources wherever and whenever we find them? Upon this question depends the future of northern native people and their environment.

Maurice Strong, Chairman of Petro Canada, has written:

Man's very skills, the very technical success with which he overspreads the earth, makes him the most dangerous of all creatures.

One critical aspect of man's use of planetary resources is the way in which he is burning up more and more of the world's energy. . . .

We can no longer afford to plan on the basis of past and current trends in consumption. If we assume that a decent standard of life for the world's peoples inevitably requires increasing per capita use of energy, we shall be planning for an energy starved world, or an ecological disaster, or both. Rather than searching endlessly for new energy sources, we must contribute to its wiser use. . . .

At present, we are far from this ideal. We have recklessly assumed that no matter how wasteful our lifestyle, we shall somehow find the energy to support it. . . .

In the last 15 years, world use of energy has doubled. North America now uses about five times as much energy as is consumed in the whole of Asia, and per capita consumption is about 24 times higher. The United States each year wastes more fossil fuel than is used by two-thirds of the world's population. [*Edmonton Journal,* September 22, 1976]

If we build the pipeline, it will seem strange, years from now, that we refused to do justice to the native people merely to continue to provide ourselves with a range of consumer goods and comforts without even asking Canadians to consider an alternative. Such a course is not necessary, nor is it acceptable.

I have said that, under the present conditions, the pipeline, if it were built now, would do enormous damage to the social fabric in the North, would bring only limited economic benefits, and would stand in the way of a just settlement of native claims. It would exacerbate tension. It would leave a legacy of bitterness throughout a region in which the native people have protested, with virtual unanimity, against the pipeline. For a time, some of them may be co-opted. But in the end, the Dene, Inuit and Metis will follow those of their leaders who refuse to turn their backs on their own history, who insist that they must be true to themselves, and who articulate the values that lie at the heart of the native identity.

No pipeline should be built now. Time is needed to settle native claims, set up new institutions and establish a truly diversified economy in the North. This, I suggest, is the course northern development should take.

We have the opportunity to make a new departure, to open a new chapter in the history of the indigenous peoples of the Americas. We must not reject the opportunity that is now before us.

INDEX

A

Abbott, Pat, 209–10
Act of 1869, 233
Act of Union, 233
Aivilik (Igloolik), 41
Aklavik, 68, 81, 83, 84, 85, 86, 143, 151,
    152, 155, 207, 226, 260
Alaska Highway, 47–48, 65
Alaska Highway Route (Fairbanks
    Route), 77–79
Alaska Native Claims Settlement Act,
    219, 255
Albedo, 111–12
Alcohol, 205–7
Aleekuk, Isaac, 160
Allen, Colin, 152
Allen, James, 65
Alunik, Ishmael, 153
Amogoak, 90
Amourous, Fr. Jean, 120
Amundsen Gulf, 84
Anderson, James, 188
Andre, Robert, 230
Andrew, Chief Paul, 159, 235
Antoine, Chief Jim, 142, 199, 260
Apache, 41
Apple, Bruno, 197
Aquitaine, 117
Arctic National Wildlife Range, 75, 76,
    79

Arctic Red River, 84, 85, 138, 230
Arctic Village, 68
Arctic Waters Pollution Prevention Act,
    111
Arrowmaker, Alexis, 159
Asch, Michael, 156
As Long as this Land Shall Last, 220
Athabasca, Lake, 46
Athabascan group, 41
Athabasca River, 49
Atkinson Point, 93

B

Bacon, Francis, 40
Banks Island, 83, 237–38
Barnaby, George, 138, 141
Barry, Tom, 87, 97, 110
Bears, 88
Beaufort Sea Project, 92, 106, 111, 112
Beaver, 41
Big Horn Point, 96
Binamé, Fr. Antoine, 225
Biological Field Program Report: 1975,
    120
Birds, 60, 70–73, 75, 86, 87–88, 91,
    97–98, 119–20. *See also* snow geese
Bird sanctuaries, 125
Black, Harry, 224
Blackfoot, 253

Blake, Philip, 208, 259
Blondin, Liza, 147
Blowouts, 107–8
Bluecoat, Gabe, 138
Bonnetrouge, Joachim, 139
Boreal forest, 34
Bosworth, T. O., 47, 168
Breynat, Bishop, 225
British North America Act, 219, 233
Brodie, Paul, 101, 102
Brody, Hugh, 157–58, 161, 174, 199–200
Bruce, Marie, 64

C

Caesar, Louis, 137
Calef, George, 68, 74
Camden Bay, 75
Campbell Hills–Dolomite Lake site, 125
Camp Farewell, 94
Canadian Arctic Resources Committee, 92
Canadian Marine Drilling Ltd. (CANMAR), 93, 103, 104
Canadian National Railway, 118
Canadian Pacific Railway, 218, 253
Canadian Wildlife Service, 83, 87, 92, 97, 98–99, 110
Canol Project, 47, 48
Cape Bathurst, 86, 154
Cape Dalhousie, 87
Cape Parry, 135
Caribou, 43, 59, 61, 62, 63, 66–70, 75, 76, 77, 78, 79, 83, 85, 89, 120, 121, 243
Carpenter, Andy, 238
Carrier, 41
Carrothers Commission, 235, 250
Cartier, Jacques, 233
Catholic Church, 129–30
Charlie, Alfred, 63
Charlie, Peter, 63
Chipewyan, 41
Chocolate, Charlie, 145
Chrétien, Jean, 171
Churchill, 158
Ciaccia, John, 254

Clement, Robert, 159
Cockney, Frank, 143
Colville Lake, 121, 135, 140
Cominco, 49, 50
Committee for Original Peoples Entitlement, 108, 146
Compressor stations, 123–24
Conroy, Henry, 222, 223–24
Constitution, Canadian, 233–34
Copper Eskimo, 41
Coppermine, 84, 169
Coronation Gulf, 84
Council of Yukon Indians, 78
Cree, 253
Crime, 203
Cross-Delta Route, 94, 97
Cruikshank, Julie, 189

D

Dawson City, 47, 50, 189
Decalta Group, 117
Defence projects, 47–48
Democracy in America, 53
Dempster Highway, 50, 68, 69, 75
Deneron, Chief Harry, 161, 244
Department of Fisheries, 122
Department of Indian Affairs and Northern Development, 89, 109
Department of the Environment, 101
Destruction City, 190
Detah, 238
Development Agencies for the Northwest Territories, 243–44
DEW (Distant Early Warning) Line, 48, 132, 135, 153, 169
Dogrib, 41, 143, 159, 224
Dome Petroleum, 93, 103, 104, 105, 106, 112
Dominion Lands Act (1872), 220
Dorset culture, 42
Drybones, Mary Rose, 197
Drygeese, Chief, 222
Dunbar, Max, 38, 93
Durham, Lord, 233

E

Eagle Plains, 75

Economy, native, 83, 174–79, 182, 189, 240–42
Ecosystem, northern, 37–40
Edgi, Agnes, 201
Education, native control of, 251
Edzo, 49
Edzo, Chief, 143
Elanik, Frank, 85
Elders, respect for, 141–42, 144
Eldorado uranium mine, 47
Elias, Alexandria, 139
Elias, Mary, 159
Ellice Island, 97
Empire and Communications, 167
Enfranchisement, 194–95
Entrenchment of native rights, 228–31
Environmental Impact Assessment, 72
Environment and Common Sense, 38, 93
Environment Canada, 92, 96
Environment Protection Board, 52, 72, 124
Erasmus, George, 144, 159
Eskimo Administration: Canada, 191
Eskimo Lakes, 86

F
Finney, George, 120
Fish, 86–87, 91, 96, 122
Fishing, 69, 84, 85, 86, 96, 122, 146, 150, 151, 153, 157, 180, 242–43
Food, communal distribution of, 139–41, 200
Food chain, 89–91
Foothills Pipe Lines Ltd., 120
Forget, Amédée, 221
Fort Chipewyan, 46
Fort Franklin, 117, 137, 140, 142, 147–50, 154, 224
Fort Good Hope, 35, 36, 46, 129, 137, 138, 145, 155, 197, 198, 201, 225, 236, 260
Fort Liard, 139, 154, 161, 223, 244
Fort McPherson, 58, 82, 84, 85, 137, 143, 146, 158, 160, 188, 189, 190, 208, 250, 259
Fort Norman, 46, 117, 118, 147, 159, 168, 198, 201, 222, 223, 235

Fort Providence, 49, 135
Fort Rae, 143, 144, 206, 224, 225
Fort Resolution, 46, 49, 188, 222, 225
Fort Simpson, 46, 49, 50, 123, 141, 142, 198–99, 250, 260
Fort Smith, 46, 189, 205, 224
Franklin, John, 115
Frost, Alice, 66
Frost, Louise, 62
Frost heave, 36–37, 51
Fumoleau, Fr. René, 192, 220, 223, 225
Fur trade, 82–84, 85, 121, 129–30, 131, 134, 138, 146, 147, 148, 151, 152, 153, 154, 157, 168, 169, 174, 180, 188, 189, 191–92, 243–44, 245

G
Gardiner, Peter, 154
Gas plant proposals, 95
Gemini North, 146
Glaciation, 41–42
Gold rush. *See* Klondike gold rush
Goose, Roy, 151
Gordon, Annie C., 84
Government, native, 132, 142–44, 236
Government, northern, 131, 159, 193–94, 234–37
Great Bear Lake, 47, 147, 154, 168
Great Bear River, 47, 118, 147, 150
Great Slave Lake, 44, 46, 49, 50, 168, 190
Great Slave Lake Railway, 50, 123
Green, Peter, 158
Greenland, Chief Fred, 260
Greenland, Jim, 143
Griper Bay, 105
Gruben, Charlie, 143
Gulf Oil, 80, 94, 95, 102, 182
Gunn, William, 72, 97

H
Halfbreed Commission, 190, 221, 230
Hardy, Rick, 223
Hare, 41
Hay River, 49, 50, 118, 123, 193, 221, 238

Headpoint, Archie, 81–82
Health and health care, native, 203–5, 209
Hecla, 105
Helm, June, 142
Herschel Island, 74
Hire North project, 198
Hobart, Charles, 156, 174, 196–97, 207
Holman, 84, 90, 146, 151–52, 160
Horsfield, Roland, 95
House of Commons Standing Committee on Indian Affairs and Northern Development, 171
Hudson Bay Railway, 69
Hudson's Bay Company, 44, 129–30, 188, 189, 191, 192, 217–18
Hunters and Trappers Association of Tuktoyaktuk, 156
Hunting, 85, 146, 149–50, 152, 153–54, 156, 157, 180, 245

I
Ice scour, 106
Igloolik, 41
Immerk, 105
Imperial Oil, 47, 80, 93, 94, 95, 96, 100, 102, 105, 117, 168, 182, 193, 222
Indian Act, 142, 195, 230
Indian Brotherhood of the Northwest Territories, 144, 146, 156, 159, 167
In-migration, 193, 247
Innis, H. A., 32, 167, 169
International wildlife range, 75–76
Inuit Land Use and Occupancy Project, 153
Inuit Tapirisat of Canada, 239, 248
Inuvialuit, 41
Inuvik, 48, 50, 82, 85, 108, 123, 151, 152, 184, 185–86, 207
Inuvik Hunters and Trappers Association, 153
Invertebrates, 89–90
Iroquois Confederacy, 217

J
Jacobson, Jerald, 72

Jakimchuk, Ronald, 69, 70
James Bay Agreement, 219, 254–55
Jean Marie River, 139
Jenness, Diamond, 130, 188, 191
Johnny Hoe River, 150
Julius, Chief, 143
Jumbo, Edward, 197

K
Kaglik, 143
Kakfwi, Noel, 235
Kakisa Lake, 135
Kaktovik, 68
Kaplansky, Kalmen, 244
KAPS Transportation Company Ltd., 49
Kataoyak, Simon, 90
Kendall Island Bird Sanctuary, 98
Kendi, Mary, 160
Kinship and the Expression of Values in an Athabascan Bush Community, 140
Kittigazuit, 154
Kitto, F. H., 222
Klondike gold rush, 47, 168, 189–90, 192, 221
Klondike River, 47
Kodakin, Chief George, 150
Kodakin, Paul, 150
Koe, Paul, 143
Koe Go Cho Society, 141, 250
Koskimaki, Carl, 124
Koyukon, 41
Kugmallit Bay, 95, 102
Kuo, Chun-Yan, 177
Kutchin (Loucheux), 41, 143

L
Labat, Fr. Felicien, 129
Lac la Martre, 144, 206
Lacombe, Fr., 253
Lamothe, René, 141, 199, 200–201
Land, native relationship with, 63, 146, 154, 157, 161, 170
Land use, native, 116–17, 125–26, 134–35, 137–38, 153, 200, 237–40, 248–49
Land Use and Occupancy Study, 146

Lang, Knut, 83
Lang, Virginia, 120
Langley Channel, 94
Language, Athabascan, 43, 157
Language, Eskimoan, 43
Laycock, Ross, 232
Lent, Peter, 68
Liard River, 123
Lonely Land, The, 56
Loucheux (Kutchin), 41, 143
Lower 51, 78
Lumber industry, 244–45

M

McCart, Peter, 96
McClellan, Catherine, 189
McGill Bay, 149
Mackenzie, Alexander, 42, 46, 47, 82, 115, 168, 188
Mackenzie Bay, 102
Mackenzie Highway, 50, 118, 123, 198, 199
Mackenzie River, 46, 49, 115–16, 123, 125
McNaught, Kenneth, 32
McTaggart-Cowan, Ian, 124, 262
Mair, Charles, 190
Mammals, 86, 88–89, 91, 120–21. *See also* caribou; muskrat; seals; whales
Manalta Coal Ltd., 117
Mangilaluk, 143
Manuel, George, 228–29
Marshall, Chief Justice John, 127, 216–17
Martell, Arthur, 83, 92
Martin, Joe, 121
Melville Island, 105, 169
Memorana, Jimmy, 84
Menioche, Betty, 198
Metis Association of the Northwest Territories, 44, 223
Metis of the Mackenzie District, 44
Middle (Reindeer) Channel, 94
Migratory Birds Convention Act, 222
Mills Lake site, 125
Milne, Allen, 92, 107, 111, 112
Mining, 47, 49, 117, 168–69, 174, 192, 226

Missionaries, 129–30, 189
Monfwi, Chief, 143, 224
Motyka, Dan, 95
Mouchet, Fr. Jean-Marie, 65
Muligak, 143
Murie, Olaus J., 68
Muskrat, 58–59, 63, 83, 84, 88, 121

N

Naedzo, Joe, 140, 142, 224
Nahanni Butte, 77, 131–32
Nahanni River, 131–32
Nasogaluak, David, 237
National Energy Board, 81
National Indian Brotherhood, 228
Natives and Outsiders: Pluralism in the Mackenzie River Delta, Northwest Territories, 154, 157
Navaho, 41
Need to Preserve the Integrity of the Mackenzie Delta, The, 97
Nerysoo, Richard, 137, 158, 188
Netro, Lorraine, 64
Netsilik, 41
Niglintgak, 95
Noksana, Mark, 85
Norman, Ethel, 201
Norman Wells, 47, 48, 49, 93, 117, 192, 222, 232, 260
Northern Canada Power Commission, 184
Northern Science Research Group, 157
Northern Transportation Company Ltd. (NTCL), 49, 184
North Star Harbour, 106
North West Company, 46
Northwestern Territory, 218, 220, 233
Northwest Mounted Police, 191
Northwest Rebellion of 1885, 44, 252–54
Northwest Staging Route, 47
Northwest Territories Act, 233
Northwest Territories Association of Municipalities, 184
Northwest Territories Chamber of Commerce, 184
Norwegian, Louis, 139

Nunaluk Spit, 87
Nuviak, Phillip, 108

O

Oil spills, 90, 92, 97, 104–5, 107–14
Okpik, Abe, 155
Old Crow, 58–66, 68, 146
Olson, Sigurd F., 56
Our Metis Heritage . . . A Portrayal, 44

P

Pacific Western Airlines, 49
Page, Robert, 253
Panarctic, 105
Parsons Lake, 95
Paulatuk, 84, 134–35, 151, 158
Paulette, François, 205
Peel River Alcoholics Anonymous, 250
Percy, Jonathon, 92
Permafrost, 35–37, 50, 51, 78
Petro Canada, 263
Piapot, Chief, 253
Pierrot, Jim, 154
Pimlott, Douglas, 92
Pine Point, 49, 50, 169
Pine Point railway, 169
Pipeline Application Assessment Group, 71
Pipeline proposals, 50–52, 94–95
Pokiak, Bertram, 138
Pokiak, Randy, 156
Porcupine River, 74
Port Radium, 47, 168
Potfighter, Alizette, 238
Processing plants, 98
Prudhoe Bay, 51, 93

Q

Qurdlurtutmiut, 41

R

Rabiska, Fred 197
Raddi, Sam, 108
Rae Lakes, 120, 145, 197

Raymond, Jack, 140–41
Recent Land-use by the Great Bear Lake Indians, 148
Regional Impact of a Northern Gas Pipeline, 195
Reindeer, 88–89
Richards Island, 80, 94
Richardson Mountains, 153
Richter, Herta, 65
Riel, Louis, 252, 253
Robertson, Jim, 184
Royal Canadian Mounted Police, 129–30
Royal Proclamation of 1763, 217
Rupert's Land, 218, 220, 233
Rushforth, Scott, 147, 148, 154, 156
Russell, Peter, 233
Russell Bay, 150
Ruttan, 243, 244

S

Sachs Harbour, 83, 84, 135, 139, 151, 152, 159, 237
Savishinsky, Joel, 140
Schwartz, Herbert, 204
Scrip, 221, 223, 230
Sea-bed permafrost, 106
Seals, 84–85
Self-government, native, 231, 233, 239–40
Sergeant, David, 101, 102
Seven Years War, 217
Shallow Bay, 94, 99, 153
Shearer, James, 92, 106
Shell Oil, 80, 81, 82, 94, 95, 102, 117, 182
Siegfried, André, 257
Sittichinli, Jim, 226
Slaney and Company, 100
Slave River, 46, 49
Slavey, 41
Slobodin, Richard, 44
Smith, Derek, 154, 157
Snow, Norman, 89, 109–10
Snow geese, 60, 71-73, 87, 97, 98. *See also* birds
Social inequalities, 207–9

Sonfrere, Chief Daniel, 118, 238
South Nahanni National Park, 77
Stager, John, 191
Statement of the Government of Canada on Northern Development in the 70s, 171
Steen, Vince, 104, 227
Stegner, Wallace, 56
Stein, Jeff, 96, 122
Stewart, Don, 193
Strong, Maurice, 263
Study of Income Distribution in the Mackenzie District of Northern Canada, A, 177
Sun Oil, 93
Swimming Point, 94

T

Taglu, 95
Tanana, 41
Templeton, Carson, 52
Territorial Council, 233, 234, 235, 236
Territorial Lands Act, 74
Texaco, 117
Thule culture, 42
Thunder River, 123–24
Tobac, Georgina, 137
Tocqueville, Alexis de, 53
Townsend, Ethel, 201
Trans-Alaska oil pipeline, 37
Transportation, 49–50
Trapping. *See* Fur trade
Travaillant Lake, 84, 123
Treaties, 218–28, 253
Robinson, 218
Treaty 1, 218
Treaty 2, 218
Treaty 3, 218, 219
Treaty 4, 218–19
Treaty 5, 218
Treaty 6, 218
Treaty 7, 218
Treaty 8, 218, 220, 221, 222, 225, 230
Treaty 11, 192, 195, 218, 220, 223, 224, 225, 230
Treaty Commission, 223
Tree line, 34–35

Trout Lake, 197
Trout River, 46
Trudeau, Pierre, 111
T'Seleie, Chief Frank, 145, 225, 243, 244, 260
Tuktoyaktuk, 84, 85, 94, 138, 143, 151, 152, 153, 186, 204, 227
Tundra, 34, 36
Tununuk, 94
Tununuk Point, 94
Tutcho, Susie, 137
Tutchone, 41

U

Unemployment, 135, 169, 179–83
United States Army, 47, 48
Urgent Need for a Canadian Arctic Wildlife Range, The, 74
Usher, Peter, 151, 153, 154, 167–68, 174

V

Villeneuve, Theresa, 199
Voices for the Wilderness, 56

W

Wage employment, 133–34, 153, 156, 165, 174, 176, 177, 178, 182, 199, 200, 203, 245
Wah-Shee, James, 229
Walker, E. R., 112
Watkins, Melville, 167, 169, 175
Watts, Rev. John, 65
Webb, Robert, 100, 101
Weeden, Robert, 75, 76
Weick, Edward, 244
Welfare, 131, 202–3
West Channel, 94
Whales, 83, 85, 86, 88, 91, 99–103
Whale sanctuary, 101–3
Whaling, 100, 167–68, 190–91
Wheeler, Ross, 205–6, 210
Whitefish Station, 84, 153
Whitehorse, 48
Wilderness Act, 55
Willow Lake (Brackett Lake) site, 125

Witty, Jack, 179, 180
Wolki, Sandy, 106
Wood Buffalo National Park, 225
Wrigley, 50, 198

Y

Yakaleya, Raymond, 260

Yellowknife, 47, 49, 50, 146, 168, 206, 238
Yellowstone National Park, 55
Yukon Gold Company, 47

Z

Zoe, Isadore, 144